THE UPSIDE-DOWN KINGDOM

THE UPSIDE-DOWN

KINGDOM

Revised Edition

DONALD B. KRAYBILL

Foreword by Tom Sine

A Christian Peace Shelf Selection

HERALD PRESS
Scottdale, Pennsylvania
Waterloo, Ontario

Library of Congress Cataloging in Publication Data

Kraybill, Donald B.
  The upside-down kingdom / Donald B. Kraybill. — 2nd ed.
    p. cm. — (A Christian peace shelf selection)
  Includes bibliographical references.
  ISBN 0-8361-3522-9 (alk. paper)
    1. Kingdom of God. 2. Bible. N.T. Gospels—Criticism,
interpretation, etc. 3. Sociology, Biblical. 4. Sociology,
Christian (Mennonite) 5. Christian life—Mennonite authors.
    I. Title. II. Series.
  BT94.K7 1990   90-33783
  231.7'2—dc20   CIP

The paper used in this publication meets the minimum requirements
of American National Standard for Information Sciences—Permanence
of Paper for Printed Library Materials, ANSI Z39.48-1984.

Scripture quotations are from the Revised Standard Version of the
Bible, copyright © 1946, 1952, 1971, by the Division of Christian
Education of the National Council of Churches of Christ in the USA,
and used by permission.

For those
"who have turned the world upside down . . .
acting against the decrees of Caesar,
saying that there is
another king,
Jesus"

(Acts 17:6-7).

And for
Helen Brubaker Kraybill
whose generosity—in the midst
of adversity—is boundless.

CONTENTS

FOREWORD

There is no scarcity of books, tapes, and radio broadcasts on discipleship. But many of the popular Christian teachings on discipleship are extremely narrow. They tend to limit the call to follow Jesus Christ to one small spiritual compartment of life. In all the other compartments they unquestioningly let the culture call the shots.

For example, in spite of all the popular Christian teachings about Jesus' lordship, it's commonly understood what comes first. Our careers come first. Getting our house in the suburbs comes first. Our upscale lifestyles come first. Then, with whatever time, energy, or resources is left, we can follow Christ.

But a growing number of Christians are no longer content to live the American dream with a little Jesus overlay. They want a more serious brand of discipleship, one that challenges rather than conforms to secular culture.

The Upside-Down Kingdom (revised edition) is a book for those serious about following Jesus Christ not only in the spiritual dimension but in all life. Donald Kraybill has written a book as provocative as the parables of Jesus. He shows us a discipleship in which down is up, inside is out, and failure is success. His book is so provocative because he insists that we bring Scripture to bear on all areas of life—our values, stewardship of time and money, attitudes toward the outcast, and handling of violence.

Except for the Bible, no book has been more instructive to my own discipleship than this book. I find myself constantly struggling with living the upside-down values of the kingdom in an alien world. To be honest, I find it much easier to talk and write about than to live what I have learned from *The Upside-Down Kingdom*. But I can never run far from Kraybill's probing question, "What would our lives look like if we lived out the beatitudes?"

Donald Kraybill reminds us that to be a disciple of Jesus Christ is to join a new community in which the countercultural values of God's kingdom are most fully expressed. "The corporate life of the people of God will be visible and external. These are the folks who engage in conspicuous sharing. We practice Jubilee. Generosity replaces consumption and accumulation. Our faith wags our pocketbooks. We give without expecting a return. We forgive liberally as God forgave us. We overlook the signs of stigma hanging from the unlovely. Genuine compassion for the poor . . . moves us. We look and move down the ladder. We don't take our own religion structures too seriously; we know Jesus is Lord and Master of even religious custom. We serve instead of dominate."

If you want to discover a more serious approach to discipleship in community with other sisters and brothers, I recommend two steps. Continue reading. And get a group of others to read and discuss this book with you. I hope not only Anabaptists, but people from all Christian (and non-Christian) backgrounds find the courage to read this book and join those of us struggling with the call to radical biblical discipleship in an alien world.

—Tom Sine, author of *The Mustard Seed Conspiracy*

AUTHOR'S PREFACE

This book is a study of the kingdom of God in the synoptic Gospels. As such, it is not a novel work since many other books also deal with this topic. Two aspects of my Anabaptist theological heritage accent the uniqueness of this particular treatment of the kingdom.

First, I am a theological layperson. Having been taught that one should not let theology solely up to the theologians, I have written as one layman sharing with others. Trained in sociology, I tend to read the Scriptures through the lenses of that academic discipline. Such an endeavor is quite precarious because as one wanders back and forth between the disciplines of biblical theology and sociology, one is bound to insult the guardians of both traditions. The combination of a Radical Reformation heritage and sociological training yields a perspective which may seem somewhat irreverent. I hope, however, that this approach will be both stimulating and provocative.

Second, I have taken the New Testament and Jesus in particular quite seriously. I have limited the study primarily to the synoptic Gospels because they provide us with the sharpest portrait of the life and teachings of Jesus. It will soon become obvious to the reader that I believe Jesus has a lot to say to us moderns. His words and insights bring a corrective note to our affluence, war-making, status-seeking, and religious exclusivism. There is always a tendency for Christians to want a few explicit rules to follow in their spiritual sojourn. I have attempted to deal with the biblical material in a fresh way, but those who are looking for new rules will be disappointed. The book raises a multitude of questions. The answers, I firmly believe, must be formulated in the context of small groups of God's children. I hope the upside-down perspective will provoke stimulating discussions enabling Christian believers to more accurately discern God's will for their lives.

The second edition has been completely revised, line by line and word by word. But the original argument remains intact: the kingdom of God announced by Jesus was a new order of things that appeared upside-down in the midst of Palestinian culture in the first century. Moreover, the kingdom of God in its contemporary expressions has upside-down features today as it breaks into diverse cultures around the world. The number of sociological investigations of the social world of Jesus' time appearing since the first edition is astonishing. This revised edition taps many of those rich resources. I have polished the text throughout and at places have clarified the thrust of certain arguments.

Numerous persons provided helpful counsel to the first edition. The following individuals gave constructive feedback to an early draft of the manuscript: Donald Blosser (chapters 5–6), Charles De Santo, J. Elvin Kraybill, Paul G. Landis, Beverly Lord, Willard Swartley, Eugene Witmer, and John Howard Yoder. I am grateful for the way they graciously shared their time and ideas. In addition, Gerald Bender, Zelah Bender, Ken Brubaker, Pam Brubaker, Stanley Godshall, Susan Godshall, Fran Kraybill, Ann Miller, and Park Miller read a rough copy of the first edition and gave invaluable advice.

The following persons kindly offered constructive ideas for improving the text and the substance of the second edition—Charlotte Baker-Shenk, Donald Blosser, Richard B. Gardner, Ray C. Gingerich, J. Nelson Kraybill, Ruth D. Lesher, Jay E. McDermond, Mike Medley, Lauree Hersch Meyer, Mark and Tracy Murray, Willard Swartley, and Paul Zehr. I am grateful for all their help and suggestions. Jeanette S. Martin, in her typically fine fashion, provided editorial assistance and word processing support for the entire revision. Michael A. King, Herald Press editor, polished the revised text in creative and imaginative ways. I especially thank former book editor Paul M. Schrock, now Herald Press director, for his care and support of this project over the years.

—Donald B. Kraybill

KINGDOM

1

DOWN IS UP

Flat Mountains

> The voice of one crying in the wilderness:
> Prepare the way of the Lord,
> make his paths straight.
> Every valley shall be filled,
> and every mountain and hill shall be brought low,
> and the crooked shall be made straight,
> and the rough ways shall be made smooth;
> and all flesh shall see the salvation of God.
>
> —Luke 3:4-6

John the Baptist shouted these words of Isaiah to announce the advent of Jesus. The dramatic pictures portray a revolutionary new kingdom. The Baptist describes four surprises of the coming kingdom: full valleys, flat mountains, straight curves, and level bumps. He expects radical shake-ups to accompany the kingdom. Old ways will alter beyond recognition. John warns us that the new order, the Upside-Down Kingdom, will revolutionize the prevailing social landscape. But in the painful ferment, all flesh will see the salvation of God.

Mary's Magnificat, her song of exaltation sung at the home of Zechariah and Elizabeth, clarifies her hope for the new kingdom. With John the Baptist, she expects the

Messiah's arrival to initiate an upside-down kingdom filled with surprises for all.

> For he who is mighty has done great things for me, and holy is his name.
> And his mercy is on those who fear him from generation to generation.
> He has shown strength with his arm.
> he has scattered *the proud* in the imagination of their hearts,
> he has put down *the mighty* from their thrones,
> and exalted those of *low degree;*
> he has filled *the hungry* with good things,
> and *the rich* he has sent empty away.
> —Luke 1:49-53, emphasis added

Five types of people are startled and surprised. In Mary's vision, those at the top of the social pyramid—the proud, the rich, and the mighty—topple. They are stripped of their prestigious seats, dethroned, scattered, and sent away empty. Meanwhile the poor and hungry, those at the bottom of the social hill, take a surprising ride to the top. Mary sings words of hope and judgment. Hope for those of low estate, as she describes herself (Luke 1:48). Judgment for those at the top who trample the helpless.

A poor Galilean peasant girl, Mary expects the messianic kingdom to flip her social world upside down. The rich, mighty, and proud in Jerusalem will be sent away. Poor farmers and shepherds in rural Galilee will be exalted and honored. Mary's longing and hope reflect the Jewish yearning for a messiah who will usher in an upside-down kingdom.

An Inverted Kingdom

The central theme in the ministry and teaching of Jesus is the kingdom of God, or as Matthew calls it, the kingdom of heaven.[1] This key idea ties his entire message together. The "kingdom of God" permeates all of Jesus' ministry, giving it unusual coherence and clarity. It is the core, the very essence, of his ministry.[2]

Debates on Jesus' understanding of God's kingdom have swirled down through the centuries. On the pages that follow we'll examine this notion: the kingdom of God points to an inverted, or upside down, way of life that contrasts with the prevailing social order. We can capture the idea of inversion by thinking of two ladders side by side—one representing the kingdom of God, the other the kingdoms of this world. An inverted relationship between the two ladders means that something highly valued on one ladder ranks near the bottom of the other. An inverted relationship appears in the refrain of a Sunday school song. The rain and flood move in opposite directions:

> The rains came down, and the flood came up,
> The rains came down, and the flood came up.

The Gospels portray the kingdom of God as inverted or upside down in comparison with both ancient Palestinian and modern ways.[3] The Gospels do not, however, see the kingdom as geographically or socially isolated from the rest of society. Jesus doesn't plead for social avoidance or withdrawal. Nor does he assume that kingdom and world are divided neatly into separate realms. Kingdom action takes place in the middle of the societal ballpark. But it's a different game. Kingdom players follow new rules. They listen to another coach. Kingdom values challenge patterns of social life taken for granted in modern culture. Kingdom habits don't mesh smoothly with dominant cultural trends. They may, in fact, look foolish.

The kingdom of God isn't only upside down. It's also authoritative for our situation.[4] Kingdom values address current issues and dilemmas. Kingdom ethics, translated into our modern context, suggest how we "ought" to order our lives. We certainly won't find answers in the Scriptures for all our ethical questions. The Gospels don't offer a cookbook solution for every modern ethical dilemma. But they do raise the right questions. They nudge us toward the big issues that undergird the meaning and purpose of our living.

A Relational Kingdom

What exactly is the kingdom of God? The term defies exact definition. It's pregnant with many meanings. This is its genius, this power to stimulate our imagination again and again.

Most biblical scholars do agree that the "kingdom of God" means the dynamic rule or reign of God. The reign of God represents God's government, authority, and ruling power. It isn't a territory in a spatial sense. The kingdom doesn't stand on a particular piece of ground. Nor is it static. It's dynamic—always becoming, spreading, growing.[5] The kingdom points us not to the place of God, but to God's ruling activities. The kingdom is present whenever and wherever women and men submit their lives to God's authority.

Does the kingdom occur when God rules in the hearts of people? This notion suggests that the kingdom is primarily an internal, inward experience of the mind. But the very term kingdom implies a collective order above and beyond the experience of any one person. A kingdom in a literal sense means that a king rules over a *group* of people. Social standards and group policies order the collective life of a kingdom. Agreements spell out citizens' obligations to each other as well as to their king. The king's ruling activity makes practical differences in the lives and relationships of his subjects. In the words of one scholar, "The kingdom is something people enter, not something that enters them. It is a state of affairs, not a state of mind."[6]

Kingdom living is fundamentally social. It involves membership, citizenship, loyalties, and one's identity. Citizenship in a kingdom entails relationships, policies, obligations, boundaries, and expectations. These dimensions of kingdom life supersede the whims of individual experience. Membership in a kingdom spells out a citizen's relationship to the king, to other citizens, and to other kingdoms. Living in a kingdom means sharing in its history and helping to shape its future.

Although a kingdom is a social order, above and beyond any puny person, individuals *do* make choices about kingdoms. We embrace or reject them. We serve or mock them. We enter kingdoms and leave them. We pledge our allegiance to them and turn our backs on them.

The sociological distinction between an *aggregate* and a *collectivity* clarifies the kingdom idea. An aggregate isn't a group. It's merely a collection of persons who happen to be together in time and space. They don't influence one another. A cluster of persons waiting for the "Walk" light at an intersection is an aggregate. Though they stand side by side, they usually don't interact with each other.

In contrast, the executive committee of a parent-teachers' association is a collectivity—a group whose members are interdependent. They influence each other, formulate common goals, and together decide how to reach them. A kingdom's subjects have a collective *interdependence* based on the policies of their king.

The kingdom of God is a collectivity—a network of persons who have yielded their *hearts and relationships* to the reign of God. The kingdom is actualized when God rules in hearts *and* social relationships. The kingdom isn't merely a series of independent spiritual fax lines linking the King to each subject. The reign of God infuses the web of relationships, binding King and citizens together.

How do we discover what God's reign looks like? What is the shape of the royal policies? Can we translate the lofty idea of God's reign into practical terms? The answer lies in the incarnation. Jesus of Nazareth unveiled God. We begin to grasp the meaning of the kingdom through Jesus' life and teachings. The life of Jesus was God's final and definitive Word. Through Jesus' person and ministry, God's voice clearly spoke, in a universal language understood by all.

The kingdom of God is the common thread woven throughout the fabric of Jesus' teaching and ministry. Jesus frequently introduced parables as examples of the kingdom. The Sermons on the Mount and Plain describe kingdom life. The Lord's Prayer welcomes the advent of the kingdom. The vocabulary of the kingdom is continually on Jesus' lips.

In addition to his words, Jesus' activity and behavior teach us about the kingdom. Jesus of Nazareth provides the most concrete example—the most visible expression of God's rule. His words and behavior offer the best clues to solving the riddle of the kingdom.[7] But in the final analysis it isn't *his* kingdom, nor is it *ours*. Always and foremost Jesus points us to *God's* kingdom.

Why Upside Down?

If Jesus inaugurated the kingdom of God, perhaps we should call it the right-side-up kingdom. Indeed, if we agree that the kingdom portrays God's blueprint for our lives, then surely we ought to tag it the right-side-up kingdom. But let me retain the inverted, upside-down image to focus several issues.

(1) *Social life has vertical dimensions.* Society has a rugged topography. In social geography there are mountains, valleys, ruts, and plains. Some people stand on high social peaks while others mourn in the valleys. The social clout individuals and groups wield varies greatly. The

chairperson of a committee musters more power than the average committee member. Lawyers swing more prestige and influence than grocery store clerks. We don't play the "game" of social interaction on a level playing field. The "upside-down" image reminds us of this vertical dimension of social life.

(2) *We forget to ask why things are the way they are.* The "upside-down" label encourages us to question the way things are. Children quickly learn common cultural values and take them for granted. Cereal becomes the "right" breakfast food. Socialization—learning the ways of our culture—shapes the assumptions by which we live. We take our way of life for granted. We assume the way things *are* is the way they *ought* to be. Eating cereal for breakfast, day after day, makes it seem unquestionably right. We internalize the values and norms paraded on screen and billboard as simply "the way life is." If our economic system sets a minimum wage, we accept it as fair and just without a second thought. If someone trespasses on our property, we happily prosecute. After all, "that's what the law provides for." We demand an 8 percent commission on a sales transaction because "that's just the way it is."

The values, beliefs, and norms of our society become so deeply ingrained in our mind that we no longer see the alternatives. Throughout the Gospels, Jesus presents the kingdom as a new order breaking in on old ways, old values, old assumptions. If it does anything, the kingdom of God shatters the assumptions which govern our lives. As kingdom citizens we can't assume that things are right just because "that's the way they are." The upside-down perspective focuses the points of divergence and conflict between God's kingdom and the kingdoms of the world.

(3) *The kingdom is full of surprises.* Again and again in parable, sermon, and act Jesus startles us. Things in the Gospels are often literally upside down. Good Guys turn

out to be Bad Guys. Those we expect to receive the reward get a spanking instead. Those who think they are headed for heaven land in hell. Things are reversed. Paradox, irony, and surprise permeate the teachings of Jesus. They flip our expectations upside down. The least are the greatest. The immoral receive forgiveness and blessing. Adults become like children. The religious miss the heavenly banquet. The pious receive curses. Things aren't like we think they should be. We're baffled and perplexed. Amazed, we step back. Should we laugh or should we cry? Again and again, turning our world upside down, the kingdom surprises us.

Stretching a footbridge across the gulf between the pressing questions of today and the biblical record is precarious. Centuries of water swirl between the cliffs jutting from each shoreline. Detour signs hinder easy passage. Before trekking over the bridge to yesterday, we must stop and ponder four detour signs. We often use these cautions to evade the kingdom message and bypass its relevance for today.

Detour One: Jesus Is Culturally Bound

The first sign warns us that trying to bridge the gap between the first and twenty-first centuries is foolish. The cultural landscapes are simply too different. Jesus lived in a small rural village aloof from industrialization, urbanization, technology, nuclear holocaust, and global corporations. According to this detour sign, kingdom ethics might work in small villages where Simon knows Martha. In a simple folk society one can talk of loving enemies and forgiving neighbors. The kingdom blueprint makes sense for gentle shepherds and naive peasants. But not for us. Jesus' teaching is trapped in a rural culture. We can't transport it across the footbridge to our modern life in a complicated global system.

According to this caution, we can study the Scripture

to learn about biblical ethics. We can describe the "oughts" for living in New Testament times. But we shouldn't try to drag them across the bridge as "oughts" for today. This detour sign tells us to construct our own Christian ethics from scratch. It tells us to ground them in common sense for the ancient biblical foundation is irrelevant.

It is irresponsible to jump blindly from isolated Scripture texts to the modern era. But if we identify the meaning of a biblical text within its own cultural setting, we can then transport that meaning across the bridge to the modern world. Certainly we must understand the values, norms, and intergroup relations of the ancient setting to grasp the full meaning of a text. We must recognize that Galilean peasant society was strikingly different from modern society.

Nevertheless, similar human habits persist on both sides of the historical chasm: nationalism, racism, economic oppression, greed, violence, abuse of power and arrogant individualism. In short, evil lurks within the social structures of both yesterday and today. As we unravel the meanings of the Gospel stories within their cultural setting, we find that they *do* indeed address the burning issues of our time as well.

The Gospels' ancient setting is no handicap when we take time to interpret them in cultural context. Precisely then, in fact, is when the biblical stories become relevant. Contrary to typical thinking, Jesus' relevance would decrease if his life and ministry had floated above culture. His grounding in a particular culture increases his relevance for today. The cultural rootage of Jesus clarifies rather than hides the message of the kingdom.

Detour Two: Jesus Goofed on the Timing

The second detour warns us Jesus himself was mistaken about the timing of the kingdom's arrival. According to this argument, he goofed in thinking that the kingdom would arrive during his lifetime. Thus we can't take it seriously today, and it certainly can't tell us how we ought to live.

The issue of the kingdom's timing is one of the stickiest problems in synoptic studies. It has provoked heated scholarly debates.[8] When will the kingdom arrive? Has it already come, or do we still wait? Is the pie in the sky or already made?

Many scholars think Jesus expected the final consummation of the kingdom during his own lifetime.[9] In Matthew 10:23, for instance, Jesus tells those he is sending out, "truly, I say to you, you will not have gone through all the towns of Israel, before the Son of man comes." In Luke 9:27, after discussing the disciple's cross, Jesus says, "But I tell you truly, there are some standing here who will not taste death before they see the kingdom of God." These and other passages suggest that Jesus himself expected the kingdom to come soon.

Thus the radical character of Jesus' life makes sense. Expecting the world to end in a few years, he offered his ethical teachings as temporary guidelines. They were applicable *only* to the short interim between his life and the imminent arrival of the kingdom. If you expect the world to end and the kingdom to burst in at any moment, it makes sense to love your enemies and give away your cloak. According to this liberal school of interpreters, Jesus designed his teachings for this short "interim" only. They certainly aren't reasonable for long-term and enduring social relationships.

In contrast, other theologians argue that Jesus thought the kingdom was present in his own ministry. Jesus said, "The kingdom of God has come near to you" (Luke 10:9) and "The kingdom of God has come upon you," (Luke 11:20). Jesus must have understood that the kingdom was already present in his ministry. This line of scholarly interpretation stresses the presence of the kingdom in the incarnation and in the later growth of the church. However, it downplays a future consummation.[10]

A third position, the dispensational view, relegates the kingdom to a future and literal reign of Christ on earth. In this perspective, Israel rejected the offer of the kingdom at the first appearance of Christ. This forced God to delay the kingdom's actualization until the return of Christ. The futuristic bent of this conservative view dilutes serious interest in applying the teachings of Jesus to our lives today. Interestingly, both liberals and conservatives reach the same conclusion: kingdom ethics taught by Jesus are meaningless today.

Other scholars stake out a fourth position. They argue that the kingdom of God in Jesus' teachings integrates both present and future. One scholar notes, "There is a growing consensus in New Testament scholarship that the kingdom of God is in some sense both present and future."[11] There are at least four meanings of the kingdom in the Gospels. (1) An abstract meaning of the reign or rule of God. (2) A future apocalyptic order into which the righteous will enter. (3) The presence of the kingdom already on earth. (4) A realm which persons are entering now.[12]

It's helpful to think of the kingdom of God as a *general* symbol rather than a *specific* one.[13] Symbols point us to something beyond themselves. The written word "dog" is a symbol. As we read the word "dog" it reminds us of a certain kind of animal.

A *specific* symbol is one with only one referent—it reminds us of only one thing. A black, female cocker spaniel puppy points us to a specific kind of dog.

In contrast, *general* symbols have multiple meanings and many referents. The word "animal," for example, suggests many kinds of creatures.

If we think of the kingdom of God as a specific symbol,

this limits us to one meaning. If the kingdom is merely a single event, we're forced to ask whether or not the event has occurred—yes or no. A single concrete historical act can exhaust such a specific symbol.

Viewing the kingdom as a general symbol offers us many referents with multiple meanings. A general symbol is elastic. It stretches forward and backward, wide and far, to cover many meanings. Thus instead of asking questions about time, we ask what the kingdom evokes or represents. For what does it stand? Toward what does it point us? Furthermore, a general symbol isn't invalidated simply because a specific event doesn't occur. The kingdom is more than an ancient or a future event. To see the kingdom as a general symbol enables us to appreciate the many ways God is king of our lives.

This study embraces the kingdom's *diverse* meanings: The Old Testmanent's hope for it. Its inauguration in the ministry of Jesus. Its power at Pentecost. Its durability in the lives of believers throughout the centuries. And its final future consummation.

Kingdom signs burst forth whenever persons submit their wills and relationships to the way of God. To quote the title of a book, the kingdom is *The Presence of the Future* among us already.[14] The kingdom of God is present today as the Spirit of God rules in the lives of believers. The members of the kingdom even now are those who obey the Lord of the kingdom. Those who follow in the way of Jesus are already part of the kingdom movement. No, Jesus didn't goof on the timing. He was simply talking about a kingdom that transcends our human understanding of time.

Detour Three: Ponder the Spiritual Meaning

A third detour prevents many of us from lugging practical ethical instruction across the bridge from ancient Palestine. This detour encourages us to soften Jesus' hard social teaching by spiritualizing it. Certain words in our language take on sacred meanings. We sort words into holy and profane boxes. We contrast hot and cold, big and small, in and out. In religious circles the term "spiritual" tops the sacred ladder. By contrast, the word "social" often hangs on the bottom rung.

Spiritual realities, the logic goes, come from God. They are holy. Human effort, on the other hand, drives social affairs. Being far from God's heart, social realities are suspect. Spiritual is better than social. We hope a certain church activity doesn't become "just a social event"— implying it would have no spiritual meaning. This unfortunate split between spiritual and social often detours us around kingdom ethics.

Spiritual realities involve great metaphysical truths. They include our beliefs about God, salvation, and the mysterious working of God's Spirit in our lives. Social realities, on the other hand, point us to earthly, mundane concerns—housing, fellowship, salary, recreation, and our social needs for approval, love, creativity, and satisfying relationships.

This false split between spiritual and social leads to a warped reading of the Scripture. It tempts us to turn Jesus' hard sayings into sweet, spiritualized syrup. This dilutes his teaching, making it harmless. We marvel at the atoning death of Jesus but forget he also demonstrated a new way of living.

Any gospel which isn't social isn't gospel. God's love for the world produced social action. God didn't just sit in a great theological rocking chair and muse about loving the world. God acted. God entered social affairs—in human form. Through Jesus, God lived and interacted in a real social environment. Jesus, in essence, disclosed God's social habits. In the incarnation, the spiritual became social.

To put it another way, this definitive social event was a

spiritual word. It communicated God's spiritual mysteries to us in a practical social form. Word and deed blended into a single reality in the incarnation. In these last days God has spoken to us not through Greek or English but through a Son—a social event (Hebrews 1:2). The genius of the incarnation is that spiritual and social worlds intersect in Jesus Christ. To separate them is to deny the incarnation. Social and spiritual are inextricably woven together in the Gospels' account of Jesus' life.

One scholar argues that repentance "is a purely religious ethical act . . . an act involving only on oneself and God and neutral regarding other human beings and the world."[15] This view mistakenly assumes repentance is a personal spiritual experience with no social implications. Moreover, why is Jesus relevant for repentance if not for ethics? Such a cleavage misrepresents the gospel. We don't have two gospels. We don't have a spiritual *and* a social gospel, a salvation *and* a hunger gospel. We have a single, integrated gospel of the kingdom. *This* gospel fuses social and spiritual realities into one.

Jesus binds the spiritual and social into an inseparable whole. On the one hand he says true faith is anchored in the heart—not in tithing, sacrifice, cleansing, and other external rituals. In this sense he spiritualizes religious faith.

On the other hand, Jesus argues that faith in God is always expressed in tangible social acts of love for the neighbor. He was, in short, smashing our categories of social and spiritual. In Jesus' view they're inseparable—a seamless fabric.

A pastor once spiritualized the story of Zacchaeus. After telling the story he reminded the congregation that Jesus can help us out of our spiritual trees. If we are spiritually "treed" we can by Jesus be freed. The sermon overlooked the profound economic dimensions of the story. It trivialized the social impact of the encounter with trite spiritual applications. A realistic reading of the text discovers a greedy tax collector who meets Jesus, repents, and immediately corrects his economic wrongs. Spiritual repentance and social retribution form *one* story, a story Jesus describes as a "visit by salvation."

To ferret out the social implications of the gospel isn't to depreciate or neglect spiritual insights. It's rather to assert that spiritual insights always have social ramifications. The integration of social and spiritual into a whole isn't a humanistic way of doing theology from below. It affirms an incarnation that moved beyond the holy of holies in the Jerusalem temple to the social realities of Palestinian society.

When we spiritualize biblical texts we extract them from practical human experience. We dilute their social meaning. When, on the other hand, we explore the social context of a biblical text, its cargo of meaning becomes pertinent to our situation today.

Detour Four: Only Change Your Character

The next barricade tells us that the kingdom only makes a difference in our personal character. In other words, the teachings of Jesus help build private character and personal—but not social—ethics. One scholar concludes that Jesus primarily desires righteous character. Conduct, he notes, should be a manifestation of such righteous character. But "it is of course true that there is little explicit teaching on social ethics in the Gospels."[16]

The distinction between personal and social ethics is tidy. But it's also problematic. It suggests that personal decisions and actions do not have social consequences. And it assumes that individuals operate in a social vacuum, detached from social forces.

Jesus, according to this view, was concerned with the private matters of the inner life. He cared primarily about character, attitudes, motives, emotions, personality traits.

Hence the ethics of Jesus apply only to inner feelings which have little impact on others. What Jesus touches is our emotional outlook—our sense of hope and inner peace.

The problem with a personal/social split is that virtually all behavior is social. Are any actions purely "personal"? Perhaps scratching one's leg would pass the test. But even this creates problems. The proper way to scratch a leg is learned in a social context. Cultural norms determine the time and method of scratching. Woe to national leaders who scratch their legs during press conferences!

Even ideas, values, and character traits have a social origin. They don't just fall from the sky. They're learned in a social context: discussions with friends, reading a book, listening to tapes, observing parents for fifteen years. This doesn't mean the individual contributes no originality or creativity. Nor does it mean individuals are culturally programmed robots. Our minds are the crucible in which a variety of influences are processed and mixed together. Each person blends these social influences in his or her own beautiful and unique way.

Not only do inner feelings and motives have social roots, they have social ramifications. Feelings of despair affect how we interact with others. The attitudes Jesus pinpointed were social attitudes—feelings directed toward other persons. Hating someone in your heart is equivalent to murder; sexual lust is tantamount to adultery.

Inner feelings and emotions aren't sealed off from others. They emerge out of social experiences and direct themselves toward others. It's difficult to think of any so-called character traits outside of a social context. Someone stranded on a desert island might ponder the meaning of integrity, honesty, and meekness but would find it an empty and frustrating experience apart from other people. If Jesus had cared only about internal character, he could have spent all his time in the wilderness lecturing the stones on the virtues of inner harmony.

The fact that ideas and feelings have social origins and consequences doesn't negate the role of the Holy Spirit. God created us as social beings and his Spirit uses others to minister to our needs and to stir our caring for the needs of others. Beliefs and thoughts may be social products with social implications, but that doesn't mean our inner life is meaningless—just the opposite. To see its linkage with others around us is to understand just how important it is. Thoughts *do* influence behavior. Jesus stressed the need for genuine internal righteousness in contrast to hypocritical ritual. He also knew the inner life yields social fruit.

Kingdom social ethics, taught and lived by Jesus, *can* be transported over the bridge linking the first and twenty-first century. This book resists the notion that Jesus should return to his own time since "He does not provide a valid ethic for today."[17] By contrast, the following pages echo the concern of other scholars that Christian social ethics be tied to the kingdom of God.[18] The Gospels don't offer a full-blown system of formal ethics to cover every conceivable situation. I don't espouse a sentimentalist mentality of simply "walking in his footsteps." But the Gospels do provide us with episodes, stories, and pictures rife with insights applicable to our modern situation.[19] The pictures of the *good* and the *right* lodged in the kingdom stories aren't impossible possibilities or romanticized ideals. They intersect at ground level with the knotty problems of human existence today.

The kingdom vision outlined in the Gospels doesn't spell out a specific program for social ethics or political action. The New Testament vision does, however, clearly tell us what the kingdom is *not*. It also introduces us to basic principles of the right and the good that undergird the kingdom. The specific applications, of course, are the work of the church—over the centuries—as directed by the Holy Spirit.

The remarkable thing about our attempts to understand the kingdom is the way we dice it into categories. Our questions and categories fragment the kingdom into bits and pieces. Is it present or future? we ask. Personal or social? Abstract or concrete? Earthly or heavenly? Spiritual or political? Tied to the church or encompassing the world? A gift from God or enacted by us?

Our human propensity to pull the kingdom apart into logical, manageable categories shatters its integrity. The kingdom of God should instead shatter our puny human categories. It's not an either/or, a yes/no. It's all the above—both/and. It is indeed God's kingdom, not ours!

We want to understand it, examine it, and analyze it. But God enjoins us to enter it. God calls us to turn our backs on the kingdoms of this world and embrace an upside-down home. Underlying all Jesus' teaching about the kingdom is a call to respond.[20] He invites us not to study but to join; not to dissect but to enter. How will we respond?

Questions for Discussion

1. What do John the Baptist's and Mary's prophecies regarding the kingdom tell us about the nature of the kingdom?

2. In addition to the ladder and the ball game, what other images might help us to visualize and symbolize the upside-down kingdom?

3. What difference does it make to view the kingdom of God as an aggregate or a collectivity?

4. Which detours provide the easiest bypasses for avoiding biblical teaching?

5. What other detour signs prevent us from applying biblical ethics today?

6. Provide other examples of "spiritualizing" that weaken the concrete social meaning of the gospel.

2

MOUNTAIN POLITICS

The Three-Pronged Temptation

The synoptic writers report that, before Jesus launched his upside-down kingdom, three right-side-up kingdoms lured him. His temptation was a forty-day ordeal. The number "forty" represents trial and oppression in Hebrew history. The flood lasted forty days and nights and the Hebrews wandered in the wilderness for forty years. Moses was up on the mountain forty days and nights. Goliath taunted the Israelites for forty days.

Mark gives no information about Jesus' test, but Matthew and Luke (both in chapter 4) agree Jesus struggled with three alternative kingdoms. They were symbolized by the mountain, the temple, and the bread. These three distinct but interrelated options formed the legs of a stool. Upon it Jesus could have sat as a bona fide political Messiah.

The temptation episodes point to a right-side-up kingdom. They embody three social institutions of Jesus' day: political (mountain), religious (temple), and economic (bread).[1] Social institutions are established patterns of social behavior. They organize the life of a particular segment of society.

Economic institutions, for instance, are a web of social rules that govern financial activity by specifying rates of interest and the rights of creditors and debtors. Members of a social system take these "rules" of the economic game for granted. They make financial behavior predictable and orderly. Social patterns become deeply ingrained in the life of a society. As in the financial sector, a cluster of social norms also organizes educational, recreational, religious, and other social spheres.

The triad of temptations offered Jesus *real* social detours. The three-fold test promised to fulfill Jewish hopes for a Messiah who would defy political oppressors, feed the poor, and bask in miraculous approval from above. Luke says the devil departed from Jesus "until an opportune time." This suggests that these enticing shortcuts didn't evaporate after forty days in the wilderness. They continually plagued Jesus.

When Peter rebukes Jesus for talking about suffering, Jesus emphatically declares, "Get behind me, Satan!" (Mark 8:33). The use of violent force, apparently continued to lure Jesus. In the midst of a squabble over power, Jesus reminds the disciples they have continued with him in his *trials* (Luke 22:28). Throughout his ministry Jesus faced political alternatives which threatened to derail his upside-down mode of nonresistant suffering.

To grasp the nature of the upside-down kingdom, we must consider the right-side-up alternatives: mountain, temple, and bread. Only as we see what Jesus rejected can we know what he affirmed. This chapter and the next two grapple with the temptation story in the *political, religious,* and *economic* context of Jesus' time. The temptations enable us to review the social setting of Jesus' ministry. Each chapter deals with one of the tempter's offers. We'll begin with the political temptation, then turn to the religious and economic ones.

Jesus the Great

According to Matthew (4:8), the setting for the political temptation was a very high mountain. Luke reports that the kingdoms of the world, with "all this authority and their glory," were offered Jesus. This was Jesus' chance to be a new Alexander the Great, his opportunity to wield political power throughout the splendor and glory of the Mediterranean world. Once again Israel would be supreme, a light and a power to all nations. God's vengeance would roll across the empires of the Middle East. The pivot of world authority and influence would shift from Rome to Jerusalem. Caesar could no longer tax and insult Jews, for Caesar himself would serve Israel.

From that mountaintop Jesus pictured himself holding worldwide political power. Not only would he rule, his throne would sit upon the world's highest peak of power, and the crowds would chant their acclaim. This right-side-up way contrasted starkly with the humble servant role. Why was this enticing? Why should Jesus care about the Roman occupation?

A short historical detour is necessary to understand Jewish political hopes in Jesus' time.[2] The Old Testament ends with the Hebrews under Persian control. The Persians had allowed the Hebrews to return home in 538 BCE,[3] after fifty years in Babylonian captivity. A peaceful coexistence with the Persians permitted the rebuilding of the temple under Zerubbabel. The situation changed rapidly as a young Greek, Alexander the Great, jumped to fame. He conquered the Persians in 334 BCE. By 332 BCE all Palestine had fallen under his control as he rampaged into Egypt. He hoped to usher in a worldwide civilization unified by the Greek way of life (known as Hellenization).

For the first time Greek traders and the Greek language made themselves at home in Palestine. After a fever killed Alexander at the age of 32, his empire fell into the hands of his squabbling generals. Palestine turned into a buffer zone shuttled back and forth between his quarreling generals some five times in ten years. One of the generals, Ptolemy, governor of Egypt, along with his successors, finally gained control of Palestine for over 100 years. Ptolemy supposedly entered Jerusalem on a Sabbath day under the guise of offering a sacrifice, only to capture many Jews and export them to Egypt.[4]

The Madman

In 198 BCE Syria captured the Jewish kingdom from the Egyptians. By 175 BCE the Syrian king, Antiochus IV, came to power and created havoc for the Jews. Nicknamed "the madman," he called himself "the illustrious." He promptly set up policies to indoctrinate Jews into Greek life. Foreign Greek culture sprouted in Jerusalem. A gymnasium was constructed for athletic training. Young Jewish males became ashamed of their circumcision, openly revealed in nude athletic contests held in the gym. Many underwent operations to hide their circumcision. They also wore Greek clothing, particularly a fashionable broad-rimmed hat associated with the god Hermes.

The Jewish writer of 2 Maccabees 4:14 laments that Jewish priests had deserted their sacred responsibilities to watch sporting events—wrestling, discus throwing, horse racing. The Greek language became prominent in Jerusalem. The Hebrews resisted Hellenization, but they couldn't stop the vicious tactics of Antiochus IV.

Twice the Syrian madman plundered the Jewish treasury to support his war activity. He carried precious furnishings from the temple—the altar of incense, the seven-branched lampstand, and the table shewbread—off to Antioch in Syria. One scholar describes his policies:

> The walls of Jerusalem were torn down and a fortress was built on the hill of the ancient city of David. The Jews

were forbidden, on pain of death, to keep the Sabbath and to circumcise their children. The king's inspectors traveled throughout the country in order to supervise the fulfillment of these decrees. In Jerusalem a pagan altar was erected on the site of the altar of burnt offering, and sacrifices were offered there to the supreme god, the Olympian Zeus in 167 BCE.[5]

During the madman's reign, two successive Jewish high priests bribed him for their positions with large sums of money. To carry a copy of the Holy Scripture meant death. The erection of an altar to Zeus ended sacrifices to Yahweh. Ten days after the altar's completion a pig was sacrificed on it. This was a horror to Jewish ritual purity. The temple sanctuary was smeared with blood and soldiers committed the grossest indecencies in the sacred temple courts.

In addition, there was economic oppression. The madman's greed for taxes included the following:

taxes on the salt mined at the Dead Sea; taxes amounting to a third of the grain harvested, to a half of the all too scanty fruits; poll taxes, crown taxes, temple taxes, to say nothing of the sovereign right to seize cattle and stores in the name of military conscription—all this fomented unrest.[6]

If their culture, worship, and identity were to survive here in their homeland, Jews thought they would need to fight.

The Hammerers

Although the high priests and many of the people welcomed Greek culture, a small group of traditional Jews resented the foreign influence. This conservative element, the Hasideans (meaning pious), protested the Jewish embrace of Greek culture. But they didn't revolt against the policies of the madman.

Rebellion came in the countryside. An old priest named Mattathias and his five sons lived in a small village about twenty miles northwest of Jerusalem. When one of the king's inspectors entered the village to force Jews to offer pagan sacrifices, Mattathias refused. He killed the inspector. Calling all who were zealous for the law to follow, father and sons fled to caves in the Judean hillside. There pious Hasideans, who were finally willing to fight to rid the land of Syrians, joined them. From their wilderness base the Jewish rebels directed hit and run campaigns into villages to destroy pagan altars and harass apostate Jews.

On one occasion some rebels, out of respect for the Sabbath, refused to retaliate against Syrian troops. The rebels were attacked and massacred. Full-scale resistance and offensive attacks began. Mattathias soon died and his son Judas the Maccabean ("the Hammerer" in Hebrew) organized a successful military campaign and hammered the Syrians. Eventually the Maccabeans regained control of the temple in Jerusalem. In 164 BCE, three years after the temple had been defiled by swine's blood, it was re-dedicated. Still today Jews celebrate Hanukkah, a feast of dedication in memory of this event.

Although Jews regained supervision of the temple, Syrians retained control of the nearby fortress in Jerusalem. With the temple restored, the pious Hasideans stopped supporting the revolt; they had little interest in political freedom. This group eventually formed the cradle of the Pharisee movement.

Another emerging group, the Sadducees, insisted on political independence. They finally achieved their goal under Simon (one of Mattathias' five sons) in 142 BCE. He declared himself priest, military leader, and spokesperson for the people. This began an eighty-year period of political independence monitored by the so-called Hasmonean family. During this era the same person often ruled as king and high priest. Coins were minted, and the Jewish state conquered Moab, Samaria, and Edom.

Conflict between the Pharisees and Sadducees forced them to side with quarreling factions in the Hasmonean family. A military stalemate between the rival groups opened the door for the Romans in 63 BCE. Pompey, the Roman general, besieged Jerusalem for three months. Finally, on a Sabbath day, the Romans took the last stronghold, the temple. Over 12,000 Jews were massacred. Pompey intruded into the sacred holy of holies, opened only to the high priest once a year, and to his amazement found it empty. The Roman general's profane act insulted faithful Jews, who viewed it as God's judgment.

After nearly 100 years of political freedom, the Jewish state was once again under the thumb of a foreign power. For centuries it would be a tributary of the large Roman Empire. Thus in the 500 years of history before the birth of Jesus, the Jewish people were batted back and forth in a game of political Ping-Pong. They were tossed among the great powers of the Middle East: Babylon, Persia, Greece, Egypt, Syria, and finally Rome.

Rome dominated Palestinian politics after 63 BCE. Nearly a generation of turmoil followed Pompey's conquest as rival factions fought for control. In their sweeping conquest and in later repression of popular resistance, the Roman armies were brutal. In some cases they burned and destroyed entire villages. At times they crucified, butchered, or enslaved entire populations. But the fire of freedom, ignited by Judas the Hammerer, couldn't be extinguished. It flared again and again in the era of Jesus until Rome finally smothered it for good in 135 CE.

Great Herod

In 37 BCE Herod the Great came to power as a Roman puppet king. A symbol of oppressive tyranny, he ruled until his death in 4 BCE. He held a tight rein over the people by hiring foreign soldiers, building strategic fortresses, and orchestrating a network of secret informers. He was ruling when Jesus was born. This Herod approached the wise men and then killed the male children in Bethlehem because he was threatened by the prospect of a new king.

Under Herod the territory of Palestine almost doubled. Herod struck a delicate balance between Roman power and Jewish nationalism. He could keep his crown only as long as he pleased Rome. He didn't have to pay taxes to Rome but was required to send troops in time of war. He could maintain his own army as long as it didn't pose a threat to the empire. Above all he was to maintain peace and govern the territory efficiently.

The outstanding mark of Herod's 33-year reign was a lavish building program. Although he didn't force Greek culture on the Jews, Herod's architecture followed Roman patterns. He constructed temples, gymnasiums, cloisters, aqueducts, and amphitheaters on an enormous scale. He built several new cities, including Caesarea, with its artificial harbor on the Mediterranean coast. Fortresses and palaces sprang up throughout the countryside. Huge construction projects, including pagan temples, were also carried out in the Gentile lands of Sidon, Tyre, Nicopolis, Sparta, and Athens, to name just a few.

Because Herod likely had some Gentile ancestry, Jewish leaders never completely trusted him. To gain their confidence he began a renovation of the temple in Jerusalem in 20 BCE—the eighteenth year of his reign. The Jews feared he would tear down the existing temple built by Zerubbabel and never replace it. To prove his sincerity he provided a thousand wagons and hired ten thousand workmen. Moreover, he trained 1,000 priests as masons and carpenters, so unconsecrated feet wouldn't desecrate the holy shrine during the reconstruction. He doubled the size of the old temple area. The magnificent new

Time Line and Key Events

BCE	538	End of Babylonian captivity
	332	Alexander the Great
		Egyptian Control
Before		198 Syria
the	175	Antiochus IV "The Madman"
Common	164	Maccabees gain control
Era	63	Pompey, Roman General

BCE	37–04	Herod the Great
	05	Birth of Jesus
	04	Death of Herod the Great
	04	General uprising and revolt
	04	Division of Herod's Kingdom
		Herod Antipas
		Philip
		Archeleus

CE	0	
The	06	Archelcus deported
Common	06	Direct Roman Control (Procurator)
Era	06	Roman taxes
CE	25–28	Jesus' ministry
	26–30	Pontius Pilate
	66–70	General uprising and revolt
	70	Rome destroys the temple and Jerusalem
	132	Bar Kochba uprising
	135	Roman destruction of Jerusalem

structure was Herod's pride and glory. In operation during Jesus' life, it was later destroyed by the Romans in 70 CE—seven years after its completion.

Herod's insatiable ambition made him both ruthless and sympathetic to Jewish concerns. He had to maintain Jewish stability to receive Rome's continuing smile. Thus he dared not allow political rivals or Jewish nationalism to gain ground. Although he distributed free corn during a famine and reduced taxes during hard times, his building projects strapped the people with heavy taxes. Some of these revenues went to the new temple, which of course received Jewish approval. Other taxes—used to subsidize lavish pagan temples in faraway places—irritated Jewish leaders. Under Herod the Great the taxes "were ruthlessly exacted, and he was always thinking out fresh ways of subsidizing his vast expenditures."[7] There was bitter popular resentment because Herod squandered much of the common wealth, sucking the lifeblood of the people with his oppressive taxes.

Herod usually tolerated Jewish worship and ritual. But occasionally there were direct confrontations. Out of courtesy to Rome, Herod placed a golden eagle, the empire's royal symbol, over the great east gate of the city. This so enraged some forty pious Jews that in defiance they tore the eagle down. Herod then burned them all alive.

In his later years, the Pharisees refused to sign an oath of loyalty to him and the Roman emperor. They were harshly punished. Although the kingdom had grown, Herod wasn't popular. Resentment seethed throughout the land. Suspicion centered around his vicious treatment of his family. His several wives—ten in all—lived in his palace. Over the years he killed two of them, plus at least three sons, a brother-in-law, and other relatives. The Roman emperor reportedly remarked, "Better is it to be Herod's pig than son."[8]

Soon after Jesus' birth, Herod lay dying. To keep his seething people from celebrating his death, he ordered leading Jews imprisoned in the Jericho arena and executed upon his death. He wanted to ensure that Jewish tears would flow, even if not for him.[9] Fortunately the prisoners were freed immediately after his death. The demise of the brutal tyrant triggered a widespread popular uprising that swirled around Jesus' childhood.

The Roman Connection

Herod's kingdom was divided into three parts. His son, Herod Antipas, ruled the district of Galilee west of the lake, including Jesus' hometown of Nazareth. The two Herods are frequently confused. Herod the Great, described above, ruled at the time of Jesus' birth but died shortly after. Herod Antipas, his son, was a contemporary of Jesus. It was Herod Antipas who executed John the Baptist and whom Jesus called a fox (Luke 13:32). During his trial, Pilate sent Jesus to Herod Antipas, who happened to be in Jerusalem at the time. After ruling for 42 years, Herod Antipas was banished into exile by the Roman emperor.

Philip, a second son of Herod the Great, received the territory northeast of the lake of Galilee. He reigned peaceably over this political turf for 37 years but receives little notice in the Gospels.

Herod's third son Archelaus governed the third and southern portion of Herod's kingdom. Jerusalem was its center. Joseph, returning from Egypt with the baby Jesus, was afraid to go to Judea when he heard that Archelaus had succeeded his father. So Joseph settled in Nazareth, ruled by Herod Antipas (Matthew 2:22).

The three brothers—Herod Antipas, Philip, and Archelaus—had to meet the Roman emperor to confirm their father's will and legitimate their power. Archelaus was in trouble even before he left Jerusalem to receive the emperor's blessing. He removed the Jewish high priest and appointed a new one. Riots broke out during the Passover feast in Jerusalem. The crowds demanded lower taxes, called for the release of political prisoners and protested the removal of the high priest. Archelaus sent a cohort of troops to quell the protest. The mob rushed the soldiers and stoned most of them to death. Archelaus promptly killed three thousand rioters, sent the rest of the pilgrims home, and left for Rome.

Fervent Jewish patriots could take no more. Insurrection spread. Rebel leaders arose throughout the country. Beyond Jerusalem, in the outlying districts of Galilee, Judea and Perea erupted in bloody disorder.[10] One of Herod's former slaves, named Simon, led guerrilla attacks on the Herodian palaces and estates of the wealthy.

In Judea a former shepherd named Athronges and his four brothers led a resistance against Archelaus for a number of years.[11] In Galilee, a Judas, whose father Hezekiah had been killed by Herod the Great, became a flaming revolutionary. Judas led the revolt from the town of Sepphoris, an hour's walk northeast of Jesus' hometown, Nazareth. He plundered Herod's arsenal at Sepphoris. These rebel leaders in various sections of the country ruled as self-proclaimed "kings" for several weeks. Athronges, in Judea, ruled for several months.

But the power of imperial Rome would not be mocked. Rome would smash the stubborn Jewish peasant kings. Since Archelaus was still in Rome during the uprising, the Roman commander in Syria intervened from the north. He moved his armies south into Palestine. He burned Sepphoris to the ground and sold its population into slavery. Continuing south, the Roman commander killed two thousand rebels, leaving the people in the countryside stunned and sullen.

In Jerusalem, diehard Jewish patriots engaged in hand-to-hand combat with Roman soldiers commanded by

Sabinus. The rebels hurled missiles down on the soldiers from the top of the temple walls and tried to set fire to a fortress protecting the Romans. Some of the royal soldiers deserted to the rebels. In the end the Romans won. Soldiers set fire to parts of the temple and plundered its treasury.

Archelaus soon returned from Rome and regained control of the countryside. The fuse on the political-religious bomb in Palestine was smoldering. This revolutionary turmoil framed the context of Jesus' early childhood. It would explode again in 66–70 CE in a massive Jewish revolt—some 30 years after his death.

Little is known about the short reign of Archelaus (4 BCE–6 CE). He antagonized Jewish sensitivities, especially by marrying a woman divorced from her second husband. Jewish indignation and hatred was so strong both the Jews and the Samaritans sent a delegation to Rome to plead for the removal of Archelaus. Surprisingly, the Emperor Augustus agreed and sent him into exile in 6 CE, during the childhood of Jesus.

This changed the political organization of Judea for the worst. Instead of being ruled by a quasi-Jewish king, it now for the first time became a Roman province. A Roman procurator (sometimes called a prefect or governor) supervised Judea directly. A procurator such as Pilate was responsible to the Roman emperor. The Roman empire had two types of provinces:

(1) The more important and wealthy areas received a governor of senatorial rank called a *legate*. The Syrian legate, Quirinius, controlled Syria to the north of Palestine with a standing army of several legions, each having up to 6,000 foot soldiers.

(2) Minor provinces like Judea required fewer troops to keep order. They received a Roman governor called a *procurator*, from a lower social class than a legate.

The procurator was directly responsible to Caesar and

had full military, judicial, and financial authority. Judea had auxiliary troops recruited from the Gentile population. The Jews, however, were exempt from military service because they wouldn't fight on the Sabbath. The procurator had five cohorts of 600 men each under his command and maintained garrisons throughout the country. A cohort of 300–500 soldiers was permanently stationed in Jerusalem in Fort Antonia overlooking the temple area to prevent riots. The procurator, Pilate, lived in Caesarea on the Mediterranean coast. But during Jewish festivals he brought extra troops to Jerusalem to prevent bedlam among the thousands of pilgrims.

Dagger Men

The first Roman procurator was sent to Judea in 6 CE to replace Archelaus some nine years after the widespread revolt. Along with direct Roman control came Roman taxes, of course. Thus the Roman commander Quirinius went to Jerusalem to take a census of the population for tax purposes. Passionate Jewish nationalists who wanted a free homeland strongly resisted Roman taxes. The switch from the puppet King Archelaus to direct Roman rule inflamed an already tense situation. Zealous Jewish patriots obstructed the census. They argued that the land belonged to God. Hence all taxes belonged also to him. Land taxes and head taxes were, in their eyes, new forms of bondage and idolatry.

The Zealots, named for their zealous love of Jewish law, longed for freedom from oppression and the establishment of an independent Jewish state. The Roman census of 6 CE enraged them.[12] Only God was king, they said, declaring it blasphemous to call the emperor "king" and "lord." In their mind, this violated the first commandment prohibiting the worship of other gods. Some thought paying taxes to the emperor was sheer idolatry. Super zealots wouldn't even touch a coin minted with the emperor's image. As one scholar notes, "Of all the peoples within the Roman empire, none so persistently and steadfastly resisted, both politically and spiritually, the Roman occupation rule as did the Jews."[13]

Jewish resistance against Rome erupted in many ways in the first 60 years of the new century. In addition to the religious zealots, roving bandits lived in caves in the countryside. At least seven popular prophets or messianic pretenders of one sort or another led popular movements. They hoped that God, in miraculous ways, would eradicate the Romans and establish divine rule as in bygone days.

There were also political rebels such as Barabbas, released at Jesus' trial. In several cases, Jewish intellectual leaders led nonviolent protests to resist the profane treatment of sacred objects and places. During Jewish festivals unruly crowds and mobs protested Roman rule. The resistance movement pulsated among common folk everywhere. In contrast, the upper crust of Jewish leaders, living in Jerusalem, often collaborated silently with the Romans.

The momentum of the resistance turned more violent in the years after Jesus' death. In the 50's and 60's CE, dagger men (Sicarii) appeared. Their cutthroat tactics involved selective assassinations and kidnapping. Their targets: high priests and other top Jewish leaders in cahoots with the Romans. An organized Zealot faction emerged in 67–68 CE and plunged into armed combat in Jerusalem. Several other political revolutionary factions, ready to slit Roman and Jewish throats, rose to the fore in the 60's. Together these rebel groups led the massive Jewish revolt of 66–70 CE.

Much of the resistance in the 60 years preceding the revolt targeted the Romans. But growing internal squabbles among rival Jewish factions also fueled the unrest. In any event, two scholars conclude that the whole period of direct Roman rule (6–66 CE) "was marked by widespread discontent and periodic disturbance in Palestinian Jewish society."[14]

Thus as Jesus began his ministry about 25 CE, Palestine was a churning caldron of revolution. Philip, Herod the Great's son, ruled the northeast region as a quasi-Jewish king. Herod Antipas, another son, ruled the Galilee area in similar fashion. A Roman procurator directed the Judean affairs in the southern region from his office on the seacoast port of Caesarea.

Pontius Pilate

Pontius Pilate was appointed the fifth Roman procurator of Judea in 26 CE. Compared with Jewish leaders, Pilate appears neutral toward Jesus in the account of Jesus' trial. But there is another side to Pilate. Brutal excess and ruthless rule characterized his administration and offended Jewish sensibilities.

Shortly after he arrived, Pilate ordered troops to go from Caesarea to Jerusalem. They entered the city under cover of night and posted banners bearing the picture of the Emperor Tiberius. This violated Jewish law, which forbade an image in the holy city. In the morning, the idolatrous banners were discovered. Incensed Jews flocked to Caesarea demanding that the scandalous images be removed. On the sixth day of the demonstration Pilate herded the mob into a race track, surrounded them with soldiers, and threatened to kill them. When he realized the mob would rather die than violate their law, he ordered the offending banners withdrawn.

On another occasion in Jerusalem, Pilate dedicated some shields containing the inscription of the Emperor Tiberius. Jewish leaders who wanted Jerusalem consecrated exclusively to the worship of Yahweh were of course insulted. The Jews protested to the Roman emperor, who instructed Pilate to move the shields to the temple of Au-

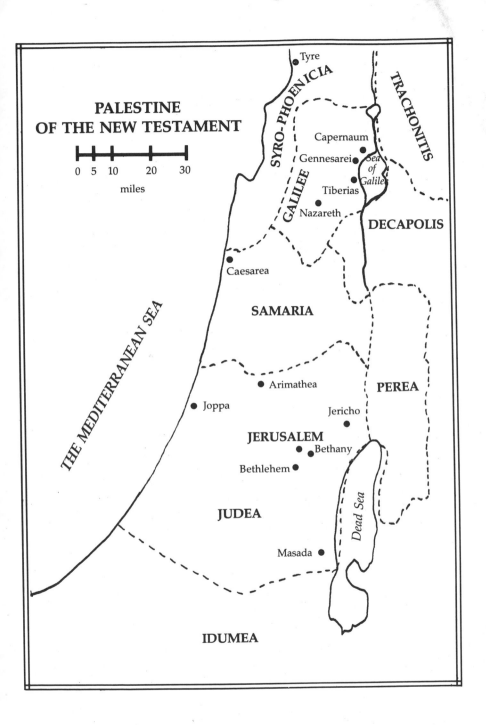

PALESTINE
OF THE NEW TESTAMENT

0 5 10   20   30
miles

Tyre

SYRO-PHOENICIA

TRACHONITIS

GALILEE

Capernaum

Gennesarei

Sea
of
Galilee

Tiberias

Nazareth

DECAPOLIS

Caesarea

SAMARIA

THE MEDITERRANEAN SEA

PEREA

Arimathea

Joppa

Jericho

JERUSALEM

Bethany

Bethlehem

JUDEA

Dead Sea

Masada

IDUMEA

gustus in Caesarea. In these ways Pilate aggravated the Jewish temper.

Even his one positive contribution yielded trouble. Pilate began constructing an aqueduct to bring water to Jerusalem from 25 miles away. The water system benefited the temple, which needed huge quantities of water to purify the sacrifice of large animals. Pilate thought the temple treasury should help to pay the bill. Temple authorities protested this secular use of money dedicated to God. Pilate insisted. Crowds of angry Jews gathered to protest the sacrilege. Pilate's troops dispelled them and killed many.

Pilate's career ended in 36 CE, after his troops attacked a group of Samaritans assembled on their holy mountain (Mt. Gerizim). The faithful had gathered to follow a self-acclaimed Samaritan messiah. After the Samaritan incident Pilate was recalled to Rome and lost his procuratorship. Philo of Alexandria described the conduct of Pilate's office as marked by "corruption, violence, degradations, ill treatment, offenses, numerous illegal executions and incessant, unbearable cruelty."[15]

Suicide at Masada

Roman and Jewish relations continued to deteriorate from 36 to 66 CE. Jewish freedom fighters living in caves frequently attacked Romans and pro-Roman Jewish aristocrats.

The crisis came to a head in 66 CE when the Roman procurator, Florus, stole seventeen talents from the temple treasury. Indignant Jews walked around Jerusalem begging for money for "poor Florus." Enraged, Florus sent his soldiers to plunder the city. The temple priest refused to make the daily animal sacrifice on behalf of the Roman emperor's welfare. Insurgent Jews occupied the temple area, challenging Florus to retreat to Caesarea. Meanwhile Zealots under the leadership of Menahem, son of Judas of Galilee, captured the Roman fort at Masada. The fort sat on the top of a well-protected peak near the Dead Sea.

Bitter clashes between Jewish freedom fighters and Roman soldiers broke out in Jerusalem. The violent conflict also pitted the Jewish aristocracy against the freedom fighters. By the end of the summer of 66 CE, Jewish revolutionaries had driven all the Roman soldiers out of the country. It took Rome a year to reconquer Galilee and three more years to retake Jerusalem.

Zealots from Masada and Galilee converged on Jerusalem for a final stand against the brutal Roman forces. After the Roman forces recaptured Galilee they moved south to Jerusalem. Systematically destroying villages, they either slaughtered or enslaved the people in their path. During the Passover season of 70 CE the Roman general Titus, with an army of 24,000 men, launched an all-out attack on Jerusalem. The brutal Roman power crushed the freedom fighters.

Before fire destroyed the temple, Titus grabbed the seven–branched candlestick and the table of shewbread as trophies for his triumphant return to Rome. The Holy Temple lay in smoldering ruins. A few rebels entrenched themselves in the Masada fortress until 73 CE. When the Romans finally gained access to the top of the summit, only several women and children were alive. The zealous patriots preferred suicide to defeat!

The Jewish historian Josephus mentions at least five Jewish military messiahs who led insurrections against the Roman occupation from 40 BCE to 73 CE. Luke reports that Barabbas, released in exchange for Jesus, was in prison for starting an insurrection in the city (Luke 23:19). The Masada defeat didn't extinguish the flame of Jewish nationalism. In 132 CE, in response to a Roman edict forbidding circumcision, it burst forth again under the leadership of Bar Kochba. With a force of 200,000 men he set up an independent Jewish state which lasted three years. The Romans lost 5,000-6,000 soldiers before finally cutting Bar Kochba down.

In the end, the Romans smashed 1,000 villages, executed 500,000 people, destroyed Jerusalem, and sent thousands away as slaves. The destruction of Jerusalem in 135 CE altered the later course of both Jewish and Christian history.

The Low Mountain

Although the Jews could perform their prescribed sacrifices during the Roman occupation, there were underlying irritants. Since Herod the Great's era, the political rulers hired and fired the high priests. Thus even the high priest was ultimately a Roman puppet. Furthermore, the eight-piece uniform the high priest wore to symbolize the essence of Jewish faith was guarded by Roman soldiers in the Fortress Antonia to prevent possible uprisings. They gave it to the high priest only on festival days. Finally, a daily sacrifice was offered in the temple to Yahweh on behalf of the Roman emperor.

This turbulent political context frames Jesus' face-off with the devil on the high mountain. A revolutionary climate fills the valleys below. The Palestine of Jesus' childhood was not serene; it was a caldron of revolutionary fervor. Only against this backdrop can we grasp the reality of his political temptation. The possibility of a political kingship was not an idle offer. It was the fervent goal of many of the messianic prophets with whom Jesus surely was familiar.

The temptation Jesus rejected was not merely an invitation to join the ranks of Jewish patriots. It was not only a temptation to unshackle Roman control. It was also a lure to endorse violence—the accepted mode of governing.

On the high mountain Jesus rejected brute force as the proper mode for governing others. The rules of political power sanctioned force, violence, and bloodshed. Jesus rejected this right-side-up institution of coercive political power. He chose, rather, to demonstrate a new power, a new way of ruling. He refused to play the game by the old rules, for his was an upside-down kingdom. But in the end his way so threatened the old kingdoms that he was crucified as "King of the Jews."

The mountain scene in the temptation symbolizes divine power.[16] It was on the mountain that God met his people through Moses (Exodus 24). Preaching on a mountain, Jesus characterizes his new power as merciful, meek, pure in heart, and peaceful (Matthew 5). The disciples received their call on the mountain (Luke 6:12-13).

After feeding the five thousand Jesus returned to the mountain for prayer and rejuvenation (Mark 6:46). The divine confirmation "this is my beloved Son" came from a cloud at the top of a high mountain (Mark 9:2, 7). From the Mount of Olives Jesus began his kingly descent into Jerusalem on a donkey (Matthew 21:1). He was arrested a few day later on the same Mount of Olives because he didn't resist capture (Luke 22:39). After the resurrection the disciples met him on a mountain in Galilee (Matthew 28:16). And on the Mount called Olivet the risen Jesus told his followers: "You shall receive power when the Holy Spirit has come upon you" (Acts 1:8, 12).

The mountain symbolizes the strength of divine power and the nearness of God. Jesus redefined the meaning of power when he refused to use force. It's hard to toss the lure of force aside. Matthew and Mark report three occasions when Jesus spoke of suffering as the new form of messianic power. Each time the disciples argued over how much power and authority they would have in the kingdom. In all three cases, Jesus responded by teaching them about suffering discipleship.

He made one thing clear: the heroes of the upside-down kingdom are not warrior kings riding in chariots or

peasant kings carrying pitchforks. The heroes of this kingdom are children and servants. These lowly ones carry
the flag of the servant regime. They operate not by the
power of might and force but by the sustaining power of
the Holy Spirit flowing from the mountain of God.

Did Jesus Use a Dagger?

Was Jesus a violent revolutionary?[17] Some argue he
was. He supposedly espoused the bloody tactics of the
dagger men. Proponents of this position argue that the
Gospels, written some forty years after Jesus' death, deliberately camouflaged his violent streak so early Christians wouldn't threaten Roman authorities.[18] In other
words, Gospel writers masked Jesus' violence with images
of a peace-loving shepherd.

Several reasons are given for placing Jesus with the
zealous rebels.[19] He instructed the disciples to sell their
clothing and buy swords at the Last Supper (Luke 22:36).
With a whip he drove the money changers and their
sheep and oxen out of the temple (John 2:15). The Romans, considering him a political seditionist and agitator,
crucified him as "king of the Jews"(Luke 23:38).
Barabbas, a known rebel, had led a political insurrection.
But considered less dangerous than Jesus, Barabbas was
released, whereas Jesus was killed (Luke 23:25).

Jesus himself said he came to bring not peace but a
sword (Matthew 10:34). Like other zealous prophets, Jesus did proclaim a kingdom. He criticized kings who
ruled over people (Mark 10:42). He even called Herod a
fox (Luke 13:32). At least one of his followers, Simon,
was called "the Zealot" (Luke 6:15). Some use these facets of Jesus' ministry to align him with violent revolutionaries.

In the Gospel accounts we find that Jesus was indeed a
revolutionary—of sorts. He did defy the ruling religious,
political, and economic powers. His statement that the

law of love supersedes the dictates of human institutions made him a revolutionary. But he hardly was a violent one.

Without refuting the charge that Jesus was a zealous rebel point by point,[20] let me note several bits of evidence which suggest Jesus wasn't among the violent rebels of his day. Zealous rebels thought humans should help God usher in the kingdom. In contrast, Jesus told his followers, "Fear not, little flock, for it is your Father's good pleasure to give you the kingdom" (Luke 12:32). Although Jesus leveled a strong social criticism against the rich, he always did so in the context of Mammon's threat to supplant God. His teaching on wealth would have also threatened Roman interests and would likely have been erased by Gospel writers had they merely been trying to appease Roman officials. Pilate may have thought Jesus was a political revolutionary; that doesn't mean he acted in violent ways.

Purging the temple of money changers wasn't a mandate for violence. Jesus was certainly dramatic and forceful. Had a major riot erupted, the 600 Roman soldiers on alert in Fort Antonia overlooking the temple would have quickly intervened. The temple purge was a prophetic condemnation of the profiteering money changers and a sign that the temple should be opened for Gentile worship. The prophetic Word—not action—stood at the center of the temple purge.

Jesus severely rebuked the ear-cutting resistance of his disciple when he was "captured" in Gethsemane. If the disciples had been heavily armed, a major clash would have likely developed. Had the disciples been deemed a violent threat, they would certainly have been captured and crucified, not allowed to flee into the darkness.

Perhaps the most convincing evidence that Jesus wasn't in the violent revolutionary camp was his warm embrace of tax collectors and publicans. Zealous rebels hated tax collectors, those traitors who pressed fellow Jews under Roman oppression. The rebels were willing to kill Jewish tax collectors. Instead, Jesus embraced them. He even invited them to join his disciple band. Jesus taught that the radical call of kingdom membership weakened the tug of other human loyalties. The message of joyous detachment from the pressures of human institutions stood in sharp contrast to the coercive and sometimes violent tactics of the zealous subversives.

The final evidence that Jesus' way transcended violence lies in his teaching and life. As we've already seen, he rejected the political temptation on the mountain. He instructs us to love enemies, do good to haters, bless cursers, forgive up to 490 times. He calls us to serve, not rule. He shows the way of love in parables where enemies help enemies. The paramount lesson is his own example on the cross. Though violated he refused retaliation. With nails searing his flesh he refused to curse. He asked, instead, forgiveness for those who "know not what they do."

Jesus was a revolutionary in violating Sabbath laws, criticizing the greedy, eating with sinners, and provoking the Pharisees. His message of the kingdom threatened the power of vested interest groups. The Romans considered him a threat to their false political tranquillity. The right-wing Sadducees hated his condemnation of their lucrative temple operation. Progressive Pharisees decried his disrespect for their laws. And the freedom fighters couldn't stand his talk about suffering. The temptation to use violence was difficult to shove aside. But to endorse violence would have negated his platform of suffering love.

Jesus was revolutionary when he attacked the root of the problem—the evil which often laces human intentions and institutions. He called for repentance. He pleaded for love. He announced that only God should be worshiped. He admitted before Pilate that indeed he was Lord of this new kingdom. But his upside-down revolution replaced force with suffering and violence with assertive love.

Jesus did threaten the status quo. He rocked the cozy boats of Sadducees, Romans, Pharisees, and rebels alike. In some ways he looked like the social insurrectionists of his day. But his revolution was upside down. It touted acts of compassion, not daggers. Love was the new Torah, the absolute norm of his upside-down kingdom.

Questions for Discussion

1. In what ways were the temptations of Jesus "real" temptations?

2. Did Jesus have the freedom to truly accept or reject these temptations?

3. What was the most significant aspect of the political history of Palestine before Jesus' time?

4. What modern situations resemble the revolutionary situation in Palestine at the time of Jesus?

5. What nationalistic movements today are comparable to the zealous rebels?

6. Why were the disciples so slow to understand Jesus' rejection of the use of force?

7. What does it mean to say that Jesus was a revolutionary? In what ways was he? In what ways not?

8. What sort of political temptations do we face today?

3

TEMPLE PIETY

A Heavenly Parachute

Ruling the world by force wasn't the only enticement Jesus faced. There was religion itself to contend with. The devil's next trick invited Jesus to embrace institutionalized religion. There were many righteous Jews in the first century. Some aspects, however, of institutionalized religion had become stale. Rituals were often empty and self-serving. A complex religious code—interlaced with do's and don'ts, pilgrimages, and sacrifices—encompassed much of Jewish life, from civil law to national festivals.

Religious fervor ran deep and strong. Jesus' upside-down way would clash with the religious heavyweights who guarded the sacred rites of Hebrew ritual in God's name. The authorities would rage as Jesus demolished their cherished assumptions and practices. Their teeth would grind at the blasphemous suggestion that God was in their midst, upsetting tables in the holy temple—the very apex of their entire religious system.

A miraculous appearance, a sudden bolt from heaven, would certainly convince even the most skeptical Sadducee of Jesus' divine authority. And so the devil offered Jesus an attractive option: why not ask God to miraculously certify his mission? This would eliminate all harassment by the religious leaders. A miraculous, divine blessing near the sacred temple would erase any doubts about Jesus' messianic authority. The masses would quickly follow if the scribes and wise men embraced the newcomer. Parachuting into the temple court would make Jesus an instant messiah.

And so the devil taunted, "Come on, Jesus, go for it. Bypass the anger of the Pharisees. Forget the poverty and disease. Don't stir up the anger of the rich. Why worry about a cross? Go for it Jesus. Just parachute in."

Thirty Acres of Piety

What lay beneath the temple temptation? The temple was the pinnacle of religious life, the very heart of Jewish worship, ritual, belief, and emotion. The temple at Jerusalem stirred passions. It was shrouded in mystery and awe. It was the seat of wisdom, law, and Scripture. It housed the *one* Jewish altar on which the high priest performed the sacrificial rites of atonement *once* a year for the entire Jewish world. In *one*, and only *one* holy of holies, the high priest entered the presence of God. The holy of holies was the literal home of God. Jerusalem was the "city of the temple." The arteries of Jewish religion pulsated with the heartthrob of the temple. It was the obvious place for the cunning devil to test Jesus.

Moderns may visualize the temple as a contemporary church building. A modest shopping mall is a better comparison. Magnificent marble colonnades and towering walls ranging from 100 to 300 feet in height covered the thirty acre temple area. Some of the large stones in the walls weighed more than 70 tons. The temple itself was about 100 feet long, 35 feet wide, and 60 feet high. Gold and silver covered much of the structure, including the roof and furnishings.

The temple wasn't used for public worship. It was rather the "house of God." Worship, sacrifice, and ritual took place in the large open courts surrounding the temple. From the distant countryside it appeared as a snowcapped peak on the holy mountain. There was so much gold in the temple that after its destruction and plunder in 70 CE, the province of Syria was glutted with gold, halving its value.[1]

A Hebrew proverb exclaimed, "He who has not seen the holy place in its detailed construction has never seen a splendid building in his life."[2] Even the disciples of Jesus were impressed. They remarked with awe, "Look, Teacher, what wonderful stones and what wonderful buildings!" (Mark 13:1). About 18,000 workmen lost their jobs when the temple reconstruction was finally completed in 62 CE.

Roughly 18,000 *priests* and *Levites*, divided into twenty-four groups called "courses," were involved in the temple operation.[3] These lay priests and Levites lived in the countryside of Galilee and Judea and came to the temple for week-long tours of duty twice a year. They also came during three annual festivals attended by Jewish pilgrims from many countries. When the temple veil was purified, 300 priests were needed to dip it in a tank of water. Two hundred Levites were required each evening just to close the temple doors. Dozens of money changers sold pilgrims "pure" money for tithes and livestock hucksters peddled animals for sacrifice.

An elite group of chief priests administered the whole operation. The temple treasury functioned as a huge national bank. It held the tithes and offerings required of Jews throughout the world and owned much property. The temple was an elaborate operation that generated the major source of revenue for the city of Jerusalem.

Devout Jews living beyond Palestine came to the temple three times a year to celebrate religious festivities. In springtime the Feast of the Passover celebrated the deliverance from Egypt. About fifty days later the Feast of Pentecost offered thanks for the first fruits of the harvest. In the fall the Feast of Tabernacles included a solemn march around the altar in gratitude to God for the completed harvest. In addition to the pilgrim feasts, the great Day of Atonement was celebrated in autumn. The high priest sacrificed a goat for his own sins and sent another one into the desert for the sins of the people.[4] During these pilgrim festivals, Jerusalem's normal population of about 25,000 swelled upwards to 180,000 people.[5]

The temple stood as a monumental reminder that God's elect people had direct access to him through their sacrificial ritual. Each morning and each afternoon, day after day, the "continual" burnt offering of an unblemished lamb was sacrificed on behalf of the community. An offering of incense mixed with spices burned daily. Devout Jews also offered private sacrifices. The priests had various duties. They removed ashes from the altar, prepared firewood, killed the lamb, sprinkled blood on the altar, cleaned the lampstand, and prepared the meal and drink offering.[6]

The temple was the centerpiece of Jewish faith. It symbolized God's living presence on earth. Folks came to the temple to pray, believing that from this site their prayers went directly to the ear of God. Here both Nazarite and Gentile convert offered sacrifices. Here was brought the wife suspected of adultery. Here the first fruits were offered. Here mothers presented purification offerings at the birth of each child. From all over the Mediterranean world flowed Jewish temple taxes. Three times a year the people themselves flooded here for festivities.[7] This was home to the 70-member Sanhedrin, the final Jewish authority in religious, political, and civil matters. Here resided the high priest. In all these ways the temple throbbed with the worldwide heartbeat of Jewish faith.

Sanitized Ritual

The high priest, priest of all priests, was the symbolic head of both priesthood and nation. He wore a splendid eight-part outfit, each piece thought to have power to atone for specific sins. The high priest was the only person allowed to enter the holy of holies once a year on the Day of Atonement. He officiated at sacrifices on the Sabbath and during pilgrim festivals. Even his death had atoning power. Slayers who fled to a city of refuge after accidentally killing someone could return home upon the high priest's death.

The high priest was subject to strict laws of ceremonial purity. He couldn't touch a corpse nor enter a house of mourning. "Arab spittle" once contaminated a high priest on the evening before the Day of Atonement. Thereafter, high priests were required to undergo a secluded, seven-day purification before officiating at the Day of Atonement. No one was to see the high priest naked or when shaving or taking a bath. His pedigree had to be immaculate. It required direct ties to the family of Aaron. Strict marital rules permitted him to marry only a twelve-year-old virgin, the daughter of a priest, Levite, or Israelite of pure descent. Many priests married the daughters of priests.

The high priest's role wasn't merely pompous and ceremonial. He wielded considerable power as president of the 70-member Sanhedrin. This august council had complete judicial and administrative authority in religious and civil matters. Its judgment on religious issues was respected far beyond the borders of Judea. It was a self-perpetuating body composed of chief priests, scribes (usually from the Pharisee party), and nobility. Although lower courts met in various districts of Judea, the Sanhedrin was the supreme Jewish authority. The power of the high priest grew considerably under the Roman procurators. He became the key Jewish spokesperson, not only for ceremonial matters, but also for political negotiations with the Romans. Sixteen of the eighteen high priests between 6 CE and 67 CE came from five prominent and wealthy Jerusalem families.[8]

An extensive pecking order of religious officials stretched below the high priest and the Sanhedrin. The captain of the temple was responsible to conduct worship and manage the temple staff. He ranked next to the high priest since he often helped the priest perform solemn duties. On the next rung were twenty-four priests who directed twenty-four groups of some 7,200 ordinary priests. They lived throughout the countryside and participated in temple ritual at least five times a year. Next were 156 priests who served as daily managers of the priests assigned to temple duty for that particular day.

The temple's administrative affairs were the responsibility of seven permanent overseers. Next in line came three treasurers who managed the temple treasury by collecting taxes, purchasing sacrificial materials, and supervising the sale of animals to pilgrims. They also maintained the ninety-three gold and silver vessels used for daily rituals and managed the land and property owned by the temple. Next in rank were the approximately 7,200 ordinary priests. Zechariah, John the Baptist's father (Luke 1:5), was one of these. They lived in the countryside and trekked to the temple five times a year to perform their sacred duties.

At the bottom of the ladder stood almost 10,000 Levites. Living in surrounding villages, they were responsible for temple work when their weekly shift was on duty. The Levites were inferior to the priests. Singers and musicians formed the upper level of the Levite crust. The rest did the temple's dirty work—gatekeeping, security watching, and sweeping the open parts of the temple area.[9]

Laying Down the Law

Jewish piety and passion were rooted in temple, Torah, and land. At the heart of temple activities and at the core of Jewish religion was the Torah.[10] Usually known as the "law," it's more accurately translated "doctrine" or "religious teaching." Technically it referred to the five books of Moses—the Pentateuch. Gradually, however, students of the Torah composed oral interpretations, a commentary on the Torah. This oral "fence around the Torah" translated the Torah into practical guidelines for daily living. So in a general sense the Torah was not only the five books of Moses but also the elaborate oral commentary which grew up around it.

The Torah, Jews believed, contained God's absolute and unquestionable will. To obey God was to obey it. A cult of worship developed around the Torah, personifying it as the "well beloved daughter of God." It was said that Yahweh devoted leisure hours to the study of the Torah, even reading it aloud on the Sabbath. Jews saw it as the absolute standard for all aspects of religious life. It was *the* source of God's truth.

Continual reading and discussion of the Torah was the prime sacred activity. In the oral commentary that encrusted the Torah, pious Jews could discover whether it was lawful to eat an egg laid on the Sabbath. They could learn if water, poured from a clean bucket into an unclean one, contaminated the clean one from which it had been poured. The Torah guided sacrifice in the Jerusalem temple and worship in village synagogues.

As we've seen, *priests* and *Levites* provided the expertise and labor to operate the temple. By contrast, the *scribes* explained the Torah's secrets.[11] There were likely a variety of clerical or, as we might put it today, "secretarial" roles the scribes played—copying documents, writing letters and agreements, recording taxes, and drawing up legal papers. The better educated and upper level scribes unraveled the complex traditions surrounding the Torah. Carefully trained, scribes were also known as "doctors of the law." They were reverently called "rabbi," "teacher," "master," and "father." The scribes wore a special robe, a long mantle reaching to their feet, etched with a fringe. Scribal status caused people to rise respectfully when these men of wisdom passed by. The highest seats of honor in the synagogue were reserved for them.

In their early teens young men would embark on a scribal career by taking a regular course of study for several years. The young student would apprentice with an older rabbi for several years until he had mastered the fine points of the Torah and its commentary. At about 40 years of age, the student was ordained as a full-fledged scribe with all the rights of a wise scholar. After ordination he could make decisions on religious legislation and ceremonial purity, as well as on criminal and civil proceedings. Only ordained scholars could transmit and create the traditions of the Torah.

Except for high priests and those from noble families, scribes were the only persons who could sit on the powerful Sanhedrin. Young Jews from around the world streamed to Jerusalem at the time of Jesus to study with esteemed scribes. Jerusalem was the intellectual and theological center of Judaism. The scribes, in short, "were venerated, like the prophets of old, with unbounded respect and reverential awe as bearers and teachers of sacred esoteric knowledge; their words had sovereign authority."[12]

Party Politics

In our exploration of Jewish religion we've scanned the formal roles of priest, Levite, and scribe. We've looked briefly at the temple, Sanhedrin, and synagogue. In addition to these roles and organizations, there were two religious political parties—the *Sadducees* and the *Pharisees*.

These parties developed in the second century BCE because of religious and social differences.

The watershed dividing them was their understanding of the Torah. The Sadducees considered the written Torah, the five books of Moses, their authority. They rejected the Pharisees' oral commentary on the Torah,[13] the tradition of the elders (Mark 7:3). The Sadducees also denied the resurrection, personal immortality, and the future life. Moreover, they were skeptical of demons and angels. In short, the Sadducees represented the conservative element of Judaism. They were the defenders of the *true* faith of Israel handed down by Moses.

The Sadducees lived primarily in Jerusalem. They were drawn from the governing class and the wealthy aristocracy. Some of the chief priests were members of the Sadducean party. They were closely involved with temple operations and dominated the Sanhedrin. In short, the Sadducees steered the religious and social affairs of the wealthy Jerusalem upper class. The Sadducees supported both the political and religious status quo in Jerusalem. They welcomed Roman political control as long as sacrifices to Yahweh could be made on the temple altar and they could retain their privileged status.

In contrast, the Pharisaic party represented the progressive wing of Judaism.[14] They were neither radical freedom fighters nor *Essenes* who withdrew to the desert. As progressives in the pursuit of holiness, they applied the Torah to practical, everyday issues. The Pharisees, or "separated ones," had developed the oral tradition which applied the teachings of the Torah to almost any situation a Jew might face. The Torah spelled out rules of purity for officiating priests. The Pharisees extended these rules, these habits of holiness, to the everyday life of the common people. By encouraging average people to be pure, pious, and holy, they hoped to mold all Israel into a holy priesthood—a kingdom of priests, a holy nation.

The Pharisees are often confused with the scribes. Many scribes joined the Pharisee party while other scribes affiliated with chief priests and Sadducees. Other Pharisees, however, came from an assortment of pious common folk. The Pharisees operated in the rural countryside, as well as in Jerusalem, promoting their doctrine in local synagogues. As champions of holiness for the common people, they stood in opposition to the rich Sadducean elite.

Although they enjoyed widespread support, the Pharisees numbered only about 6,000. This was due, most likely, to their strictness. Prospective members had a probationary year to prove their compliance with the meticulous laws of purity. The Pharisees did buck the ruling establishment in Jerusalem. But they also disdained common people who were careless about ceremonial purity and tithing. Strict legalists they were, yes, but also receptive to new applications of doctrine, ever seeking to apply the Torah to new situations.

Messianic Wishes

At the birth of Jesus, messianic hopes were alive in the Jewish community. Hopes for a messiah who would usher in a peaceable kingdom of God had intensified in the century before Jesus. There were many stripes of hope. But the deepest yearning was for a new ruler anointed by God. He would reestablish the Davidic throne in all its former glory. The Psalms of Solomon, written the century before Jesus, picture the Messiah as overthrowing the rude Gentiles who intrude in God's holy place. He'll expel those corrupt priests who pervert worship of Yahweh. He'll reassemble the scattered tribes in the Promised Land. He'll bring blessed days. Under him Jerusalem, the holy city of God's presence, will reign supreme—"a place to be seen in all the earth."[15] In Luke 1:32-33 the angel Gabriel offers Mary a fresh vision of the messianic reign.

> He will be great, and will be called the Son of the Most
>   High;
> and the Lord God will give to him the *throne* of his father
>   David,
> and he will *reign* over the house of Jacob for ever;
> and of his *kingdom* there will be no end.

A similar refrain comes from the mouth of Zechariah, the father of John the Baptist, recorded in Luke 1:68-72.

> Blessed be the Lord God of Israel,
> for he has visited and redeemed his people,
> and has raised up a horn of salvation for us
> in the house of his servant David,
> as he spoke by the mouth of his holy prophets from of
>   old,
> that we should be saved from our enemies,
> and from the hand of all who hate us;
> to perform the mercy promised to our fathers.

It was uncertain how the Messiah would appear. Some thought he would come from the skies, riding a cloud. Others expected him to be human-born, but suddenly revealed in a decisive disclosure. Jerusalem, home of the sacred temple, was the site where such messianic texts were carefully studied and debated.

The temptation account doesn't specify exactly where the devil wanted Jesus to jump. Over the edge of the temple wall, falling hundreds of feet into the Kidron Valley below? Or was he perhaps to plummet into the courtyard at the temple's entrance? Regardless of the mode of divine parachuting, the temptation was to certify, beyond all reasonable doubt, the Messiah's miraculous arrival. It was to take place at the center of Jewish religious life where things were done properly, in exact compliance with the law. The scribes, the Sanhedrin, the high priests—all the religious heavyweights—would be sacred witnesses. They would accredit the Messiah's arrival.

Such miraculous certification would end bitter confrontations with the religious establishment. All opponents would fall silent. The Jerusalem aristocracy would welcome the new miracle worker. Jesus could avoid wandering among poor peasants in Galilee. There could be no doubt—no question about it. Jesus the Messiah had arrived!

Upside-Down Messiah

The thought of basking in the religious establishments' doting approval must have tantalized Jesus. But he turned away. He rejected right-side-up religion. The temptation nagged him, nevertheless, right up to the crucifixion. As the guards arrested him in Gethsemane, he reminded the ear-cutting disciple that he could call a cloud of angels to defend him. But he didn't. Instead of succumbing to institutionalized religion, Jesus uprooted its very foundations. His parables wreaked harsh judgment on Jewish leaders. He willfully violated sacred Sabbath laws. "Blasphemer!" cried the religious leaders when he chased merchants from the temple and called the holy shrine a den of robbers.

Yet he didn't completely spurn established religion. He taught in synagogues and in the temple. He endorsed the Torah. He asked cured lepers to show themselves to the priest, according to tradition. He directed Peter to catch a fish to pay the temple tax. He was a Jew. He supported the virtues of the Law and the piety of genuine Hebrew faith.

But when religious practices grew stale he turned them upside down and inside out and called them to their original reason for being. He refused to bless religious structures which ranked people by pious deeds. He replaced the machinery of formalized religion with compassion and love. Jesus, the upside-down Messiah, would become the new high priest. The Holy Spirit would move the sacred holy of holies from the temple to the heart of each believer. No longer would people worship God in the holy temple or on a sacred mountain. Now they could approach God in spirit and in truth (John 4:23). Now the Spirit would live in the temple of each believer. Worship would be freed from elaborate buildings and complicated ritual. In the words of the Gospels, "Something greater than the temple is here" (Matthew 12:6).

Jesus would be the final and definitive sacrifice. He would be the unblemished lamb of God slain for the sins of the world. Jesus would reveal the secrets of the Torah of love, which superseded legalistic detail. This Torah would make ceremonial cleansing, washing, and sacrificing obsolete. Jesus affirmed the new, upside-down religion when he told a scribe that he was close to the kingdom of God if he placed love for God, self, and neighbor above *all* the burnt offerings (Mark 12:34). In Jesus we see upside-down religion—no building, no program, no professional clergy. In Jesus we have a final sacrifice, a definitive offering, a new temple in each believer's heart, and the supreme Torah—the law of love.

Jesus rejected the temptation for spectacular display. He preferred the messianic secret. Throughout his ministry, he was slow to disclose his identity. He spoke in riddles and parables. Those he miraculously healed he forbade to speak. This was no arrogant, horn-blowing Messiah. This was no magician performing special signs so the crowds could clap. His life itself was the sign. Care for the lost, compassion for the poor, love for all. These were the messianic signs.

The new heroes were the throwaways of institutionalized religion. They were the repentant sinners and publicans, the tax collectors and harlots. And what of the old heroes, the scribes and the priests, the Pharisees and Sadducees, the guardians of the old sacred way? They now were the villains, dethroned, brought low. No wonder they killed him.

Questions for Discussion

1. How does the description of the temple in this chapter compare with your previous knowledge of the temple?

2. What parallels, if any, exist between institutionalized religion in Judaism and institutionalized religion today?

3. If you had been living in Jesus' time, which of the religious groups might you have joined? Why?

4. Do we have an "oral law" today which serves as a commentary on the Scripture?

5. Why was Jesus so cautious about his messianic identity?

6. If we had been Mary or Zechariah, what kind of Messiah might we have expected?

7. In what ways are we tempted to engage in elaborate religious display?

8. Who are the heroes and the villains today?

4

WILDERNESS BREAD

Welfare King

Was Jesus tempted to turn stones into bread merely because he was hungry? This interpretation may hold a grain of truth. But the fuller significance of the temptation lies in the economic plight of Palestine's masses. Bread symbolizes the heart of material life. The core of many diets, it appears on tables meal after meal, week after week. In the Lord's Prayer—"give us this day our daily bread"—it represents life's basic necessities. Through his literal hunger, Jesus identified with the thousands of poor peasants whose daily existence revolved around the search for bread. His gnawing appetite stirred him to act on behalf of others who shared his pain.

Jesus' temptation, however, isn't to gobble down boulders of bread to relieve a forty-day fast.[1] Thinking of bread reminds Jesus of God's manna freely distributed during the Hebrews' forty-year roam in the desert. Perhaps memories of hometown Nazareth also come to mind. He sees ruthless creditors pushing poor peasant farmers off their land and a system of double taxation oppressing the masses. He hears the lepers, the blind, and the poor—trampled on by the pious and greedy—crying for help. Why not miraculously feed the masses and throw a divine banquet for his followers? Free food would surely bring a groundswell of public support in Galilee. "Feed 'em, Jesus, feed 'em," the tempter whispers, "You have the power. Go ahead. Use it!"

Even the religious authorities were afraid of the masses. The nighttime arrest of Jesus was prompted by their fear of the crowds. Jesus himself realized that a well-fed mob could seize him and make him king by force (John 6:15). Bread was the quickest way to the heart of the crowd. Mark peppers his Gospel with references to multitudes (numbering in the thousands) following Jesus. Luke (12:1) notes that the surging multitudes once squeezed together so tightly they trampled each other. Neither Pilate nor the high priest could defuse the contagious frenzy of mob action. Feeding the crowds offered Jesus a shortcut for galvanizing their political support.

The bread temptation involved more than abuse of power. It would reduce God incarnate to a welfare king. The enticing thoughts flow on: "Lessen their poverty without suffering." "Let the religious authorities continue their idolatry." "Don't preach God's judgment on the greedy—just distribute bread to the hungry." "Don't criticize economic injustice, the temple system, and the Roman occupation—just toss bread to poor Galilean peasants and let the rest of the world go by." Such devilish suggestions would have reduced humans to soulless organisms—mere bread-eating animals.

Very Rich and Very Poor

Most members of developed societies belong to a large middle class. In sharp contrast, first-century Palestine had basically two economic classes: *upper* and *lower*.[2] In peasant societies rooted in agriculture, 90 percent or more of the people are usually farmers. Wealth is based on land ownership.

So it was in Palestine. A small *upper class* accounted for 10 percent or less of the population. These were the landowners, hereditary aristocrats, appointed bureaucrats, chief priests, merchants, government officials, and various official servants who served the needs of the governing class. The rest of the people—likely 90 percent or more— were in the *lower class*. Living precariously, hand-to-mouth, they were at the mercy of weather, famine, pestilence, bandit raids, and war.

There were distinct subgroups within the lower class. Near the top were craftsmen, carpenters, masons, fishermen, and traders. Most, however, were farmers. Some were tenant farmers or sharecroppers on large estates owned by absentee landowners. Others farmed their own plots. Still others were day laborers picking up work wherever they could. On the fringe of the lower class were persons involved in "unclean" occupations such as tanning. At the financial bottom were the outcasts— peasants forced off their land, wandering vagabonds, beggars, lepers. These down-and-outers may have numbered some 10 percent of the people.

In Galilee, where much of Jesus' ministry took place, the middle class was also largely absent. One historian describing Galilee says, "It can be safely concluded that there existed both the extremely rich and the miserably poor, the latter being the lot of the majority of the people."[3] The parables and sayings of Jesus assume a two-class system of rich and poor. In spite of many small distinctions, one stark reality dominated the economic landscape: the *few* lived in luxury while the *many* lived in harsh poverty.

Plush Aristocrats

Jerusalem wasn't only the highest religious peak. It towered above the country in social and economic prestige as well. An elite aristocracy made up of the chief priests, wealthy landowners, merchants, tax collectors, and the Sadducean Party called Jerusalem home.[4] The upper class—those living off the rent from their estates, skilled artists, clever traders, and poets—all migrated toward the city housing the great temple.

Extravagance oozed from the affluent elite. Gold bindings were wrapped around the palm branches they carried to festive ceremonies. They brought their offering of firstfruits in golden vessels on Pentecost. A city ordinance prohibited their covering their phylacteries with gold. Two men reportedly wagered the equivalent of more than a year's salary on being able to anger one of the leading rabbis.

Many of the rich in Jerusalem derived their wealth from vast country estates farmed by slaves and hired men or rented to tenants. One of Herod's chancellors owned an entire village. It was said that another person had inherited 1,000 villages, 1,000 ships, and so many slaves they didn't know their master. According to the sages, a wealthy man was one who had a hundred vineyards, a hundred fields, and a hundred slaves. Some of the special artists working in the temple received the equivalent of 300 dollars a day. Unskilled workers in Jerusalem received their food and about 25 cents a day.

On the Day of Atonement, everyone was required to go barefoot. To protect her feet, the wife of a high priest carpeted the path from her house to the temple. A snobbish attitude permeated Jerusalem's elite. They wouldn't sign a document as a witness unless they were sure the other witnesses were also well-to-do. They accepted dinner invitations only if the other guests matched their own high status. The arrogance kept the elite from mingling with common people, except to employ them as servants.

The rich gave large dowries when their daughters married. One dowry exceeded a million gold denarii (a single denarius was the equivalent of a day's wage). A village

man who took a Jerusalem bride was required to give his
weight in gold as a betrothal gift. A country bride also
brought her weight in gold to her city groom. Joseph of
Arimathea (Matthew 27:57), a rich man, no doubt belonged to this rich upper crust. Jerusalem also had a sizable middle class of retail traders and craftsmen as well
as a poor segment.

The Poor Masses

The poor masses were called "people of the land." At
one time this simply meant *common people*, or served to
distinguish between rural and urban folk. But it later became a taunt hurled at those who observed religious laws
carelessly.[5] The Pharisees, avoiding contact with such
folk, even refused to eat with them. The religiously careless were so scorned that they couldn't testify in court
nor be appointed guardian of an orphan. Pharisees
wouldn't marry them and considered their women unclean vermin.

Galilee, sixty miles to the north of Jerusalem, was the
center for the common folk. Rich in resources, Galilee
was the most densely populated area of Palestine. Before
the reign of Herod the Great, many Gentiles bought land
there. But in the years before Jesus' birth, Jewish immi-
grants resettled it. By the time of Jesus' birth, Galilee was
predominantly Jewish. Herod Antipas, the ruler of the
area, built the capital city of Tiberias along the Sea of
Galilee. The region, however, still carried its former stigma: "Galilee of the Gentiles."

The Galilean population of some 350,000 included a
large number of slaves and some 100,000 Jews who had
absorbed some Greek culture. Most Galileans were poorly
educated and were ignorant of the finer points of religious law. They did, however, have a synagogue in each
village, although this likely wasn't a building devoted
solely to worship.[6] Overwhelmed with making a living,

they had little time to worry about minute details of ritual purity. The following words of a Pharisee must be taken lightly, but they do show the Pharisaic disdain for the unorthodox people of the land.

> A Jew must not marry the daughter of the people of the land for they are unclean animals and their women forbidden reptiles. And with respect to their daughters the Scriptures write, "Cursed be he that lieth with any manner of beast" (Deuteronomy 27:21). . . . Said R. Eleazar: one may butcher a people of the land on a Day of Atonement that happens to fall on a Sabbath (when any kind of work such as butchering constitutes a violation of a double prohibition). His disciples said to him, master, say "slaughter" (instead of the vile word butcher). But he replied "slaughtering requires a benediction, butchering does not."[7]

Although exaggerated, this attitude reveals the hatred of some of the religious aristocracy toward the common people. The feeling was mutual, for it was said that the "people of the land" hated the Jewish scholars more than the heathen hated Israel. Another rabbi, once a person of the land himself, said:

> When I was a people of the land, I used to say, "I wish I had one of those scholars, and I would bite him like an ass." His disciples said, "You mean like a dog." He replied, "An ass' bite breaks the bone; a dog's does not."[8]

It was from these backward people that the fierce streak of Jewish nationalism burst forth some years after Jesus' death. This revolutionary fervor, directed at the occupying Romans, was also targeted on the rich Jerusalem aristocracy who courted the Romans. Nazareth, a village in the heart of people-of-the-land country, was Jesus' home. It was situated in a fertile farming area of Galilee with a major fish exporting enterprise. But the masses lived in dismal poverty. Most had to get along with one set of clothing. There was a saying that "the daughters of Israel are comely but poverty makes them repulsive."

Oppressive economic factors fed the political turmoil and restlessness in first-century Galilee. The social ferment was stirred not only by Roman rule and strident nationalism, but also by harsh economics. Taxes had been high during the era of Herod the Great, although much of the revenue was funneled into the magnificent temple at Jerusalem and consecrated to God. At Herod's death a delegation of Jews complained to the Roman emperor that Herod derived too much of his wealth by confiscating land and goods. Herod may have privately owned one half to two thirds of his kingdom.[9]

Much of Galilee was divided into large estates owned by wealthy merchants and Sadducees living in Jerusalem, as well as Gentile landowners living outside Palestine. The parables of Jesus refer to absentee landowners who placed a steward over their property and laborers. Some peasant farmers owned small plots of land. But rising debt was pushing them off their land. They were forced to mortgage their property to pay taxes amounting often to half their harvest. Tax collectors and estate owners then snatched the land from the deeply indebted peasants.

Peasant families were often trapped on the plot, working as day laborers for wealthy and absent landholders. One writer describes the situation.

> Within a few decades, small and middle-sized plots of land had disappeared, whereas the properties owned by the temple and the imperial crown grew beyond proportion. . . . Driven to misery, many peasants abandoned their land and joined bands of robbers that survived by pillage and lived in caves in the mountains.[10]

The Roman IRS
The poverty was intensified by a double system of tax-

es: *civil* and *religious*. It's impossible to calculate the exact proportion of taxes. Most scholars agree, however, that 30 to 70 percent of the peasant's annual income eventually fell in the hands of various tax collectors and creditors.[11] The tax bite was much worse than the typical tax burden in modern nations.

Along with Rome's direct rule came crushing taxes. The efficient Roman bureaucracy collected taxes on people, houses, animals, sales, and imports and exports. First a land tax took about one-fourth of the crop. Then a poll, or per capita tax, was levied on each male over age fourteen and each female over age twelve.[12] The taxes were gathered by Jewish tax collectors appointed by the Roman government from within the ranks of well-to-do families. The police who accompanied the tax collectors were sometimes guilty of abuses. Fraud abounded.

There were also many other tariffs and tolls, including import duties, bridge and road tolls, and market fees. The collectors of these tolls were known as publicans. They exploited the public's ignorance of toll fees and were seen as utter deceivers.[13] Publicans worked for a "tax farmer" who had paid the Romans the highest bid for the toll income of a certain district. Most tax farmers were Jews who worked for the Romans. The tax farmers collected the designated Roman taxes, then added their own additional fees. Zacchaeus was likely a tax farmer. The produce market in Jerusalem was given to a "farmer" who taxed the produce merchants.

The bite of Roman taxes was particularly irksome in Jesus' time because, as political taxes, they were no longer used to rebuild the temple as they had been under Herod the Great. Now they were financing a foreign army and the luxuries of a faraway empire.

Since the Jews never regarded Roman rule as legitimate, they viewed Roman taxes as outright robbery. They saw Gentile rulers in Palestine as robbers without rights over the land or its people.[14] The rabbis made no distinction between tax collectors and thieves. Even the Gospels portray tax collectors as sinners. The taxation was so oppressive that Syria and Judea begged for a reduction in 17 CE. When Jewish Zealots gained control of Jerusalem in 66 CE, they burned all the debt records stored in the Jerusalem archives. They hoped to prevent future retaliation by the rich.

God's IRS

Two dozen or so religious tithes and offerings were required of the devout Jew. Religious taxes were prescribed by Jewish law. Jewish males over age twenty paid a temple tax each year. The equivalent of two denarii, or two days' wages, this half shekel tax was due at the beginning of the Passover month each spring. A few weeks before Passover, tax collectors traveled to outlying districts to gather the tax from those who would miss the Jerusalem Passover. In Matthew (17:24) these collectors ask Peter for the half shekel tax. Used for operating and maintaining the temple, this tax could only be paid in high quality Tyrian silver. The Roman denarius, however, was the common currency. Money changers at the temple made a profit by exchanging Tyrian silver for the common denarius.

Jewish farmers also gave an offering of the first fruits of their crops in gratitude for the coming harvest. They also gave a tithe of the harvest itself and a tithe of the herd to support the Levites. In the time of Jesus, the priests in Jerusalem sometimes took the tithe by force at the expense of the Levites. A second tithe supported the poor. An additional tithe was possibly collected for the poor every third year.

Farmers were required to leave gleanings on their fields for the poor. On top of this came the sabbatical year practice of letting land lie fallow every seventh year.

This "involved the loss of at least a year-and-a-half of agricultural produce in every seven year cycle—a crushing burden, indeed, upon a people which was unable in any year to save a substantial part of the crop."[15] In addition, there were many personal contributions—peace and sin offerings as well as offerings for the dedication of a child. The Pharisees at the time of Jesus were tithing herbs from their gardens—a practice Jesus mocked in light of their neglecting justice and mercy (Matthew 23:23).

The religious tithes and taxes were not viewed as free will offerings. They were seen as divine ordinances commanded by God. There was, however, no legal way to enforce them. The exorbitant taxes tempted many rural people to let their religious tithes slide. Such carelessness infuriated religious leaders, especially the Pharisees, who viewed obedient tithing as essential to holiness. One scholar contends that the press of Roman taxes forced this "crisis of holiness." It solidified the Pharisees' insistence on careful observance and spurred their disgust toward nonobservant peasants.[16]

The Carpenter's Son

We find Jesus growing up in this peasant setting. Two additional shreds of evidence place him with the poor peasants of Galilee. Mary describes herself as a person of "low estate" in her song of exaltation (Luke 1:48). The prescribed offering for the dedication of a child in Jerusalem was a lamb and a dove. But Mary and Joseph brought only two doves, a practice acceptable for poor families unable to afford a lamb.

Although these bits of evidence suggest Jesus came from a poor family, he probably didn't spring from the poorest of the poor. His father was no day laborer or landless tenant. He was a craftsman—a skilled worker, likely a mason, carpenter, or cartwright.[17] Joseph probably belonged to the higher ranks of Galilee's poor class—as did Jesus, also a craftsman. Among Jesus' followers were independent fishermen and tax collectors. Thus Jesus and at least some of his followers came from the upper levels of Galilean peasantry.[18]

Even though he was a skilled craftsman, Jesus identified with the poorest of the poor.[19] He told enthusiastic followers that he had no place to lay his head. The foxes and birds were better off than he was (Luke 9:58). His disciples were caught on a Sabbath shelling wheat in the field. Such grain was left for the benefit of the poor according to the Deuteronomic code.

When grilled about paying Roman taxes, Jesus asked for a coin, showing an empty pocket. He held no job after beginning his ministry. As with other rabbis, he wasn't paid for his teaching. He had no formal support beyond the pittance given by several women along the way (Luke 8:3). Jesus and his followers were a band of wandering itinerate preachers who lived hand-to-mouth. Their ethical radicalism led to their homelessness, meager possessions, and distance from family.[20]

Although he grew up in poverty-ridden Galilee, Jesus parted with his cultural background by refusing to join the zealous rebels who endorsed violence for political purposes. The rebels captured the imagination of bright youngsters growing up in the midst of economic oppression. They dreamed of someday burning the record of debts in the Jerusalem archives. Jesus grew up in the midst of revolutionary rhetoric—but left it behind. His message wasn't simply a reaction to economic oppression. Although he despised economic injustice, his primary passion was the inauguration of a new kingdom—one that would grapple with poverty in a new way.

Living Bread

Jesus' bread temptation involved more than easing personal hunger. He was tempted to go back to Galilee and miraculously feed the masses. We can't second guess all the dimensions of the test. Perhaps he thought of picking up the mantle of Judas the Galilean and joining other freedom fighters to resist Roman taxes. Perhaps like other bandits of the day he dreamed of raiding the stockpiles of rich estates. If he had the miraculous touch, why not use it to feed the masses in one grand smorgasbord? Why not achieve economic justice in one bold stroke?

But Jesus finally rejected the live-by-bread-alone option. A miraculous feeding was a short-term solution. Hunger would return with the miracle baker's death. Avoiding the quick and temporary fix, Jesus offered a new alternative. His life, his way, his teaching would form a new foundation for living. This would be a permanent bread of life. As persons digest this new bread, it fills them with new spirit and vision. And those blessed with surplus material bread begin to share it in new ways.

Near the midpoint of his ministry Jesus fed the five thousand and the four thousand with loaves and fishes. This was the sign: Jesus himself was the living bread, the long awaited Messiah (Mark 6–8). The breaking of the bread came just before the scene at Caesarea Philippi where Peter confesses that Jesus is the Christ. The crowd feeding wasn't a ploy to establish Jesus' identity as a miracle worker. Indeed, a few days later Jesus told the crowd the only reason they followed was because they were fed (John 6:26). He understood that miraculous feedings didn't cultivate serious disciples. The feeding sprang from his compassion for the crowd's hunger (Mark 6:34; 8:2).

Through breaking the bread Jesus did, however, disclose his messianic identity, not as miracle worker but as initiator of an upside-down kingdom. In John 6, Jesus declares, "I am the bread of life . . . the living bread which came down from heaven. . . . If anyone eats of this bread, he will live for ever."

As he prepared for a violent crucifixion, Jesus ate the Passover meal with his disciples and breaking bread told them, "This is my body" (Luke 22:19). After the resurrection, the Emmaus road walkers suddenly recognized Jesus in the breaking of bread (Luke 24:30-31). His messianic identity as Savior of the world was revealed not by turning boulders into loaves but by allowing his life to be broken for others.

When the values of Jesus' upside-down kingdom become our bread of life, the economic institutions of society lose their grip. Rich folks who accept the eternal bread freely share their mundane bread. This is an upside-down way of feeding the hungry. It's neither revolution by angry peasants nor miraculous baking. Rather, those with abundance, moved by God's mercy, stop hoarding and give generously.

If the upside-down way of Jesus pulled the rug from under conventional politics and religion, it yanked even harder at the carpet under economic oppression. Again and again, story after story, Jesus preaches against economic injustice. "Woe to you that are rich. . . . Blessed are you poor" (Luke 6:20, 24). His teaching condemns economic practices that trample the poor to make the rich even richer. As we shall see in the next chapters, the heroes of Jesus' upside-down kingdom aren't the wealthy landowners relaxing in Jacuzzi's in Jerusalem but the poor, the maimed, and the weak.

Jesus challenged the major social institutions of his day: politics, religion, and economics. As often happens, the three were woven together. The rich aristocracy—chief priests and Sadducees in Jerusalem—owned large estates in Galilee which trapped small tenant farmers. This ruling elite controlled the mighty Jewish supreme court—the Sanhedrin. This body, in turn, controlled the temple ritual and religious regulations. This same upper crust of Jerusalem was in cahoots with the Romans. They welcomed the Roman occupation, which protected them against bandits enticed by their wealth.

This ruling Jewish elite cheered when the Romans crushed zealous freedom fighters. The religious leaders were likely part of the crowd that shouted, "Crucify him, crucify him." They knew Jesus was more dangerous than the rebel leader Barabbas. One bandit could be caught again and killed. But a new teaching, a new way of living which overturned the political, religious, and economic tables was too dangerous for Jerusalem's ruling elite.

And so the mountain, the temple, and the bread symbolize the three social institutions with which Jesus struggled in the wilderness. His upside-down way sliced through prevailing assumptions and social structures. The temptations were invitations to affirm conventional politics, conventional religion, and conventional economics. If indeed Jesus' mission was to embody new modes of living for God's people, it makes little sense to view the temptations as merely personal enticements. He was wrestling with the big issues of his day. This reading of the temptations lets us appreciate the anguish Jesus must have felt as he grappled with the forces of politics, religion, and wealth. It also reminds us that God was introducing a new upside-down kingdom—based on a new power, a new temple, and a new bread.

Questions for Discussion

1. Evaluate the suggestion that the bread temptation was larger than Jesus' personal hunger.

2. Does it "spiritualize" a serious problem like poverty to say that "Jesus is the bread of life"?

3. Why is *bread* such a prominent symbol throughout the New Testament?

4. How do our economic arrangements today help to produce hungry masses?

5. Which socioeconomic situations today are similar to

those surrounding Jesus' ministry?

6. Is Jesus' bread temptation irrelevant for those of us who find ourselves in comfortable situations?

7. In what ways do we encounter modern forms of Jesus' three temptations?

8. How might someone in dire poverty interpret the bread temptation differently from someone living in affluence?

5

FREE SLAVES

Hometown Boy Lynched

Jesus gave an emphatic "no" to the three right-side-up kingdoms. But what was this upside-down kingdom all about? Mark (1:15) and Matthew (4:17) report that following his temptation, Jesus announced the arrival of the kingdom of God. Luke (4:16-30) begins his account by describing Jesus' appearance in his hometown of Nazareth. Although Matthew (13:53-58) and Mark (6:1-6) agree the audience was stunned by Jesus' appearance, they place the event later in their sequence of his ministry. Luke sees greater significance in this hometown ruckus. For Luke, Jesus' inaugural sermon in front of familiar faces unravels the mysteries of the new kingdom.

The decisive moment arrives. Jesus strides to the front of his hometown synagogue. The leader hands him the scroll. Jesus turns to Isaiah.[1] But he doesn't read. He quotes forcefully from memory. The hometown folks can't believe their ears. The carpenter's son, Joseph's boy, declares *he* is the anointed one. He is God in flesh. He is the long-awaited Messiah, standing before them.

In a terse quote from the prophet Jesus summarizes his identity and mission.

> The Spirit of the Lord is upon *me*,
>> because he has anointed me to
>> preach *good news* to the *poor*.
> He has sent me to proclaim *release* to the *captives*
>> and *recovering* of *sight* to the blind,
>> to set at *liberty* those who are *oppressed*,
>> to proclaim the acceptable year of the Lord.
>> —Luke 4:18-19, emphasis added

Proclaiming liberty. Setting free. Announcing the favorable year of the Lord. These words ring Jewish bells. The people know what Jesus means. They've heard these phrases again and again. Releasing, liberating, letting go, forgiving, restoring. Yes, yes! These are images of messianic hope. This is what the Messiah, "the Anointed One," is all about.

Three elements stand out in Jesus' use of Isaiah's passage (Isaiah 61:1-2). First, Jesus reveals *he* is the Messiah. Second, his role is to bring liberating news to the poor, the blind, the slaves, and the oppressed. Third, this is the proclamation of God's favorable year. Then Jesus concludes with dynamite: "*Today* this scripture has been fulfilled in *your* hearing." The messianic announcement is alive today in your presence. You are living witnesses to it. You are seeing it fulfilled before your very eyes! I am more than Joseph's boy, *I* am the *Messiah!*

The reaction of Jesus' friends and neighbors to his message is fascinating. As the full impact of his words sank in, they were astonished. So astonished they tried to kill him by chasing him out of town and shoving him off a cliff. Why this murderous reaction to the hometown boy? What did he say that goaded them to violence?

In his simple announcement of the outbreak of God's reign, Jesus omitted a phrase at the end of the Isaiah passage concerning a Day of Vengeance when God would punish the wicked. Indeed, several stories at the end of his sermon confirmed just the opposite. God would extend mercy and liberation even to the wicked. This upside-down announcement infuriated the crowd (more on their reaction later).

The usual reading of Jesus' inaugural sermon completely spiritualizes its meaning. We often understand Jesus as proclaiming release to the captives of sin, giving sight to the spiritually blind, and offering liberty to those oppressed by spiritual bondage. Although this is true, the Old Testament background of the text expands its meaning by rooting it in practical social realities. The "acceptable year of the Lord" refers to the Old Testament Jubilee. Jesus thus links his messianic role to the Hebrew Jubilee.[2] The sermon is, in essence, a Jubilee proclamation.

Is Jesus calling for a concrete program of social and economic reform? New Testament scholars don't agree on this point.[3] What is clear, however, is that the social values heralded by Jesus suddenly take on new meaning in the Jubilee perspective. The Jubilee vision offers an interpretive framework, a metaphor that enables us to understand the teaching and ministry of Jesus in new ways.[4] But what was the Jubilee?

A Hebrew Turnover

Three Old Testament books—Exodus, Deuteronomy, and Leviticus—describe the Jubilee. We're familiar with a weekly cycle of six workdays followed by a *sabbath*. This pattern emerged from the creation story when God relaxed on the seventh day. The Hebrew calendar didn't stop with the weekly cycle. It counted six work years and then celebrated the seventh as a year of rest. This seventh, or "Sunday" year was called a *sabbatical* year. Scholars aren't sure if the *Jubilee* actually fell on the forty-ninth or fiftieth year; either way, the year of Jubilee celebrated the end of the seventh seven-year period[5]. To summarize:

The Sabbath ended a week of six days.
The sabbatical year ended a "week" of six years.
The Jubilee ended a "week" of sabbatical cycles.

The term Jubilee means "a ram's horn." A special horn, taken from a mountain goat, was blown on the Day of Atonement. This signaled the start of Jubilee festivities. The priests blew the special horn only on the Jubilee year. Other years they used an ordinary ram's horn. The sabbatical and Jubilee years established a chronological rhythm for Hebrew society. The vibrations of this rhythm could turn social life upside down. In brief, three shake-ups were expected in the seventh, or sabbatical, year.

(1) *Land* was given a vacation in the seventh year. Crops weren't to be planted or harvested. Unplanted "volunteer" plants were to be left for the poor. The Lord promised a plentiful yield in the sixth year, large enough for both sixth and seventh years. As the people rested on the Sabbath after six days of work, so also they granted the land a vacation after six years of productivity (Exodus 23:10-11; Leviticus 25:2-7).

(2) *Slaves* were released on the seventh year. Some folks became slaves because of rising debts. After working for six years as a hired servant, the Jubilee freed them in the seventh year. It's not clear if slaves were always released on the sabbatical year, but the principle of freeing them after six years of labor certainly existed (Exodus 21:1-6, Deuteronomy 15:12-18).

(3) *Debts* were erased in the sabbatical year. Since Israel had an agricultural economy, debts were mostly charitable loans to needy persons not commercial ones. Charging interest on loans to other Hebrews was prohibited. The principal of any debt was also canceled in the sabbatical year (Deuteronomy 15:1-6).

(4) On the fiftieth, or Jubilee year, greater shake-up occurred. The ownership of *land* returned to the owners who held it at the beginning of the 50-year period.

> And you shall hallow the fiftieth year, and proclaim
> liberty throughout the land to all its inhabitants; it shall
> be a jubilee for you, when each of you shall return to his
> property and each of you shall return to his family
> (Leviticus 25:10).

This 50-year turnover preserved the original pattern of
land ownership. The Jubilee prevented greedy barons
from buying up more and more land at the expense of
the poor. Although land was bought and sold throughout
the forty-nine years, the Jubilee restored land ownership
at least once in each generation. The Hebrews really
didn't *buy* the land in the intervening years; they pur-
chased its *use*. As the Jubilee approached, the cost of using the land dipped because fees were calculated according to the number of harvests remaining before the Jubilee (Leviticus 25:13-16).

It's difficult to know if the sabbatical and Jubilee practices were followed conscientiously. Historical references
outside the Scriptures suggest that the practice of letting
the land idle on the sabbatical year continued until the
destruction of the temple in 70 CE and perhaps even later. It's uncertain how often slaves, debts, and land were
restored. Some evidence suggests at least partial observance of these practices. During the reign of Zedekiah,
before Jerusalem fell to Babylon in 586 BCE, the rich released their slaves but soon recaptured them. Jeremiah
fumed at their disobedience.

> You turned around and profaned my name when each of
> you took back his male and female slaves, whom you had
> set free according to their desire, and you brought them
> into subjection to be your slaves. Therefore, thus says the
> Lord: You have not obeyed me by proclaiming liberty . . .
> behold, I proclaim to you liberty to the sword, to pesti-
> lence, and to famine, says the Lord. I will make you a
> horror to all the kingdoms of the earth (Jeremiah 34:16-
> 17).

Jeremiah viewed the sabbatical violation as one of the reasons for the impending destruction of Jerusalem (Jeremiah 34:18-22).

About 423 BCE Nehemiah (5:1-13) rebuked the people for not observing the Jubilee after returning from captivity. He told the nobles and officials to free their slaves and return their land to its original owners. In the last chapters of Ezekiel, the prophet calls for reestablishing the Jubilee (Ezekiel 45:7-9; 46:16-18).

Although many scholars think the Jubilean land reform was never practiced, others believe it was periodically observed. There is firmer evidence that debts were released. A leading Pharisee, Hillel, living about the time of Jesus' birth, started the *prosbul*.[6] This legal device ended the devastating effect of canceling debt every six years. Creditors were slow to lend money when they knew the approaching sabbatical year would wipe out their loans. In short, people refused to lend money because they would never see it again. The *prosbul* allowed lenders to deposit a certificate with the courts when the loans were made. This paper prevented debts from being erased on the sabbatical year. Borrowers also knew that their debts would be binding, despite the sabbatical teaching.

The need for the *prosbul* to bypass the sabbatical suggests debts were indeed being canceled. Despite erratic practice, the sabbatical and Jubilee were important symbolic markers of Hebrew time. Above all, they embodied key theological values.

Level Pyramids

More important than the details of the Jubilee are the theological principles undergirding it. There can be no question that the Jubilee vision called for social upheaval, for upsetting the social order. As the social blueprint for the people of God, the Jubilee touched three factors which generate inequality. (1) Control of the land represents access to natural resources. (2) Ownership of slaves symbolizes the human labor necessary for production. (3) Borrowing and lending money involves the management of capital and credit.

The use and distribution of these resources—natural, human, and financial—tilts the balance of justice in any society. In the modern world, technology is a fourth variable in the equation. By controlling these resources, some become wealthy as others slide into poverty. The Jubilee principles highlight the divine vision for the age-old problem of social injustice.

1. *Divine Ownership*. A bold message reverberates through the Jubilee Scriptures: God *owns* the natural and human resources.

Why shouldn't the land be sold perpetually? Because "the land is mine; for you are strangers and sojourners with me" (Leviticus 25:23).

Why should slaves be released periodically? "For they are my servants, whom I brought forth out of the land of Egypt; they shall not be sold as slaves" (Leviticus 25:42, 55).

The land and the people are the Lord's! We are not to abuse nor carelessly use them. We who manage land and people are not *owners*. We are *stewards* accountable to God, the true owner. We dare not use land and people selfishly to build economic pyramids, create social dynasties, or feed greedy egos. Giving the land a vacation in the sabbatical or seventh year fits this understanding. Since the land is the Lord's, it shouldn't be abused. On the seventh year it's given back—restored to God—its original Owner. A theology of stewardship underlies the entire Jubilee vision. Natural, human and financial resources are, very simply put, *God's*. These resources are ours only on loan. As short-term stewards of them, we are accountable to God for their proper use and care.

2. *God's Liberation*. Why were God's people called to

participate in this unusual vision? Why were the people to forgive debts, liberate slaves, and restore land? Was this some human concoction to prevent rebellion and revolution?

Not at all. God's liberation is the driving motivation. God's decisive act in the Egyptian exodus provides the theological base for the Jubilee. Let no one forget: "You shall remember that you were a slave in the land of Egypt, and the Lord your God redeemed you; therefore I command you this today" (Deuteronomy 15:15). "I am the Lord your God, who brought you forth out of the land of Egypt to give you the land of Canaan, and to be your God" (Leviticus 25:38).

"For 450 years" God is saying, "you worked as slaves carrying bricks for the Egyptian taskmasters. Not long ago you were whipped and beaten slaves. You too cried out for freedom. I, the Lord your God, intervened on your behalf. I liberated and redeemed you from Pharaoh's enslavement. I freed you from bondage and brought you back to the Promised Land."

Time and again the memory of God's liberating acts flash across the pages of the Old Testament.

3. *Jubilee Response.* The Jubilee was a response to God's gracious liberation and deliverance. As the people recalled how God freed them from slavery, their joyous response was to pass that freedom on by forgiving debts, releasing slaves, and redeeming the land. To the modern mind, releasing a slave sounds like a noble act. But the Jubilean prescription didn't stop with a self-righteous pat on the back. Simply freeing a slave wasn't enough. "And when you let him go free from you, you shall not let him go empty-handed; you shall furnish him *liberally* out of your flock, out of your threshing floor, and out of your wine press" (Deuteronomy 15:13-14a, emphasis added).

Why such generous mercy? Isn't it enough to free the slave? Why this extra dose of goodness?

The biblical refrain is clear. "As the Lord your God has blessed you, you shall give to him" (Deuteronomy 15:14b).

As God liberally redeemed you out of Egypt, so you ought to graciously liberate your brothers and sisters.

Jubilee acts of social justice aren't motivated by heavenly badges of merit. They're the natural and joyful response to the good news of God's liberation.

4. *Jubilee Compassion.* The Jubilee response has one eye on history, on God's gracious acts of deliverance. The other eye is on the less fortunate. Jubilee behavior responds to God's acts in history and to the cries of those crushed by social injustice. The sight of trampled outcasts reminds the Hebrews of their own slavery in the past.

The poor are the reason the land lies fallow. God commands that "the seventh year you shall let it rest and lie fallow, that the poor of your people may eat" (Exodus 23:11).

God promises that "There will be no poor among you . . . *if* only you will *obey* the voice of the Lord your God, being careful to do all this commandment which I command you this day." Then God adds, "You shall not harden your heart . . . against your poor brother, but you shall. . . lend him sufficient for his need. . . . You shall open *wide* your hand to your brother, to the needy and to the poor, in the land" (Deuteronomy 15:4-5, 7-8, 11, emphasis added).

God warns the people not to refuse loans to the poor just because the sabbatical year is near. The debt may not be repaid because of the sabbatical cancellation; *nevertheless*, "you shall give to him *freely*, and your heart shall not be grudging when you give to him; because for this the Lord your God will bless you in all your work and in all that you undertake" (Deuteronomy 15:10, emphasis added).

There is a double motive in Jubilee forgiveness: a gracious response to God's liberation *and* compassionate eyes that see human hurt.

5. *Upside-Down Revolution*. The Jubilee envisions a social revolution. But it's certainly a unique one. Revolutions usually erupt at the bottom of the societal ladder. Exploited peasants, angered by their oppression, grab pitchforks or machine guns and lash out at rich oppressors. If successful, they gain power. More often they're crushed. Successful revolutionaries of today often become the oppressors of tomorrow as they continue to use the same violent weapons.

Jubilee is upside-down revolution. Here the flame of revolution burns at the top. God's grace moves those in seats of power, the rich and influential. They now see with compassionate eyes and join the Jubilee by redistributing natural and human resources. This flattens socioeconomic pyramids. Those at the top begin freely giving as God has given them.

6. *Institutionalized Grace*. The Jubilee concept is rooted in a keen awareness of human sin and greed. Without social controls, economic pyramids rise. Without constraints and periodic leveling, the weak at the bottom are stamped into the dirt. Societies must have special provisions to defend and protect the helpless. Without periodic and regular levelings power and wealth consolidate in the hands of a small elite.

The Jubilee is a splendid example of a social—yes, an institutional—plan to harness personal desire and ambition. Benevolence can't be left to the personal whims and wishes of the rich. Such giving makes the rich feel better. But it doesn't alter those evil structures which perpetuate opulence at the expense of the poor. Jubilee builds a regular and periodic leveling into the fabric of social life. It makes justice a rule of the game.

The Jubilean vision doesn't squelch individual initiative. It doesn't call for communal living nor prescribe legalistic equality. It allows personal aspirations their place. But it knows such things easily get out of hand. So it wisely mandates structural change at regular intervals to equalize the disparities which would otherwise run rampant. As we've seen, the Bible understands such institutionalized grace as a response to the grace of a God who has already taken the initiative. Divine grace stirs economic change.

In true biblical fashion, the Jubilee integrates spiritual and social dimensions. It weaves religion and economics into one fabric. Pulling the two apart prostitutes the biblical truth. Refusing to participate in the economic turnover constitutes flagrant disobedience.

Meanwhile Back at Nazareth

Good news for the poor. Release for the captives. Sight for the blind. Liberty for the oppressed. God's favorable year! The old words ring with new meaning as Jesus quotes them in hometown Nazareth. Some New Testament scholars think Jesus may have preached these words in a sabbatical year.[7] One scholar even argues it was the actual year of Jubilee.[8] In any event, the Old Testament background embellishes Jesus' use of these words. Now they strike us with new meaning. The Hebrew word for liberty is used only seven times in the Old Testament—but each time with the year of liberty.[9] The literal meaning of Jubilee was certainly good news in Nazareth. The poor could say good-bye to their debts. Those driven into slavery because of debts could return home. Peasants forced to sell land would see it returned once again to their family. No question about it—this was *very good news!*

But there's more. Jesus wasn't just making another Jubilee proclamation. "The Lord has anointed me." This is a messianic announcement. It's remarkably similar to Jesus' response when John's disciples asked if he was indeed the Messiah. Jesus didn't say yes or no (Luke 7:22-23). Rather, he said "the blind receive their sight, the lame walk, lepers are cleansed, and the deaf hear, the dead are raised up, the poor have good news preached to them." These are the same folks that Jesus mentions at Nazareth.

This isn't the first time such a list appears. In fact, we find the same catalog in the messianic prophecies of Isaiah 29:18, 35:5, and 61:1. What do these images mean? They're all age-old descriptions in the East for the time of *salvation,* when crying, sorrow, and grief will end.[10] Jesus surprises us by adding lepers and the dead to the list of the saved. Both are missing from Isaiah's passages. Alert listeners would have heard Jesus using messianic code words from the Old Testament. They would have heard him saying, "The Messiah is *here!* Salvation is dawning. The kingdom of God is *near.* It's no longer far away in the clouds. God's presence has broken in among you *now.* It's happening before your very eyes!"

The theme of restoration links together the Jubilee, Jesus' Nazareth sermon, and his reply to John's disciples. Things will be restored, returned to their original state. Images of paradise—no debt, no poverty, no slavery— shine forth. These images of the garden take us back to Genesis and creation. Enacting the Jubilee vision will restore things to their original garden perfection.

Jubilee talk clarifies the role of the Messiah, the one who announces God's release. The Messiah lets us go, forgiving our debts, redeeming our sins. Jesus Christ remolds us into the image of God. He cuts the chains of sin. Our eyes open. The handcuffs of evil drop off. This is true liberation. We repent and turn back to the garden, rekindling harmonious ties with God—finding a home once more in the family of God.

And so at Nazareth Jesus announced God's acceptable year of salvation. But his punch line insulted Jewish pride: God used Gentiles in Old Testament days. The Jubilee restoration wasn't only for Jews but for *all*—even Gentiles. Jesus offered the Gentiles words of grace instead of vengeance. There would be no more favorites. The Jubilee proclaimed by Jesus was universal. It knew no ethnic barriers, no ethnic favorites. This was the startling news that incited rage in the Nazareth crowd. Instead of a day of God's vengeance against Gentiles, Jesus announced a day of universal mercy and forgiveness.[11] There could be no doubt about it. Jesus, Gentile-lover, was a false prophet. And so they chased him out of town and tried to shove him over a cliff.

The Jubilee Habit

A redemptive rhythm emerges from the Jubilee. It echoes from garden to empty tomb. The drummers of holy history pound out a four-beat message which vibrates down through the ages:

Garden—Egypt—Exodus—Jubilee
Perfection—sin—salvation—mercy
Freedom—oppression—restoration—forgiveness.

The first beat reminds us of God's perfect creation. The second beat recalls oppression in Egypt. God's mighty intervention brings restoration and salvation. Finally, we can respond to God's salvation by extending mercy and forgiveness to others.

Once we were oppressed. Once we were captives. Now, the Jubilee reminds us, we're forgiven debtors. We're released slaves. What should be our response? Suddenly the reciprocal rule from Deuteronomy 15:14 strikes home: "As the Lord your God has blessed you, you shall give to him." It points to the New Testament chain reaction. Forgive as I have forgiven. Be merciful as I have been merciful. Love as I have loved. Give freely as I have given to you. God's graciousness moves us to forgive others.

God's mercy nudges us to cancel debts. We release our slaves because God released us. In short, we pass the Jubilee on.

Just as the Hebrew response to God's liberation had real social consequences, so must ours. It's not enough to sit and ponder the theological beauty of this. We must act. The biblical model calls us to start forgiving not only interpersonal insults but financial ones as well. We lower rents and raise salaries. In the words of the Lord's Prayer, "forgive us our debts, as we also have forgiven our debtors" (Matthew 6:12).

Two points stand out here. One is that granting and accepting forgiveness are linked. We're eligible to accept God's forgiveness as we repent and forgive others. The other is that the word *debts* as used in the Lord's Prayer may refer either to sins or to financial debts.[12] Are we to forgive not only bad feelings but also financial debts? In any event, couched in the center of the Lord's Prayer we find the Jubilee principle.

The parable of the unforgiving servant (Matthew 18:23-35) also underlines the Jubilee posture. A king forgives a servant's large debt. The forgiven servant grabs a fellow servant by the throat and demands repayment of a small debt. When the friend can't pay, the forgiven servant locks him in prison. When the king hears this, he angrily throws the forgiven servant in jail until he can pay the original debt. The story concludes tersely with the Jubilee moral: "So also my heavenly Father will do to every one of you, if you do not forgive your brother from your heart" (Matthew 18:35).

The principle of reciprocal forgiveness embedded in the Jubilee pervades new Testament teaching. Even the economic teaching of Jesus makes sense in the context of the Jubilee model. In this framework his words take on new meaning. They invite us to respond concretely, in economic ways, to God's liberating initiative.

The Dog's Tail

We've seen how Jubilee links spiritual and social spheres. Although tied together, they represent different starting points. In fact, the way they mesh has stirred much philosophical controversy. Social scientists argue that our beliefs are often shaped by our social and material environments. Hence the chicken and egg question. Do our ideas influence our economic lifestyles or vice versa?[13] Philosophers and theologians tend to line up on one side. They contend our beliefs do shape our economic behavior.

On the other side, many social scientists argue that our convictions are mere reflections of our economic status. In this view, our economic niche shapes the beliefs we hold dear. For instance, a person born into a wealthy family will likely believe affluence is a sign of God's blessing. In contrast, those born poor are more likely to believe God will bless them in heaven with divine pie in the sky. Peasants eking out a harsh and meager living will likely dream of God's future heavenly blessing while their rich oppressors view the here and now as already heavenly. The songs of American slaves, for example, focus on the future hope of crossing Jordan's stormy banks to enter the Promised Land. Whereas today's affluent upper crust drive luxury cars and need no heavenly escape from financial woes.

At stake here is the relationship between religion and economics, spiritual and material, our faith and our pocketbook. This raises the question of the dog and the tail. Does our faith wag our wallet, or does our bank account wag our convictions? What controls what? This oversimplifies, of course. There is no simple relationship between pocketbook and piety.

But economic factors do powerfully shape the way we look at things. Salary, the income of our friends, the value of our house, and our social status—all these factors shape our thinking. They provide a set of lenses that filter our view of the world. We cling to theological beliefs that support and legitimate our economic status. Financial factors filter our Bible reading and tint our religious lenses so our beliefs conveniently support our economic lifestyles.

In short, our wallets too often wag our beliefs. This contradicts the biblical pattern. The scriptural vision calls for a faith which opens pocketbooks. Economic forces shape us all. We can't jump out of our social environments. But we can hear and obey the biblical message which urges us to place our economic decisions *under* the jurisdiction of faith.

The Jubilee provides the Old Testament solution to this dog-tail problem. Faith in a God who graciously delivered from slavery motivated people to open *wide* their hand of mercy. God's saving acts in holy history moved the community to forgive debts, free slaves, and return land. The Hebrews did sometimes balk at practicing the Jubilee. This simply attests to the grip of economic loyalties over faith. The biblical model, nevertheless, is clear: faith should wag wallets. This Old Testament principle undergirds the teaching of Jesus, which we will explore in the next chapters.

Christian obedience today doesn't mean duplicating the historical details of the Jubilee. We no longer live in a theocracy where civil and religious legislation are interwoven under God's direct kingship. A small band of Christians can't impose their brand of economic philosophy on the larger society. Restoring land to its original owners won't help families who have never owned land in the first place. Land redistribution won't correct modern injustices flowing from unequal distribution of technology, information, capital, natural resources, and other non-land resources. Allowing wheat to stand every seventh year in Nebraskan fields won't feed the hungry in

New York and Bombay. Although many of the *details* aren't applicable today, the theological *principles* of the Jubilee do offer a biblical framework for Christian economic practice.

The Jubilee vision weaves together social and spiritual, political and personal, inward and outward. It also blends God's initiative with ours. Prodded by divine liberation, we forgive. As we forgive, so we are forgiven. As we are merciful, so we receive mercy. These truths lie at the heart of the Jubilee. And the Jubilee vision permeates Jesus' teaching, not only at Nazareth but throughout his ministry.[14] Mercy, liberation, freedom, compassion, release. These are the code words of Jubilee. And these are Jesus' words. They energize his parabolic pictures. They shape his social acceptance and forgiveness of the poor and outcast.

The vision is theological but its consequences are practical. For the Jubilee declares God's kingship. And God's decree brings release from enslavement to old authorities, forgiveness from indebtedness to old kingdoms, and liberty to those in spiritual *and* social bondage. This indeed is Jubilee. It is the acceptable day of the Lord, the day of liberty, the day of salvation. And it is Jesus of Nazareth who articulates and embodies it.

Questions for Discussion

1. How do the principles of Jubilee economics mesh with modern economic systems?

2. In what ways are Jubilee principles relevant to our financial involvements today?

3. List examples of spiritual and economic integration in your own life.

4. Identify ways our economic concerns control or wag our religious beliefs.

5. What differences should our faith make in our financial affairs?

6. What is the difference between ownership and stewardship? *P95*

7. How might you apply Jubilee principles to the economic life of your parish, congregation, or fellowship?

— Benevolent fund
— Pastor same standard of living as majority in parish.
— Give instruction

6

LUXURIOUS POVERTY

Perpetual Jubilee

Jesus holds up the Jubilee model as the new way for his disciples. People on the way with him respond to God's gracious love by sharing with the needy around them. Jesus pays an astonishing amount of attention to wealth. Particularly in Luke's Gospel, Jesus makes economic conversion basic to the new kingdom. We'll follow Luke's record with cross-references to the other Gospels.

Jesus didn't condemn private property. He didn't call for a new Christian commune. His message did, however, harshly judge the greedy practices of both Galilee and Judea. Wealth doesn't simply drop from the sky. It's a commodity in a system of social rules that controls its acquisition and use. In chiding the greedy, Jesus questioned those economic norms of his day which allowed the affluent to oppress the poor. He didn't say material things are inherently evil. But he did warn of their danger. They can quickly become demons which unseat the rule of God. We'll begin by exploring six dangers of wealth which, according to Jesus, undercut our allegiance to the kingdom.[1]

Beware: The Strangler

Tucked away in the parable of the sower is a sermon-ette on the threat of riches to kingdom citizens.[2] The seed is the Word of God. Its growth symbolizes the emergence of the kingdom. The seed that falls among the thorn bushes is choked. "And as for what fell among the thorns, they are those who hear, but as they go on their way they are choked by the cares and riches and pleasures of life, and their fruit does not mature" (Luke 8:14; Mark 4:18-19; Matthew 13:22). The seeds do sprout. There is growth and new life. But prickly thorns quickly smother vitality. The cares, riches, and pleasures of life suffocate the new plants.

The synoptic writers all use the word *choke*. Spiritual life is gagged. Fruit buds appear, but there is no harvest. The pods never mature. In the modern context, the cares, riches, and pleasures of life may be jobs, professional advancement, houses, resort homes, luxury vacations, exotic hobbies, financial investments, clothing, cars, and expensive leisure. These pleasures of life abort the kingdom's growth. They divert us from its work and spoil the harvest.

Beware: The Worrier

Yesterday brings guilt. Tomorrow brings worry. Jesus understood that wealth generates anxiety. Will we be secure tomorrow? What if the stock market crashes? Could the burglar alarm fail? Owning of property makes us fret about its defense and protection. In Luke (12:22-34) and in Matthew (6:19-21, 25-33) Jesus urges the disciples four times not to be anxious about food and clothing.

> And do not seek what you are to eat and what you are to drink, nor be of anxious mind. For all the nations of the world seek these things; and your Father knows that you need them. Instead, seek his kingdom, and these things shall be yours as well. Fear not, little flock, for it is

your Father's good pleasure to give you the kingdom. Sell your possessions, and give alms; provide yourselves with purses that do not grow old, with a treasure in the heavens that does not fail, where no thief approaches and no moth destroys. For where your treasure is, there will your heart be also (Luke 12:29-34).

The Greek text means "do not make anxious efforts for."[3] Pagans are anxious about material things. They worry and fret about what they will wear, what they will eat, where they will live, and how much they will earn. "The nations of the world seek these things."

Not so Jesus' disciples. They're not to worry about such things. They're to concentrate fully on the kingdom! God will care for them. In the context of the sabbatical year, when crops weren't planted, the instruction takes on new meaning. One scholar offers this paraphrase.

> If you work six days (or six years) with all your heart, you can count on God to take care of you and yours. So without fear leave your field untilled. As he does for the birds of heaven which do not sow or harvest or collect into granaries, God will take care of your needs. The Gentiles who pay no attention to the Sabbath are not richer than you.[4]

In the context of the sabbatical year these words don't prescribe sloth. Their counsel remains applicable today. Amassing *things* distracts us from the kingdom. We're not day laborers. We're not hired servants who have to worry about our job. We're children of a caring Parent. The poor are the focal point of Jesus' discourse. Hoarding is the pagan way. Giving alms to the poor embraces the upside-down way. The Jubilee principle rides again. Children of a loving God respond to the gift of the kingdom by selling their possessions for the sake of the poor.

This same spirit permeates the Beatitudes when Jesus says give to those that beg, lend without expecting a return (Luke 6:34-35; Matthew 5:42). Excessive profits don't tantalize those whose hearts the kingdom captures. When the kingdom is our treasure, we switch from hoarding to giving. When we focus on kingdom priorities we liberally share our wealth. And in the process we not only restore and liberate the poor but also ourselves! We free ourselves from anxiety and the bondage of worry.

We don't inherit worry. Possessions bring worry. Healthy children rarely worry. A four-year-old listened to a record designed to elicit emotional responses from children. A voice on the record asked, "What are you sad about?" and "What are you mad about?" Hearing the question "What are you worried about?" she came sobbing to Mommy saying, "I have nothing to worry about." A few days later, relieved, she chimed, "I finally found something to worry about." To enter the kingdom as a child, as Jesus calls us to do, is to allow God to care for our tomorrows.

The pithy saying from Matthew's Gospel sums it up. "Therefore do not be anxious about tomorrow, for tomorrow will be anxious for itself. Let the day's own trouble be sufficient for the day" (Matthew 6:34). The number of insurance contracts sold each year reflects the amount of corporate anxiety in a society. A preoccupation with possessions enslaves us to the demon of worry.

Beware: The Blinder

In one of his most stinging parables Jesus shows how the trappings of riches can blind us.[5]

> There was a rich man, who was clothed in purple and fine linen and who feasted sumptuously every day. And at his gate lay a poor man named Lazarus, full of sores, who desired to be fed with what fell from the rich man's table; moreover the dogs came and licked his sores. The poor man died and was carried by the angels to Abraham's bosom. The rich man also died and was buried; and in

Hades, being in torment, he lifted up his eyes and saw Abraham far off and Lazarus in his bosom (Luke 16:19-23).

Usually known as the story of Lazarus and the Rich Man, a better title might be, "Surprised by Hell." Jesus likely aimed the story at rich Sadducees who doubted the existence of an afterlife. It may also be Jesus' answer to incessant requests for a miraculous sign.

In any case, the teaching is clear. The rich man lives in a large house and throws parties every day. He wears fine purple robes and the most expensive Egyptian underwear. He's not a robber or cheat. He hasn't gained his riches illegally. He has simply and legally taken advantage of the economic system of his time. His wealth may have come through inheritance, family connections, hard work, or chance. In any case, he was an upright and decent rich man, perhaps a Sadducee, but certainly not a swindler.

At the edge of the rich man's estate lay a poor beggar suffering from a skin disease. Lazarus, the only character named in any of Jesus' stories, means "God helps."[6] Day after day he reaches out for tidbits of bread. Household guests toss leftovers to him after wiping their hands with them while feasting. The Greek word for *beggar* is related to the word for *spit*. Lazarus was a "spit upon" person despised by the revelers. The beggar embarrassed the rich man and spoiled the decor of his party.

Only the dogs had no favorites. They licked the wounds of poor Lazarus. The dogs symbolized the unsaved, the Gentile outcasts. The upside-down moment dawned. The rich, religious Sadducee spit on the beggar in contempt. But the dogs, of all things, showed compassion. Instead of spitting, they used their saliva for healing. They licked the sores of poor Lazarus. What a stinging punch line—dogs with more compassion than rich Sadducees.[7]

Suddenly the world turns upside down. The rich man roasts in hell and old spit-upon Lazarus sits at Abraham's right hand. He sits in the place of honor, the most prestigious seat in the congregation of the righteous.[8] The tables are turned. High and low reverse. Lazarus had reached up to the rich man, begging for crumbs. Now, roasting in hell, the rich reveler reaches up to Lazarus and begs for a drop of water. Echoes of Mary's Magnificat ring in our ears. "He has filled the hungry with good things, and the rich he has sent empty away" (Luke 1:53).

The message is clear. The rich man, blinded by luxury, refused the Jubilee and now faces a scorching end. The huge gulf symbolizes his distance from God. Almighty God had not forgotten weak, spit-upon Lazarus. But this isn't a story to comfort beggars.[9] The parable doesn't ask the poor to patiently await their reward in the sky. No, the ending of the story focuses on the five rich brothers who are still living.

In the heat of the moment, the rich man feels compassion. He begs Abraham to let Lazarus rise from the dead and warn his brothers. Abraham refuses. Again the rich man begs for a miraculous messenger to rise from the grave and warn his brothers. Each time Abraham says, "They have Moses and the prophets; let them hear them. . . . If they do not hear Moses and the prophets, neither will they be convinced if some one should rise from the dead" (Luke 16:29, 31).

In other words, they've known about Jubilee since their childhood. Their ears have heard the Jubilee laws read aloud Sabbath after Sabbath in the synagogue. The harsh conclusion is obvious. No special messenger will warn the rich. Judgment will singe those who refuse to practice Jubilee and flagrantly violate God's reign. Scrumptious feasting and a lavish lifestyle blinded the rich man. Wrapped in the good life, he couldn't see the sores or hear the nearby cries of despair. How much more serious is the blindness of those who have not only Moses and the prophets, but also Jesus, Paul, James, and church history. Those that have eyes to see let them see!

Beware: The Boss

In another parable Jesus informs us that riches not only blind, they also boss. A rich man has a steward managing his estate (Luke 16:1-9).[10] The owner discovers the steward is dishonest. Thus he asks for a complete inventory of his goods before firing the cheat. The shrewd manager, sensing impending doom, quickly calls in his master's debtors and reduces their debts. A surprised boss commends the steward for his swift action.

This story has perplexed commentators. The Jubilee perspective and knowledge of the financial practices of the time clarify the riddle.[11] At the heart of the story is the fact that the steward was charging interest on goods he had loaned to the debtors. Interest, considered usury and against God's law, was forbidden in the Old Testament. The Pharisees, however, had concocted ways to charge a hidden interest condoned even by Jewish civil courts.

When loaning grain, wine, and oil, hidden interest *could be charged* if the loan was not of "immediate necessity." Most loans weren't considered of "immediate necessity." Thus interest was typically charged, violating the law of God. For example, if a woman had one drop of oil and wanted to borrow more oil, a loan was *not* of "immediate necessity." She already had *one* drop of oil! Thus her creditor could charge interest on her loan.

The rule of "immediate necessity" applied primarily to commodity loans like wheat and wine. Monetary loans were often translated into commodity values so hidden interest could be charged. The interest, however, was never written into the contract, for that would have directly violated God's law.

Back to the story. The steward is in a crunch. He'll soon be jobless, lacking references. His reputation will be smudged. In a jam, he decides to forgive the borrowers the interest he had *unjustly* added to their loans. He likely made the loans in commodity values—oil or grain—to hide the interest he would collect for himself. By canceling the illegal interest, he lost a considerable sum. He didn't have the power to forgive the entire debt since the principal was owed to the master. "Our steward, then, lending at interest to Jews was *morally* a transgressor but *legally* secure, so long as his contracts hid the fact that the loan was usurious."[12]

The steward acted righteously by releasing the interest on the loan. According to the law of the land, the steward could have forced the debtors into slavery if they defaulted on their interest payments. But the interest wasn't the property of the master according to Old Testament law. The master, in fact, may not have known the steward was charging interest. Under the oral law of the Pharisees, if the steward forgave interest without the owner's authority, the owner had to accept the steward's decision. Indeed, the owner had nothing to lose and all to gain. He would now appear to be a caring and forgiving creditor and wouldn't have gained the interest anyway since it was headed for the steward's wallet.

The steward, in the end, modeled righteousness by forgiving unjust debts. Moreover, by granting favors to the indebted farmers, he can expect favors in return from them. They will offer very welcome hospitality and support when he loses his job. The owner commends and ratifies the decision of his steward to follow the Old Testament law and act righteously (Luke 16:8). Then comes the upside-down saying: "the sons of this world are more shrewd in dealing with their own generation than the sons of light."

The Pharisees, supposedly the sons of light, had devised these ingenious ways to skirt the law of God because they were "lovers of money."[13] The worldly steward acted righteously by canceling the interest. The unrighteous mammon is likely the forbidden interest. If the Pharisees can't be faithful in a little thing like loaning money, how can God trust them to handle larger wealth faithfully?

According to Luke, the parable launched Jesus into a biting sermon: "'No servant can serve two masters; for either he will hate the one and love the other, or he will be devoted to the one and despise the other. You cannot serve God and mammon" (Luke 16:13). The Pharisees, lovers of money, heard this and scoffed at him.

But Jesus said to them, "You are those who justify yourselves before men, but God knows your hearts; for what is exalted among men is an abomination in the sight of God" (Luke 16:15).

The steward was caught between two masters. The law of God forbade interest, but the law of the Pharisees permitted it. The two masters contradicted each other. The fraudulent steward realized the impasse and chose to obey God's law. In upside-down fashion, the scoundrel turns hero.

Mammon, an Aramaic term, means "wealth, money, property, or profit."[14] The striking truth here is that Jesus sees mammon claiming divine status. In his view it competes directly with God. Wealth, more than anything else, can act like a god. Jesus doesn't grant deity status to knowledge, skill, appearance, occupation, nobility or nationality. It is wealth, he says, which clamors to control and boss us like a deity.

Fluctuations of the stock market can become our obsession. We easily become engrossed with new gadgets and begin serving them. As new toys captivate children, so material pursuits can captivate grownups. We bow down and worship at the altar of materialism. Luxuries begin to manipulate and dictate our lives. Mammon turns into a god. We can't serve God and wealth simultaneously. We can use wealth to serve God's ends, but that's quite a different thing than serving wealth itself.

Particularly irksome is the profit addict who hides beneath a veneer of pious religious slogans. When Jesus sanitized the temple, he struck at profiteering that oppressed the poor in the name of religion. "Is it not written, 'My house shall be called a house of prayer for all the nations'? But you have made it a den of robbers" (Mark 11:17; Matthew 21:13; Luke 19:46; John 2:16). The merchants operating in the temple weren't acting illegally. They were exchanging "pure" money for offerings and selling animals for sacrifice at a high profit. They had concocted a "legal" system that robbed the poor. Jesus called them "robbers," for they engineered a system that exploited the poor in the name of religion.

The Pharisees, engaged in their own version of fraud by charging secret interest, sneered at Jesus' rebuke. He declared that amassing wealth to impress others is a downright abomination in the eyes of God (Luke 16:15). The pursuit of profit, an easy buck, and secure financial status top the modern success ladder. But they fall to the bottom of the upside-down kingdom. Mercy and compassion are the new yardsticks for measuring success in God's inverted kingdom.

Beware: The Damner

Wealth can have a damning effect on our lives. Jesus underscores this point in a story about a rich fool (Luke 12:13-21). Example stories like the rich fool and the good Samaritan, unlike parables or allegories, show how kingdom citizens should act.

A man in the crowd runs up to Jesus and asks for legal advice. His brother won't share the family inheritance. The man begs Jesus to reprimand his stingy brother. Jesus refuses. Instead he tells a story about barns, for he detects a spirit of covetousness in the man worried about his fair share of the family farm.

The forty-nine-year Jubilee pattern protected the inheritance rights of the poor. If land returned to former owners each generation, a family couldn't accumulate large tracts. Inheritance practices usually favor the children of the rich. Perhaps Jesus was pricking not only this man's greed but also the habits of inheritance which gave him a free farm while others had none.

Back to the story. A farmer enjoys good yields. He expands his storage space and locks up the grain. He plans a party. That night God calls him a fool and demands his soul. Jesus summarizes the inversion, "He who lays up treasure for himself . . . is not rich toward God" (Luke 12:21). The barn this fellow builds isn't a holding shed to keep grain until threshing, but a warehouse for permanent storage.[15] Rather than practicing the Jubilee by sharing his surplus, he hoards it like a fool. Not compassion for the poor but avarice moves him. This is no righteous, sabbatical storage of the sixth year's yield. This is selfish expansionism at the poor's expense. His motive is clear: "Take your ease, eat, drink, be merry"(Luke 12:19-20).

Then in the midst of the party God knocks on the door and calls him a fool. In everyday use "fool" means stupid or a little crazy. The biblical definition is harsh. The fool is one who says there is no God (Psalm 14:1). The rich man's barn is his god. A practical atheist trapped by riches, he lives as though there is no God. In Matthew's Gospel (5:22) the person who calls his brother a fool is worthy of hell. When God dubs the farmer a fool, God damns him. The fool's refusal to practice Jubilee, his captivity by wealth, damns his soul. Stacking up his own treasures makes him a pauper in God's sight. Again inversion strikes. Those who pile it up down here are poor in God's kingdom. The rich in God's kingdom give gener-

ously. In so doing they save their souls from wealth's
damnation.

Jesus warns, "Beware of all covetousness; for a man's
life does not consist in the abundance of his possessions"
(Luke 12:15). Again we find an inversion between kingdom values and societal standards. After the coffin is buried, the gossipers ask, "How big was his estate?" "How
much did she leave?" "Successful" folks leave large financial holdings. The seductive voices of our age proclaim that financial success *does* determine significance.
Life *does* consist of possessions. Abundant possessions *do*
equal abundant life.

Other values govern the upside-down kingdom. Here
investment portfolios aren't acceptable yardsticks for
measuring a person's life. Here the matter is clear: covetousness, being glued to excessive profit and privilege, is
wrong. The mind-set which selfishly builds bigger barns
is clearly named: it's greed, not prudent investment.

Beware: The Curse

The Beatitudes sharpen the contrast between rich and
poor. Here Jesus, in upside-down fashion, awards the
poor and spanks the comfortable. In normal social life we
applaud those who uphold social norms. We give them
awards, diplomas, trophies, or stars on their chart for eating vegetables. We spank deviants who break social rules
with incarceration and fines. Since we value monetary
success, we give the successful enticing rewards. We
shower them with private estates, public citations, prestigious positions, glamorous attention, and access to political power. We assume, as did Jesus' contemporaries, that
wealth equals blessing from God.

Jesus demolishes our assumption by flipping it upside-
down. "Blessed are you poor, for yours is the kingdom of
God. . . . But woe to you that are rich, for you have received your consolation" (Luke 6:20, 24). Instead of re-

buking the poor for being lazy, Jesus exalts them. He makes the despised, the forlorn, and the weaklings the recipients of God's happy blessing. The rich, whom we applaud, Jesus curses.

Does all this mean that raw poverty is a virtue? Is Jesus suggesting that the poor automatically enter the kingdom? Likely not. The term *poor* in the biblical context has at least three meanings. First, it refers to the materially poor—destitutes living in squalor with meager food, housing, and clothing. The term occurs more than sixty times in the Old Testament and usually refers to material poverty.[16]

Second, in a broader sense, the poor in the Bible are the oppressed. They are the captives, the slaves, the sick, the destitute, and the desperate. They are the down-and-outers, the outcasts who can't defend themselves. Those living on the fringes of society depend on the mercy of the powerful. The multitudes following Jesus often consisted of the disreputable, the uneducated, and the stigmatized. Their social blemishes blocked any hope of salvation by the Pharisees' formulas.[17] Jesus' followers were often called the "little ones," and "the least ones."

The third connotation of poor comes out of an Old Testament tradition. Here the poor are the humble in spirit—those who are poor toward God. Regardless of their economic status, they stand before God as beggars with outstretched hands. They plead for mercy with contrite and broken spirits. It was this poorness in spirit—this humility—which Matthew highlighted in his version of the Beatitudes, "Blessed are the poor in spirit, for theirs is the kingdom of heaven" (Matthew 5:3). Matthew underscored inner spiritual poverty while Luke clearly had the materially poor in mind.[18] Luke's Beatitudes consist of a quartet of blessings and woes. (See Luke 6:20-26.)

Blessed are	Woe to
You poor	You that are rich
You that hunger now	You that are full now
You that weep now	You that laugh now
You when men hate you	You when all men speak well of you

What does all this mean? Luke is clearly thinking of those who are indeed financially poor, really hungry, actually crying, actively persecuted. Those at the bottom of the social ladder, discarded on the human trash pile, have not, however, been discarded by God. Almighty God hasn't thrown them out. Indeed God's blessing falls on them. Meanwhile the rich who refuse to practice Jubilee may be indicted for snubbing the law of God. And those who find release from the demonic grip of possessions will have new riches in the kingdom.

But is Jesus applauding sheer poverty? Is he saying that the destitute are automatically in God's kingdom just because they are poor? Probably not. More likely he is making it clear that the poor have God's unconditional welcome. Moreover, in many ways the poor are closer to the kingdom than those caught in the bondage of wealth. It's easier for the poor to enter the kingdom because they aren't entangled in property and prestigious reputations. The grip of mammon distances the rich from the kingdom. As we shall soon see, riches often block the pathway to the kingdom. The outcasts—sinners, prostitutes, children, uninvited guests, publicans—enter the kingdom more readily than the sophisticated, the righteous, the strong, the rich, and the pious.

The poor understand dependence, simplicity, and cooperation. They know the difference between needs and luxuries. Having fewer entanglements, they're freer to abandon all else for the kingdom. They have little to give up. They simply walk in. And are grateful. They know what it's like to be forgiven. The haughty, the arrogant, and the rich find it difficult to stoop in humility at the kingdom's door, acknowledging their dependence on God.

Jesus offers good news to the poor. Their poverty isn't a sign of divine disapproval, a common Jewish view of the time. He signals salvation by transforming the destitute. The blind see. The lame walk. The deaf hear. The lepers are cleansed. The oppressed are released (Matthew 11:5; Luke 4:18-19; 7:22). God welcomes the poor through Jesus Christ. Social outcasts they are, yes, but no longer bums in God's sight. Their poverty is no divine spanking. They're just as welcome in the kingdom as anyone else. That is good news indeed!

It was probably this good news to the poor that required Jesus to add: "Blessed is he who takes no offense at me" (Matthew 11:6; Luke 7:23). Healing lepers and curing the sick carried little offense. But Jesus insulted Pharisaic ears when he blessed the poor and welcomed the destitute into the kingdom.[19] Jesus made it clear that the rich were also welcome—if they shucked off the shackles of wealth, obeyed God's economic laws, and practiced Jubilee.

Jubilee Refused

We've surveyed six warnings of Jesus about wealth. Now we turn to three biblical characters. The rich young ruler, Zacchaeus, and the widow with a coin.

We often lift the story of the rich young ruler (Luke 18:18-30) out of context. Jesus' dialogue with this bright fellow is sharpened when placed alongside his meeting with Zacchaeus. Side by side, Zacchaeus and the ruler dramatize opposite responses to the Jubilee.

The adjective *rich* isn't strong enough for this young upstart. He was *very* rich. He had everything that counts. He was young, wealthy, powerful. This triad sent him soaring to the top. We can only speculate about how he became rich at such a young age. Was it hard work, inheritance, luck?

Why does he stop Jesus? Is his abundant life shallow? Does meaninglessness stalk his life? What must he do to inherit eternal life? This basic question haunts him. The one other time he was asked about eternal life, Jesus responded by telling the good Samaritan story. Here again, as with Lazarus, Jesus links eternal life with proper handling of wealth. The rich ruler is sincere and conscientious, not a cunning robber. He has, in fact, been raised religiously. He knows God's commandments. He has studied in the synagogue. His attendance chart shows the proper Sunday school, Bible school, youth choir, camp, and youth group stars. He knows Scripture and denominational doctrine by heart. His theology is orthodox. He not only knows the creeds—he lives them.

Jesus answers his eternal life question by pointing out one deficiency. He must sell all his possessions before he can follow Jesus. Why should he sell all? Because the poor are hungry and needy. Wealth has captured his heart. Selling all will refocus his attention on the heavenly kingdom. Jesus not only tells him to sell but also invites him to "come, follow me."

We should accent the "follow" rather than the "sell." This is an invitation to join the people of the kingdom and selling all was, in this case, a necessary first step. Jesus didn't always counsel persons to sell all that they have. But in this case he does. The ruler's final decision isn't reported. But it was likely negative since he turns away sadly. He decides to forfeit eternal life.

Jesus summarizes the event harshly: "How hard it is for those who have riches to enter the kingdom of God! For it is easier for a camel to go through the eye of a needle than for a rich man to enter the kingdom of God" (Luke 18:24-25). Some scribes changed later versions of the manuscript to soften the hardness of this teaching. One later edition said that getting a rich man into heaven was like pulling a cord or rope through a needle. Another version said it was like getting a camel through a small gate. Neither of these are likely authentic interpretations.[20] Jesus probably *meant* a camel and a needle. Such exaggeration fits his other teachings on wealth. Today Jesus might put it like this: it's harder for the wealthy to enter the kingdom than for a casino owner to slip through the deposit slot of an automated teller machine.

The outburst of the crowd was predictable. "Then who can be saved?" The answer: "What is impossible with men is possible with God" (Luke 18:27). This doesn't mean God will miraculously drag the wealthy through the kingdom's gate. It means that God's grace can free even rich people from wealth's demonic grip. As we shall soon see, even a rich person can be converted, turned around and taught to practice Jubilee.

Luke builds a bridge between the sad ruler and Zacchaeus with two short stories. Stitched with irony, the stories surprise us: those who see are blind, and a blind man sees. Jesus tells the disciples about his impending doom on the cross. They don't understand. They're perplexed. The disciples, who should know about these things, don't. Perhaps they symbolize the blindness of the rich ruler. The next story features a blind beggar outside of Jericho. He can't see. But he understands who Jesus is and yells for mercy. Jesus heals him. Suddenly this blind one sees; the people glorify and praise God. Luke is preparing us for Zacchaeus.

Jubilee Embraced

Zacchaeus might have been short, but he ran a sizable business (Luke 19:1-10). Jericho was no small farming village. It was a large city with pools, parks, and typical Greco-Roman buildings. The surrounding area, irrigated and extremely fertile, made it wealthy. The rabbis spoke of the "fat lands of Jericho." Because of its balmy weather, Herod the Great made it his winter capital. The region had the distinction of cultivating large groves of balsam trees. They sold for an enormous price, often bringing their weight in gold.[21] Furthermore, Jericho was the gateway for a trade route that ran between Jerusalem and the whole Gentile area east of the Jordan.

Zacchaeus was rich because he was the chief tax "farmer" of the district. A team of subordinates collected the taxes for him. It was a lucrative job in a lucrative area. Zacchaeus had outbid other contenders to secure the right to collect the taxes. Tax collectors used force and fraud to make a financial killing. Tax bosses like Zacchaeus often embezzled from their employees. Tax collectors and especially the tax bosses were despised. This was not only because they were Jews working for the Romans but also because they cheated and used force to collect taxes. They were stigmatized. They weren't allowed to be judges nor could they serve as witnesses in court. Like Gentile slaves, they were even denied those civil and political rights granted to blemished bastards.[22] Money from a tax collector couldn't be given for alms because it was tainted. Eating and associating with tax collectors would contaminate the righteous.

It would have been unthinkable for a Pharisee to lunch with Zacchaeus. The people sneered at him. Perhaps they nicknamed him Zacchaeus out of contempt, for his name means "the righteous." He was anything but righteous. Yet Jesus has lunch with him. The rabbis and scribes would have joyfully spit in his face. Jesus deliberately contaminates himself by eating at the table of this outcast. They eat together in a large mansion. One of the finest in Jericho, it was built on the excessive profits Zacchaeus had squeezed from the poor.

We don't know the details of their conversation, but a

miracle happens. Jesus' care and compassion move Zacchaeus. They so move him he decides to practice Jubilee. He calls neighbors and friends together on the front lawn. Flabbergasted, they hear crabby old Zacchaeus say, "Behold, Lord, the half of my goods I give to the poor; and if I have defrauded any one of anything, I restore it fourfold" (Luke 19:8). The people cheer. They can't believe the miracle unfolding before their eyes.

We don't know the final balance in Zacchaeus' bank account. Depending on how much he returned because of fraud, it may have been empty. Or he may have had a pile left over. In any case Jesus affirms his action. "Today *salvation* has come to this house, since he also is a son of Abraham. For the Son of man came to seek and to *save* the lost" (Luke 19:9-10, emphasis added). This man has been saved! He has joined the people of God. He is in the royal family, a son of Abraham. This is what the day of salvation is all about. What is impossible with humans is possible with God. By the grace of God, a rich man has walked through the eye of the needle.

Things are quite upside down. The rich young ruler has his theology in order but lacks obedience. Zacchaeus has a lousy or nonexistent theology but practices Jubilee. The ruler calls Jesus a "good teacher." Zacchaeus, the cheat, calls him "Lord." The ruler tries to obtain eternal life but refuses to share and can't squeeze through the needle's eye. Zacchaeus probably gives little thought to life eternal, but his new care for the poor opens the needle's eye. The religious leader runs up to Jesus. In contrast, Jesus invites himself to lunch with a sinner who is moved by his compassion. In the first story economic concerns stagnate faith. In the second story faith drives the economic agenda. Here are two contradictory responses to the gospel, opposite reactions to the poor. On the one hand, good theology, no Jubilee, condemnation. On the other hand, scant theology, Jubilee, salvation.

Upside-Down Jubilee

We conclude Jesus' teaching on wealth with a case of inverted Jubilee. Near the end of his ministry, shortly after cleansing the temple, Jesus returns to it. He stands in the massive temple treasury where offerings are placed in large golden vessels. Again we find a comparison of the rich and poor.

> And he sat down opposite the treasury, and watched the multitude putting money into the treasury. Many rich people put in large sums. And a poor widow came, and put in two copper coins, which make a penny. And he called his disciples to him, and said to them, "Truly, I say to you, this poor widow has put in more than all those who are contributing to the treasury. For they all contributed out of their abundance; but she out of her poverty has put in everything she had, her whole living" (Mark 12:41-44; Luke 21:1-4).

In the verse preceding this account, Jesus condemns those "who devour widows' houses and for a pretense make long prayers. They will receive the greater condemnation" (Mark 12:40). A widow in Palestinian society was an outcast. She had no inheritance rights from her husband's property. When the husband died, the oldest son acquired the property. If there was no son, a brother of the deceased husband might marry the widow. If the brother refused or there was none, she would return to her father's house or to begging. Widows, like other women, had no role in public or religious life. They often wore black clothing to signal their plight. Moreover, the rich often oppressed widows.

Jesus condemned the scribes for devouring widows' houses. The scribes had developed religious rules which pushed widows out of their own homes. They glossed over their injustice with long and pretentious prayers. After searing the scribes, Jesus turned to highlight the widow's faithfulness. The rich—probably Sadducees and nobles from the aristocratic Jerusalem families—were putting "large sums" into the offering plate. These impressive gifts were likely pure and proper silver coins.

A poor widow comes. She drops in two copper coins worth a penny. The copper lepton was the smallest Greek coin in circulation. It took 128 of these leptons to equal one denarius—a day's wage. So the widow drops in 2/128 of a day's wage!

Jesus is impressed, so impressed he calls the disciples together for a lesson. The widow, he says, has put in more than all these rich persons together. How can this be? She put in everything she had. They just skimmed the top off their abundance. The actual amount of money was insignificant. What counted was the amount left over for consumption. The rich were still quite rich, even after a sizable offering. The poor widow gave everything, not a self-righteous tithe. The story suggests that the important thing is what proportion of our wealth we give rather than its raw amount.

Jesus affirms the Jubilee attitude of the poor widow. Certainly she could have found convincing excuses for not giving the last coins in her purse. Upside-down Jubilee occurs when the poor give more sincerely than the rich.

There is other evidence that Jesus expected the poor to give. His instruction in Matthew (5:40) to give your cloak as well as your coat is directed toward a poor person. Debtors often gave their coat as a sign of their intent to repay a loan (Exodus 22:26). If the creditor demanded repayment, a poor debtor was to give even his cloak. Jesus not only expects the rich to practice Jubilee, he also affirms the charity of the poor. They, as well as the rich, can be snared by covetousness.

The six warnings and three character studies summarize Jesus' economic message. The amount of material in the Gospels focusing on wealth is astonishing. No other concept, except for the kingdom of God itself, appears more frequently in the Gospels. We simply can't conclude that economic values are peripheral to the kingdom. They stand at the core of the new kingdom. Conversion which doesn't involve economic change isn't authentic. The values of the kingdom clash with the economic values of modern life. Jesus not only condemns greed in first-century Palestine, he calls for a perpetual Jubilee. The upside-down message reverberates again and again.

Blessed are you poor . . . woe to you that are rich. Luke 6:20.

What is exalted among men is an abomination in the sight of God. Luke 16:15.

Lazarus goes to Abraham's bosom, the rich man ends up in torment. Luke 16:22, 23.

So is he who lays up treasure for himself, and is not rich toward God. Luke 12:21.

For all the nations of the world seek these things. . . . Instead, seek his kingdom. Luke 12:30, 31.

The rich young ruler seeks eternal life, but salvation visits Zacchaeus' house. Luke 18:18—19:10.

Do not lay up for yourselves treasure on earth . . . but lay up for yourselves treasures in heaven. Matthew 6:20.

No one can serve two masters; for . . . he will hate the one and love the other. Matthew 6:24.

The teachings of Jesus emerged in the first stage of a new social movement which eventually became the church. Since leaders of new social movements are often "outside" the mainstream of society, they typically criticize institutionalized economic practices and structures. Many Christian disciples find themselves "inside" institutions concerned with continuity and self-preservation. Stable and predictable financial arrangements are necessary for organizations to continue. Protecting financial self-interest is basic to institutional survival. How, then, do we relate the economic teachings of Jesus, the "outsider," to the issues faced by "insiders" in mainstream organizations, corporations, schools, and churches? In what ways can the teachings of Jesus inform the economic life of modern organizations, without jeopardizing their survival?

Questions for Discussion

1. Identify instances when the six warnings of Jesus were applied to material possessions in your life.

2. What aspect of wealth has been most troublesome in your experience? Why?

3. What economic practices today might produce a Lazarus?

4. What is the most surprising comparison between Zacchaeus and the rich young ruler?

5. Summarize the central message of Jesus' economic teachings.

6. To what extent do Jesus' teachings about material possessions fit the Jubilee framework?

7. In what ways do our typical inheritance practices help or hinder the Jubilee vision of Jesus?

8. Identify persons and organizations which follow Jubilee principles today.

7

RIGHT-SIDE-UP DETOURS

Our commitment to the present economic order often diverts us around the biblical teaching on wealth and distorts our reading of the Scripture. We're tempted to lift verses out of their context and twist them to legitimate or "bless" our personal economic philosophy. In addition to slanting Scripture our way, we often use nonbiblical but "sacred" sayings to rationalize affluence. We'll scan ten detours—ten examples of ways our economic commitments may wag our theological beliefs. The ten bypasses permit us to slip by the substance of Jesus' message. These evasions, often based on an isolated verse or proverbial saying, enable us to maneuver around Jesus' call for economic conversion.

Detour One: What About the Parable of the Talents?

A frequent excuse clings to a familiar parable (Matthew 25:14-30; Luke 19:11-27). It's ironic that we use the parable of the talents, directly following Luke's story of Zacchaeus, to contradict Zacchaeus' behavior. The popular interpretation of the parable often runs along these lines. God has given each of us different abilities or personal talents—singing, managing, counseling, etc. The talents also refer to our financial assets—especially our ability to make money. God will hold us accountable for how we use these personal gifts and material resources. God will reward us for expanding them.

Punishment, on the other hand, will strike those who sit on their resources. Thus if making money is our gift, we should make money like mad. We should multiply capital assets and property as rapidly as possible. This logic can justify profiteering. Matthew's Gospel quotes the master telling the unfaithful steward, "You ought to have invested my money with the bankers, and at my coming I should have received what was my own with interest" (Matthew 25:27). A literal interpretation of these lines misses the point entirely.

Just because Jesus uses money as the key symbol in the story doesn't mean the parable addresses financial stewardship. The actual objects in a parable are usually not literal prescriptions for Christian behavior. Everyday symbols are used to craft a story with a deeper meaning. We don't say that the parable of the sower means Christians should actually sow grain. Nor do we say that the parable of the lost sheep implies we should raise sheep! On the other hand, example stories such as the good Samaritan *do* show Christian behavior, "Go and do likewise" (Luke 10:37).

So what's the point of the talents? A nobleman entrusts his servants with a commodity and holds them accountable for it. His unexpected return causes a crisis. The master judges the servants by how they cared for his property. The commodity in the story is our knowledge of Christian faith. Perhaps Jesus was thinking of the scribes or Jewish people in general. How had they managed the faith and Scriptures which had been given them? Jesus was now judging their stewardship of the law. How well had they handled their stewardship of the commandments? Had they preserved and interpreted the law of Moses properly? Or had they buried their knowledge of the law in the sand?

The early church thought the parable meant that Jesus, like the nobleman, was going away. Upon his return, he would judge them on how they had multiplied the kingdom. In fact, Luke (19:11) reports that Jesus told the parable *because* some disciples thought the kingdom would appear immediately when they arrived in Jerusalem. Luke likely thought Jesus would judge his followers' stewardship of the kingdom at his second coming, rather than immediately. Jesus might then ask how well they had practiced the teachings of the kingdom.

As one writer puts it, we're to "trade" or "barter" with kingdom ideas.[1] We're to invest and expand our kingdom knowledge. We're responsible for using our knowledge of the kingdom to its fullest. The more talents we have, the more we know about the secrets of the kingdom, the greater will be our accountability.

So, rather than a story which justifies the acquisition of wealth, we have the opposite. The more we know about the upside-down way of Jesus, the greater our obligation to live it. The parable of the talents echoes the story of the rich man and Lazarus. The rich man knew about Moses and the prophets. He understood the Jubilee. He had been given a talent, knowledge of God's economic way, but had buried it. He didn't feed the beggar Lazarus. So he faced condemnation.

Luke places the parable of the talents immediately after Zacchaeus. Perhaps Luke is suggesting *we* are responsible for the stewardship of the ideas of the Zacchaeus story. Will we, like Zacchaeus, allow the lordship of Jesus Christ to open our pocketbooks? A similar interpretation fits the wisdom saying at the end of the parable. "To every one who has will more be given; but from him who has not, even what he has will be taken away." The key issue here is *more* of what? This hardly means that those who have money will make more. Although that's often true, the meaning of the parable is clear. Those who invest and multiply their kingdom knowledge will be given *more*. Those who waste it may lose the kingdom completely.

Detour Two: Seek the Kingdom and Get Rich!

After teaching about anxiety, Jesus instructs the disciples to "seek first his kingdom and his righteousness, and all these things shall be yours as well" (Matthew 6:33; Luke 12:31). Does this offer biblical proof that those who pursue the kingdom will become rich? May we view riches as a sign of God's blessing? We have already seen that wealth in Jesus' eye was more of a curse than a blessing.

What does it mean that kingdom seekers will have the material things of life as well? In the context of the sabbatical year, Jesus is simply saying that God will provide an adequate six-year yield to cover needs in both the sixth and seventh years. If folks follow his command, he will care for them. The "things" God will supply are basic food and clothing—not luxurious homes and estates. God will provide the basic necessities. In the context of the sabbatical year, this passage isn't a scheme for getting rich off the kingdom. It simply offers basic survival in the seventh year.

A business venture or a household managed in harmony with Christian principles—honesty and integrity—will likely be successful. But managers and owners who truly allow the rule of God to operate in their lives won't hoard gain. They'll share it in the spirit of Jubilee. Our material stockpiles may be a barometer of our willingness to follow kingdom principles.

Matthew counsels us to seek the kingdom and God's "righteousness," which could be interpreted as God's "justice." Seeking the kingdom doesn't mean bread will mysteriously fall out of heaven. Nor does it mean we'll automatically get rich. Seeking the kingdom with the intention of getting rich perverts the kingdom's very essence.

Detour Three: Leave and Gain!

We find another evasive route near the end of the rich young ruler story. Jesus concludes, "Truly, I say to you, there is no man who has left house or wife or brothers or parents or children, for the sake of the kingdom of God, who will not receive manifold more in this time, and in the age to come eternal life" (Luke 18:29, 30; Mark 10:29-30; Matthew 19:29). Matthew and Mark include land in their list of things forsaken. Does this mean Jesus will multiply our property if we follow him?

A pastor warming up his congregation for an offering used this verse. He promised that God would literally return $100 for every dollar placed in the offering. Giving with the hope of getting rich distorts the spirit of Jubilee. Such an interpretation would also multiply wives, husbands, and parents in this age!

Jesus doesn't expect our spouses and lands to multiply. He is saying that when we join the kingdom we join the family of God. Disciples who sell property or leave homes will find a warm welcome in other Christian homes as they travel. They will discover a network of new sisters, brothers, and parents in the kingdom who welcome them with beds and teapots. Those who argue that God will double our wealth if we forsake everything for the kingdom usually are the ones who have *not* left houses or lands. They are, rather, trying to find an isolated verse to justify expansion. In contrast, Jesus says that those who make sacrifices for the kingdom's sake will receive both material and spiritual rewards now and in the age to come.

Detour Four: The Poor Are Always with You!

All four Gospels report the story of the woman pouring expensive perfume on Jesus (Matthew 26:6-13; Mark 14:3-9; Luke 7:36-50; John 12:1-8). There is considerable variation in the four accounts. All writers (except Luke) report that the onlookers condemned this waste of a year's wages. They wondered aloud why the perfume wasn't sold and the money given to the poor. Jesus said, "For you always have the poor with you, but you will not always have me" (Matthew 26:11).[2] Is this a clear example of Jesus' fatalism? He acknowledges the perpetual existence of the poor and shows the priority of worship over social concern—or does he?

Interestingly, Jesus quotes directly from Deuteronomy 15, the chapter with Jubilee and sabbatical instructions. Earlier in the passage God tells the Hebrews that if they're obedient there will be no poor in the land. God then says that if they harden their hearts, there will be poor. As long as greed and selfishness continue, the poor will be among them. Does this justify a callous neglect of the poor? Just the opposite! "The poor will never cease out of the land; therefore I command you, You shall open *wide* your hand to your brother, to the needy and to the poor, in the land" (Deuteronomy 15:11, emphasis added).

In light of his continual plea on behalf of the poor, it's hardly conceivable that Jesus now contradicts himself by telling us to neglect the poor who, after all, will always be around and there's not much we can do about it. He's rather saying that as long as greed and ambition govern the lives of people and their social systems, there will always be poor. His observation of this fact *does not* justify its perpetuation. Rather than excusing us from social obligation, Jesus is reminding us that the alleviation of poverty is a never-ending struggle.

A detailed study of Jewish law shows that pouring the perfume was an act not of worship but of charity.[3] A prostitute couldn't give her offering in the temple because her profession contaminated it. Contaminated earnings and ointment could, however, be used to prepare a corpse. Preparation for burial took precedent over feeding and clothing the poor. In the words of Jesus, "She has done it to prepare me for burial" (Matthew 26:12). The prostitute takes a tool of her trade—perfume—and uses it in an act of charity to prepare Jesus' body. She joyfully gives the perfume which once seduced other bodies to prepare the body which will be broken for the sins of the world. Splashing perfume over Jesus' body symbolized the rejection of her old ways and her spontaneous joy of forgiveness, for she had many sins. Upside down indeed!

Detour Five: It All Depends on Your Attitude!

It's tempting to summarize Jesus' teaching on wealth by saying, "It's our attitude that's important. As long as we have the right attitude, things will work out okay." Now obviously attitudes are important; they influence our behavior. Jesus taught that wrong attitudes are as bad as wrong behavior. And the poor can be as materialistic, if not more so, than the rich.

Jesus didn't say, however, that we can substitute good attitudes for good behavior. Good sentiments are a fine place to start, but Jesus clearly wants us to go beyond them. He condemns the rich fool for expanding his barn and the rich man for throwing crumbs to Lazarus. He encourages us to distribute wealth. Several times he tells his disciples to sell their possessions. He describes Zacchaeus as a child of God because his change of attitude alters his economic behavior. The rich young ruler has good attitudes, but they aren't enough to feed the poor.

Warm feelings in our heart, good intentions in our head, and proper attitudes in our mind are an essential first step. But they don't clothe and feed the poor. Behavior is the test. Jesus calls for attitude changes that produce action.

Detour Six: What About Stewardship?

Stewardship is a core concept in understanding our relationship to wealth. Sometimes we use stewardship itself to mask impious behavior. Oddly enough, the word *stewardship* isn't used by Jesus to discuss wealth. Instead, he warns of the dangers of mammon and calls for compassion. In Hebrew, steward means "man over the house." The steward is an official who controls a large household for the master. It's proper to use the term "stewardship" to describe the Christian's relationship to property. The concept reminds us that God in fact owns the property. But what do we mean by stewardship?

It's helpful to distinguish between the wishes of the owner and the wishes of the steward. The steward is responsible to manage the property according to the master's wishes, *not* the steward's. We sometimes use the term to whitewash our own desires. We make stewardship mean taking whatever resources we have, multiplying them as fast as possible, and using them for our own purposes.

This twists the biblical view of stewardship. The biblical view begins with God's vision for the use of natural and human resources. In the Old Testament Jubilee, and in Jesus' teachings, God's resources are to be widely shared. They're not to be used to elevate some people and put others down. They're to be given freely to those in need. Good stewards of God's resources generously share and distribute them. We're not stewards of God's resources when we stockpile and multiply them for personal gain. Good stewards are prudent and careful guardians of the resources that have come their way. They despise waste and callous abuse of resources. Faithful stewards are frugal when calculating their own needs and generous when responding to others.

Detour Seven: Give a Tithe!

Even tithing can serve as a self-righteous diversion around Jesus' message. It can become a mechanical rule to justify luxurious living. The New Testament doesn't explicitly instruct us to tithe. Jesus and the apostle Paul both encourage liberal giving. Liberal offerings go beyond tithing, as we've seen in the case of the poor widow. Tithes were an integral part of the Old Testament system of sacrifices and offerings. The New Testament assumes the tithe as a minimal standard for giving.

The weakness of the tithe as our only guideline for giving is obvious. A person earning $10,000 a year gives $1,000 and retains $9,000. Someone else earning $100,000 and giving $10,000 can live extravagantly on $90,000. Tithing unfortunately focuses our attention on how much we *give* rather than on how much we *keep*. In upside-down fashion, God cares more about what we *keep* than what we *give*. It's less important that one person gives $1,000 while another gives $10,000. What counts is that some struggle to make ends meet with $9,000, while others justify spending $90,000 lavishly because, after all, "we have tithed."

Token tithes don't necessarily exemplify good stewardship, compassion, or Jubilee. They easily become self-righteous maneuvers to justify opulence. Rather than using the tithe to excuse upscale living, we ought to explore ways of shrinking our standard of living so we have more surplus to give.

A graduated tithe is one way of working at this issue.[4] A family might establish a baseline budget of, say, $30,000.

It might then give a regular 10 percent tithe on this basic figure.

Five percent is added to the tithe for each thousand above the baseline.

A $31,000 income is tithed 10 percent on the first thirty thousand and 15 percent on the next thousand, and so on.

When the income reaches $48,000, all of the last thousand is given since the graduated tithe has jumped to 100 percent.

At $48,000, a family following this scheme would have given $13,350 and retained $34,650 for personal use and savings. Under the traditional tithe, they would have given $4,000 with $43,200 left over. A graduated tithe embodies the Jubilee spirit and nudges us in the direction of generous stewardship.

Detour Eight: Live Within Your Means!

A strict tithing mind-set promotes the notion that the good life is fine "if we can afford it." The popular adage of "living within our means" suggests that those of meager means must follow an austere budget. Those with larger means can, of course, consume freely. "If you can afford it; you can have it." As our means expand, so does our appetite for so-called "necessities." The things that we couldn't afford in the past become necessities as our incomes rise. Living within our means is obviously necessary—especially for lower-income families. It often, however, becomes a convenient excuse to endorse an upscale lifestyle for higher-income folks. "Live within your means" is a cultural rule of thumb that steers us away from the spirit of Jubilee.

Detour Nine: Maintain the Witness!

"Maintain the witness" is a pious argument that also evades the Jubilee model. It suggests that a high standard of living is necessary to "witness" effectively to affluent persons. To reach upper-class folks with the gospel we need to communicate with them through their own symbols. We can't witness meaningfully to the Mercedes crowd if we drive a Ford. Christians need to splurge to communicate the gospel in an affluent context. The advocates of "luxury evangelism" certainly wouldn't encourage Christians to steal as a witness to legal offenders. Nor would they encourage sexual promiscuity as a witness to prostitutes. Yet they use this logic to rationalize an extravagant lifestyle. In the process, the good news becomes diluted.

Such upscale "witnessing" calls others to a simple "yes" to Jesus in their heart with few expectations for social and economic conversion. This is cheap salvation. When the gospel becomes inoffensive, it's no longer gospel. Cheap gospel doesn't free people from the grip of social fads but calls them to a false gospel which makes service to mammon appear righteous. The gospel of Jesus Christ frees us from enslavement to other idols. Maintaining a high standard of living in order to "effectively" witness not only mocks true faith, it also leads others to a cheap gospel.

Detour Ten: Children of the King!

A final detour reminds us that we are, after all, children of a King. The Scripture promises manifold blessings to God's faithful children. Since earthly kings live in extravagant palaces, we Christians should also live luxuriously. This is how we show our membership in God's royal court. Children of a king should dress and eat in regal fashion.

Jesus is, of course, our King. But that hardly gives us license to indulge in lavish living. Just the opposite. If Jesus is indeed Lord and King of our life, we'll seek to obey his commandments to share our wealth. His kingship is upside-down in contrast to earthly kingdoms. He does promise to "bless us," to provide wholeness, peace, and joy. But he never promises to make his children financially rich.

Meanwhile Back Home

What does all this mean? The imminent rule of God in the lives of believers is the key to Jesus' economic message.[5] The nearness of God's reign robs the economic demons of their power. We've seen the Jubilee principles woven throughout the Gospels. As we experience God's forgiveness, we can in turn forgive. As we learn of God's goodness, we no longer fret about necessities. Once we were beggars, strangers, slaves, and debtors. Now God has made us new, filling us with compassion for those who remain trapped as we once were.

God's love for us transforms our economic behavior. Mercy, not accumulation, becomes our new yardstick for measuring success. Generous giving replaces conspicuous consumption. God's highest law forms the core of this upside-down way. Loving God with all our heart means loving our neighbors as much as ourselves. And this means caring, sharing, giving—valuing our neighbors' welfare as much as our own. The liberating detachment of the new way strips the old economic demons of their grip.

Jesus doesn't offer specific answers, but he does prod us toward the right questions. He pushes us beyond rules and regulations by calling for a perpetual Jubilee. He doesn't reject private property nor insist on communal ownership. Much of his teaching assumes our ownership of private property. We can't lend or give to those in need if we have no property. At times we may need to sell all, like the rich young ruler. Other times Jesus may call us to join Zacchaeus, returning our unjust profits without selling all. What Jesus asks of us may vary, but he does insist that we treat the poor as if they were us.

Although addressed to individuals, Jesus' words rocked the foundation of the Palestinian economy. His call for Jubilee shook the economic structures which encouraged huge disparities between rich and poor. Does working hard to earn money justify spending it lavishly and self-ishly? Are there times when the legal acquisition of money is immoral? Jesus warns us that wealth can turn into a powerful god, capturing our imagination, demanding our allegiance, bending our knees, and ruling our lives.

The Jubilee perspective nudges us to question cultural assumptions we take for granted. Is it morally right to pay only a minimum wage even when it's legal? Should we charge exorbitant professional fees, even though they're legal and customary? Exorbitant professional fees may hinder the Jubilee by perpetuating economic structures which keep poor people poor while rich folks feast.

Is getting the "best price" for a property or product always "good stewardship"? Selling for a lower figure to a needy person might be more in the spirit of Jubilee than demanding the "best price." Is charging the highest commission always consistent with Jesus' way? Does "good stewardship" mean squeezing the last nickel out of every deal? Is it best to charge the highest price so we can give more away? In subtle and unconscious ways our economic systems may distort our faith. We dare not assume that just because "that's the way things are," that they're ethical, moral, or Christian.

Who's Rich?

Jesus talked of the rich and the poor. These terms needed little clarification for his audience. In a two-class society the rich were obvious. It's easy to toss aside Jesus' comments about wealth because we assume we're not rich. A moment's reflection shows that the term "rich" is quite relative. A person rich in one context may be poor in another. It depends on who we compare with whom. There are simply no absolute standards to define the slippery term *rich*. Middle class folks tend not to worry about Jubilee because Jesus was talking about the *really* rich.

Social scientists note that happiness doesn't automatically rise with wealth. We're satisfied when we *feel* we have enough resources to meet our perceived needs. What we *think* we need is, of course, socially shaped by the people around us. If we don't think we need much we can be happy with little. If we think we need to match our upscale peers, a modest salary hike may leave us sulking.

When I think about rich people, I think of the Rockefellers, the Hunts, the Kennedys, and the Trumps. I think of places like Palm Springs, California, where "simple and unpretentious" homes go for several million dollars. I think of chief executives who earn several million a year. I think of the sports and film stars with multi-million-dollar salaries. These are the rich folks in my book. And I'm certainly not one of them. Or am I?

A visit to a rural church in Central America a few years ago opened my eyes. A Christian brother took me to his banana plot over a mile up the mountain. I counted as we walked. He had over fifty patches on the only pair of trousers he owned. I realized I was rich, very rich indeed, with my dozen pairs of trousers and shirts to spare.

The relative meaning of *rich* encourages us to look up the social ladder and compare ourselves with those above us. We certainly aren't rich compared to someone making $50,000 a year more than we do. No, we aren't rich beside the person with a larger house than we have. By looking up the ladder, we're *never* rich. Staring up the ladder makes us feel poor. Thus the biblical message eludes us. We may hope that the rich on the rung above us drop a few leftovers down and don't trample our fingers. But that's wishful thinking because the ones above us are also looking up and feeling poor in contrast to the rich above them. And so the feeling of poverty spirals ever upward.

The Jubilee perspective reminds us that once we were slaves, once we were captives. The reminder shifts our focus downward, where the biblical spotlight always points. Pagans look up. When we follow the biblical spotlight, we look down and realize we're rich. The Jubilee message has struck home. Few readers of this book are a Lazarus. But Lazaruses *are* in our communities. They sit, by the curb, receiving less than the daily minimum of calories. Even estimating conservatively, about half a billion—that's 500 million!—people are gradually starving. *Another* half billion receive enough calories but are short on protein. From outright starvation to deficient diets, about one fourth of the worldwide village is hungry.[6]

Compared to them, most of us are rich. We're even flab fighters. Undisciplined diets send us scampering after the perfect weight loss program. About one third of us among the world's population gobble up some 80 percent of the resources. We leave the poorer two thirds to scrap for the remaining 20 percent of the goodies. Even when respective standards of living are taken into account and "real" purchasing power is calculated, the average American is 10 to 17 times richer than the average person in many countries.[7] We can only read our Bibles as rich Christians. We are rich. Not poor.

Downscale

Where do we start? We can begin by consuming less. Many of our so-called necessities are status symbols we polish to maintain a respectable image among our peers. Incessant shopping has become a sacrificial ritual on the altar of materialism. Curtailing consumption is the beginning of responsible stewardship of God's nonrenewable resources. Materialism is a dead-end trap. The more we get the more we want.

And the more we get the more we need to maintain what we have. As soon as we catch up with a fad or fashion, someone else moves ahead. Again we're behind. Someone else always outdoes us with a bigger model, more accessories, greater speed, super convenience, or advanced styling. Advertising ever creates new needs and desires. Our cravings wrap our lives in artificial trappings and rob our souls of moral integrity. The drive for *more* of everything leaves the rich empty, the poor hungry, and scarce resources wasted.

All of us need friends for support and affirmation. Our self-image is rooted in how we *think* other people view us. The old social adage is true—I am what I think you think I am. If I think other people think I'm odd, I feel inadequate and unsure of myself. We want others to respect us and think well of us. To gain that acceptance we display the status symbols of our social group—cars, clothing, boats, books, computers, and trinkets. Outdated clothing, small cars, modest housing, and simple vacations violate the rules of middle-class etiquette. Unfortunately, fashion expectations often peak in the pew at 10:00 a.m. on Sunday morning.

Others may punish upside-down behavior with smirks, gossip, ridicule, and avoidance. This hurts. That's why we need Christian friends who also affirm upside-down values. We're all social beings who depend on others for our sense of worth and value. It's important to select and create circles of friends—reference groups—that affirm and support kingdom values. This network of Christian friends needn't have a formal structure, but it must offer reinforcement for modest lifestyles. The loving support of an alternate culture, a Christian enclave, lets us withstand the seductive and demonic forces of materialism.

Curtailing consumption isn't a panacea for world hunger. Buying less steak at the local supermarket won't push more protein into third-world pantries. As Christians, we consume less not because it's necessarily an effective solution to world hunger, but because it's the morally responsible thing to do. We're accountable not for grandiose solutions to world problems but for our personal obedience to our knowledge of the gospel. That's the essence of the parable of the talents.

It's easy to do nothing because we fear our small act won't count. It's true that one more baby, one more luxury car, and one more vacation home won't make a significant difference. However, when several million other people think and act the same way, the *corporate consequences* of our behavior are devastating. Five million more pieces of litter, 10 million more gas guzzlers, and 20 million more babies will make a whopping collective impact. The belief that "my behavior won't make a difference anyway" doesn't excuse us from moral responsibility.

On the other hand, individual acts aren't enough. We also must act together through organizations at local and international levels that make a difference. Above all we must nurture a global perspective that makes a difference on the personal and local level.

There are several simple questions those of us concerned with simplicity can ask ourselves.

If everyone throughout the world consumed as many natural resources as I do, what kind of a world would we have?

How much does my level of consumption drain energy resources and strain the environment?

Is my lifestyle this year more simplified than it was last year? Or is it more complicated, more consumptive, more stressful?

In which direction am I drifting?

Practicing Jubilee

Jesus doesn't call us away from the world of commerce and business. He doesn't teach us that managing money and property is wrong. He tells us instead that the reign of God in our lives should shape our acquisition, management, and disposal of wealth. The expression of Jubilee takes different forms, depending on our position in a particular economic structure. If we're the rich one in a relationship, it may mean sharing beyond expectation with persons below us.

As employers, we practice Jubilee by paying above-average wages with joy. Instead of trying to squeeze the maximum labor from employees at the minimum price, we share profits, provide dignity in work, and encourage stock ownership in the company. This isn't a prescription for bankruptcy, nor a carelessness about the bottom line. In fact, the long-term spin off may yield happier employees working harder and producing more for all. A commitment to the Jubilee perspective calls for distributing wealth fairly among those who help create it. Funneling all profit into the hands of a few contradicts the Jubilee spirit.

Where does profit come from?

Where does it go?

Does its distribution conform to a Jubilee vision? Or does it push a few folks to the top of the economic ladder and hold the rest at the bottom?

These are questions with which the Christian entrepreneur must struggle.

Recall the biblical injunction that people and material resources are the Lord's. We're not to exploit them. We're to value people over things. We're to use possessions, not people. A corporation, following the Jubilee vision, will employ the socially disadvantaged—ex-offenders, the deaf, the disabled, and those stigmatized in other ways. Jubilee companies will establish their own goals for hiring minorities. For those giving professional services the Jubilee approach might mean a graduated payment scale tied to client income. Or it might mean charging fees below the prevailing rates. Jubilee professionals don't exploit, even when this is legal or customary. The rich whom the biblical vision energizes share the Jubilee with those around and below them with joy.

Upside-down giving that spills beyond expectation signals our entrance into the kingdom. It's a powerful sign that King Jesus is king of our resources. We need to find creative ways to use our resources for the sake of the poor. In one community a pretrial bail association posts property bail so the poor don't need to sit in jail for months before their trial. Homeowners provide their properties as bail for this program. Property or savings can be used as collateral for disadvantaged persons lacking credit who want to buy a home or start a small business. If we love our neighbors as ourselves, will we sign our neighbor's loan application and live to pay the consequences of a default?

When we're the poor in a relationship, the Jubilee takes a different turn. Instead of banging on the boss's office door for our own raise, we might advocate on behalf of those who have less than we do. We might offer to pay beyond the established price for a product or service. We can freely tip beyond expectation. We can add a tithe to the monthly rent or mortgage as a sign of Jubilee. These aren't careless expressions of stewardship. They're upside-down witnesses to our freedom from economic bondage. Freely sharing in the Jubilee spirit isn't always possible. But as we cut frivolous extras and work toward a modest standard of living, we can give "surprise tithes." Such tithes are signs of God's love and our release from the demons of mammon.

Upside-Down Giving

There are five signs of upside-down giving. First, we funnel Jubilee sharing toward those crunched by economic disparities. Jesus again and again directs us to give to the poor. In contrast to many religious promoters, Jesus didn't plead for contributions to his cause. His passion was for the poor, not for religious propaganda. Jesus understood that the most powerful Christian witness comes when our giving isn't tied to the strings of propaganda. The Jubilee mentality gives to genuine need, not to self-serving religious programs.

Second, Jubilee generosity includes other Christians in the decision-making process of giving. Rather than wheeling and dealing to buy seats of influence and public recognition, Jubilee giving is a corporate expression of love. Rich and poor in the church share in the giving process.

Third, Jubilee giving assumes that one form of giving is not to take money from others in the first place. Taking as much as possible from others to give more contradicts the Jubilee spirit. Not taking funds in the first place, funds that might be rightfully ours, is in itself a form of giving. This in many ways protects the dignity of the individual more than paternalistic gifts.

Fourth, Jubilee giving doesn't send checks to every compassion fund picturing emaciated children. Money addresses only one type of need. Money alone isn't enough. People, time, dignity, and education must also be included in the Jubilee package. Compassion ought to be intelligent, orderly, sophisticated, and humane. It must go beyond Christmas baskets, to jobs, low-interest loans, credit, security, educational projects, and housing.

Fifth, Jubilee giving flows from the story of God's love. It attests to the biblical story of Jubilee—the story of God's compassion articulated by Jesus. Without the biblical perspective, financial aid simply pushes others up a hollow and vicious economic ladder. Jubilee giving proclaims the good news of forgiveness in Jesus Christ. Giving that doesn't bring a message of spiritual liberation is little more than do-gooder paternalism that leads to new ways of worshiping mammon.

Consider an example of modern Jubilee. Habitat for Humanity is an international organization that creatively applies biblical economics. Habitat operates in several hundred locations in more than two dozen countries around the world. The program builds low-cost, modest homes for those without homes. Prospective home owners must give some 500 hours of "sweat equity" (volunteer time) to qualify for a house. They must give some of the "sweat equity" to other projects before construction begins on their home. They can pay off mortgages *without* interest over 20 years. Contributors share money, time, supplies, and labor hand-in-hand with the poor. Habitat builds more than homes—it builds relationships and community. Above all, Habitat nurtures dignity and responsibility. It is indeed an exemplary model of modern Jubilee.

Questions for Discussion

1. Identify other detours that may circumvent the biblical teaching on wealth.

2. Which of the detours is most prevalent in your personal experience; in the life of your congregation?

3. List some typical assumptions about economic life which may clash with Christian faith.

4. Identify examples of financial practices that may be immoral even though legal.

5. Do you consider yourself rich?

6. What ways have you discovered to limit your consumption?

7. How do you respond to the five signs of upside-down giving?

8

IMPIOUS PIETY

The Oral Tradition

Why did Jesus' ministry cause a head-on clash with religious authorities? Jesus lived in an Old Testament world entrenched in the teachings of Moses. He didn't come to destroy the law or to scorn it. He embraced it and fulfilled it. If Jesus affirmed the law, why did he collide with religious leaders? The answer lies in his attitude toward the oral law. Jesus endorsed the written Torah, the five books of Moses, but he scoffed at parts of the oral law. He saw the oral law as having less authority than the Scriptures. This stirred the ire of the Pharisees. The Gospel writers likely underscored the antagonism between Jesus and the Pharisees because the early church faced opposition from the Pharisees. A brief overview of the oral law helps us grasp the nature of the conflict.

At the time of Jesus there were actually two Torahs, two types of religious law. Both Sadducees and Pharisees accepted the written Torah, composed of the five books of Moses, as the holy law of God. It contained the commandments given to Moses on Mt. Sinai. There was also an oral Torah, an unwritten law, passed on by word of mouth from generation to generation. The scribes had de-

veloped the oral law and by the time of Jesus the Pharisees followed it to the letter. The oral law evolved
through three different stages—*Midrash, Mishnah,* and *Talmud.*

The first step, or *Midrash,* emerged after the Jews returned to their homeland from Babylonian captivity. The
Midrash was a verse-by-verse commentary explaining the
written Scripture. An interpretation followed each verse.
For example, in Leviticus 19:13 the written law says,
"You shall not oppress your neighbor or rob him. The
wages of a hired servant shall not remain with you all
night until the morning." The Midrash commentary following this verse says:

> This applies also to the hire of animals, or of utensils, or
> of a hired man's wages even if the employee did not come
> to him to ask for the wages. . . . A wage earner hired for
> the day must be given pay for the following night; one
> engaged for the night, for the following day.[1]

In this fashion the Midrash provided a verse-by-verse
commentary on the five books of Moses. This vast corpus
was preserved *orally*—passed by word of mouth across
the generations, until it was written down after the time
of Jesus.

The second stage of the interpretation emerged in the
two centuries before Jesus. It culminated some four centuries later (about 200 CE) as the oral traditions were
gradually written in the *Mishnah.* This stirred fierce controversy, since many rabbis considered writing the law
the same as burning it.

Eventually this corpus of wisdom and law was expand-
ed, in a third stage, into the *Talmud.* This final collection
of oral laws became the distinctive book of Judaism comparable to Christianity's New Testament.

The oral law or "tradition of the elders" (Mark 7:5)
helped clarify and interpret the written word. At first the

oral tradition was subordinate to the authority of the
Scriptures. But over the years the authority of the oral
law grew. In time it was said that God had given the oral
law to Moses and preserved it by divine providence over
the generations. The oral tradition soon assumed equal, if
not greater, authority than the written word. The scope
and detail of the oral law is astonishing. A written compi-
lation of the Mishnah has some 700 pages of small print![2]
The scribes and rabbis memorized it. No wonder a
scribe's entire life was devoted to its study and memory.

The Mishnah is organized into six major divisions
called *orders*. Each order holds seven to twelve subdivi-
sions called tractates. These are further broken down into
some 523 chapters. Finally, each chapter contains about
five to ten legal paragraphs.[3] The Mishnah covers the
whole gamut of questions which might arise over religious and civil legislation.

Can laborers on top of a tree or wall offer a prayer?
Can one open up quarries or wells during a sabbatical
year? If one is naked and makes a dough offering from
barley in one's house, does that make the offering unclean? Is tying a knot work which violates the Sabbath?
Can a man divorce his wife for burning a meal? What's
the proper death penalty for someone who blasphemes?
Burning, stoning, beheading, or strangling? Is a man ceremonially unclean if he touches a mouse? If an unclean
bird sits on the eggs of a clean bird do the eggs remain
ceremonially clean? If a dog eats the flesh of a corpse and
then lies at the door of a house does it make the house
unclean?

On and on it goes, as the Mishnah spells out the do's
and don'ts, the fine lines between sacred and profane.
Like a holy snowball, the oral tradition had grown ever
heavier over the centuries.

Progressive Pharisees

The Pharisees, unlike the Sadducees, applied the oral law to everyday life. Their intent was good. The Pharisees believed that religious faith should penetrate all of life. By careful examination of the Scriptures, they tried to prescribe proper conduct for every circumstance. They didn't want the Law of Moses to become a sterile book, detached from life.[4] By contrast, the Sadducees affirmed the authority of the written law but didn't apply it to the real issues of their day. They were able to embrace the Roman presence and accept the influence of alien cultures because the books of Moses seemed irrelevant.

By adhering to the written word and some oral ritual regulations, the Sadducees excused themselves from everyday obedience to the law. Thus they could piously operate the Jerusalem temple even as they flirted with the Romans. The Pharisees, on the other hand, cared about faithful practice. They showed their submission to the Mosaic covenant through obeying the oral law. Carefully they followed the rules of ritual purity and tithing. Scrupulously they observed many pious regulations, hoping that someday all Jewish people would follow their example.

The Pharisaic vision, in short, was to call forth a holy nation, a nation of priests.[5] The term Pharisee carries a negative connotation suggesting hypocrisy and self-righteousness. In the context of their times, however, the Pharisees were sincere progressives! They truly wanted the Mosaic vision to blossom in Judaism's corporate life.

In broad terms four groups responded differently to the political situation in Palestine. The *Essenes* were an out-of-power priestly group. They retreated to separatist communities housed in caves near the Dead Sea. Someday they hoped to displace the Sadducees in running the temple. Patriotic *rebels* worked to violently overthrow the Romans. The *Sadducees* compromised, working hand-inglove with the Romans to maintain the status quo for financial gain. They were, in many ways, the political, economic, and religious conservatives. The *Pharisees*, meanwhile, worked seriously on the Jewish agenda of holiness. They lived in creative tension. They tried to strike a delicate balance between retreat, revolt, and compromise. Amidst the tumult they clung stubbornly to their vision of a holy, priestly nation.

Irreverent Jesus

Jesus' irreverence is a fascinating question. Why did he deplore religious ritual? Why did he scorn civil law? He broke rules of piety by working on the Sabbath, disregarding ritual cleansing, associating with disreputable persons, and cleansing the temple. We'll explore the meaning of these four provocative acts and then summarize Jesus' verbal critique of the Pharisees.[6]

Jesus' violation of Sabbath norms was most irksome. Surely he knew better! Sabbath rest was one of the Ten Commandments. A symbol of respect and worship of God, it was a distinctive feature of Hebrew faith. It set the Hebrews apart. The Jews carefully preserved it for sacred worship. Transgressing Sabbath law was a serious matter—offenders received the death penalty. Those who broke a Sabbath ordinance after receiving a warning were stoned. Jesus demolished some of the human *traditions* encrusting the Sabbath but didn't destroy the *principle* of the Sabbath. Indeed, he upheld it.[7]

All four Gospels report Jesus' Sabbath deviance. Matthew and Mark record two violations: harvesting grain and healing (Matthew 12:1-14; Mark 2:23—3:6). Luke notes four controversies (Luke 6:1-11; 13:10-17; 14:1-6). John (5:2-18) reports a Sabbath healing. Matthew, Mark, and Luke trace a five-step sequence.

First, Jesus defends his disciples for shelling grain on the Sabbath. The offense isn't stealing. Travelers and the

poor were allowed to help themselves to grain left standing in the field. The insult is working (shelling the grain)
on the Sabbath.

Second, the Pharisees discuss the violation with Jesus
and according to Jewish law warn him.

Third, they put him under surveillance (Mark 3:2) to
see if they can catch him in a second offense punishable
by death.

Fourth, even after a warning, he profanes the Sabbath
again, this time by healing. Tension rises. Mark says, "He
looked around at them with anger, grieved at their hardness of heart" (Mark 3:5).

In the fifth and final step, the Pharisees make plans to
destroy him. Jesus suddenly withdraws from the area, apparently fleeing for his life.

Luke reports two additional Sabbath healings. Why is
Jesus so bold? Why continue this disrespectful behavior?
Why play with death? Why does Jesus strike at the oral
tradition, even jeopardizing his own life? The sick had
been ill for many years. Why not politely wait *one* more
day until the Sabbath passed? Jesus knows full well the
penalties of the law. Despite a second warning, he continues to heal. Why?

Jesus' intent was to stab at the heart of the oral tradition. Although the Ten Commandments forbade Sabbath
work, the oral law encompassed a meticulous system of
rules for Sabbath observance. In written form the Mishnah contains 36 pages of rules broken down into 243
paragraphs. One paragraph lists 39 types of prohibited
work: sowing, plowing, baking, spinning, tying a knot,
writing or erasing two letters of the alphabet, putting out
a fire, lighting a fire, striking with a hammer, and on and
on.[8]

Many paragraphs discuss the prohibitions in detail. For
instance, camel drivers and sailors couldn't tie knots on
the Sabbath. But knots for hair nets, sandals, and belts

were permissible. Knots, opened with one hand, were permissible since they weren't considered knots. It was as wrong to untie a knot as to tie one. Territory was divided into four types of space: public, private, neutral, and free. Sabbath rules dictated what material could be moved from one area to another. A person throwing anything from a private to a public space or vice versa was guilty of a Sabbath infraction.[9]

Ingenious devices were created to bypass Sabbath legislation. People weren't allowed to walk more than 3,000 feet on the Sabbath. To circumvent this, they could "establish residence" at the end of their Sabbath day's walk, a day in advance. They established residence the day before by carrying two meals to a place 3,000 feet from their home. One meal they ate there and another they buried—thereby "establishing residence." On the Sabbath people could travel 3,000 feet from their permanent home to their "newly established residence" then go an additional 3,000 feet. Their legal detour doubled the length of Sabbath day journeys.[10]

The Sabbath, with its complicated ritual, symbolized the peak of institutionalized religion. By violating the Sabbath Jesus undercut the authority of religious leaders, especially the Pharisees. Jesus explained his behavior with these words: "The sabbath was made for man, not man for the sabbath; so the Son of man is lord even of the sabbath" (Mark 2:27-28; Matthew 12:8; Luke 6:5). The point is simple but profound. The Sabbath was designed to serve people—to refresh us after six days of sweat. It was intended to serve our physical, emotional, and psychological needs. The Sabbath was to be servant, *not* master.

Over the years this understanding turned upside down. As the oral law accumulated, the Sabbath also grew. It soon became a master. It enslaved people. They no longer ruled it. The Sabbath had stopped serving them. People dutifully served it by obeying hundreds of regulations. Instead of rest it provided new things to fret about. Rather than welcoming the Sabbath, people welcomed the workdays which freed them from Sabbath burdens. This religious institution, once so noble in intention and purpose, had turned oppressor.

Then came Jesus, claiming he was Lord of the Sabbath, saying he reigned over religious ritual and tradition. He refused to bow down and worship them. He called those enslaved by custom to serve God and God alone. People dare not, he said, place custom ahead of feeding and healing people. Repeatedly Jesus placed human need above religious dogma. He noted ironically that the Pharisees took better care of animals than people. They would pull an ox out of a pit on the Sabbath but prohibit a doctor from touching a sick person. For the Pharisees, religion had become ritual. Jesus turned religion upside down by turning ritual into compassion.

Dirty Hands

It's hard for us to understand the pious Jew's paranoia of uncleanness. Old Testament law divided objects, persons, places, and animals into two categories—clean and unclean. Camels, badgers, swine, vultures, eagles, and winged insects, to name a few, were all considered unclean. Cemeteries were taboo. Contact with a contaminated person or animal polluted a clean object. The Mishnah devoted 185 pages to laws of defilement and purity. Ceremonial washing before each meal marked conscientious Pharisees. They sanitized themselves without fail, hoping to engender a nation of purified priests.[11]

Jesus irritated the Pharisees by skipping ceremonial washing. Matthew (15:1-20) and Mark (7:1-23) report similar accounts. Pharisees and scribes from Jerusalem came 60 miles north to Galilee to question Jesus on this issue. Luke (11:37-38) notes that the Pharisee who hosted

Jesus for a meal was astonished that he ate without washing. The Pharisees stressed eating with the right people—those who obeyed the purity laws. They also held to the tradition of the elders that required washing hands before eating. The washing sanitized any religious "dirt" accidentally acquired during the day.

Why, the Pharisees wondered, did Jesus neglect the purifying rinse? Jesus answered. "You leave the commandment of God, and hold fast the tradition of men. . . . You have a fine way of rejecting the commandment of God, in order to keep your tradition!" (Mark 7:8-9). Quoting Isaiah the prophet, he told them that they worshiped with lips but not heart. They taught human ideas as if they were divine doctrine. In short, the Pharisees had elevated the oral tradition to divine status. They not only served but worshiped oral tradition. They gave it precedence over the Word of God and even used it as an excuse to disobey God's will.

A religious vow called corban illustrates how good things had been perverted (Mark 7:10-13). Through the corban vow, the Pharisees encouraged adult children to consecrate their property to the temple rather than using it to support their elderly parents. After the property was dedicated to the temple, it couldn't be used to support elderly parents. Cutting off financial support jeopardized the welfare of the elderly. Jesus condemned the corban vow which promoted piety at the expense of human suffering. Human words and traditions superseded the supreme law of loving one's neighbor. The religious system operating in the name of God ironically obscured God's law of love.

Jesus was harshly criticizing the purity laws when he said defilement results from things which come out of the mouth, not those that go in. Words of gossip, deceit, false witness, and slander defile a person, not food (Matthew 15:18-20; Mark 7:20-23). In a few words Jesus abolished those aspects of oral tradition that blocked the way to true holiness. Perfect cleansing, he said, occurs in acts of charity flowing from the heart (Luke 11:41).

Dirty Friends

A third aspect of Jesus' behavior which peeved the Pharisees was his fellowship with unclean persons. Tax collectors and sinners who ridiculed the rules of purity were considered filthy. The Pharisees, of course, shunned them. Jesus excluded no one. He invited sinners to meals (Luke 15:2) and joined in their parties (Mark 2:15; Matthew 9:10). This infuriated the Pharisees, who mocked him, saying, "Behold, a glutton and a drunkard, a friend of tax collectors and sinners" (Matthew 11:19; Luke 7:34). Some scholars contend that Jesus' table fellowship with sinners and outcasts was the distinguishing mark that set him apart from other religious prophets of his time.[12]

In Palestinian culture, inviting someone to a meal was a sign of honor. It signaled peace, trust, intimacy, and forgiveness; sharing a table meant sharing life. In Hebrew culture, table fellowship symbolized fellowship before God. Breaking bread around a common table brought a corporate blessing to all who joined in the meal. By eating with religious rejects Jesus embodies divine compassion for all. And he signals their inclusion around the heavenly banquet table. He thus welcomes them into the community of salvation.[13]

By lodging with Zacchaeus and his sort, Jesus challenged the norms of religious etiquette. His message was clear: people were more important than pious rules. Indeed, he said, he came to save the sick. The healthy don't need a physician (Matthew 9:12-13; Mark 2:17). Ironically, the "sick" leaders who thought they were healthy rejected the Physician. Those who knew they were "sick" and acknowledged their need were invited to the Physician's party.

Religious piety easily becomes idolatrous and exclusive. It sorts people into profane and sacred boxes. A web of pious rules shield the "righteous" from the stigmatized. Jesus blurred the fine lines which separated sacred from profane. By embracing sinners he made it clear the new kingdom welcomed *all*, regardless of past piety or sin.

Fumigating the Temple

Defiling the Sabbath, mocking ritual, and befriending sinners rankled the Pharisees, guardians of the oral tradition. Jesus' final provocation pricked a different group: the Sadducees. As we saw, this political party operated the large temple in Jerusalem. Wealthy Sadducees benefited from income generated by the temple. His defiance in the temple rebuked the temple hierarchy.[14] The temple was the hub of Hebrew worship. It was one thing to strike against the oral tradition of the Pharisees in upstate Galilee. It was quite another matter to level an attack on the nerve center of religious, political, and economic power! The Sadducees enjoyed cozy Roman connections. A cohort of 500-600 Roman soldiers stood by in the Jerusalem fortress watching for any ruckus in the temple area. Jesus had left the docile shepherds and fishermen of Galilee. Now he walked Jerusalem's halls of power.

All four Gospels report his decisive act. Fully aware that the Sadducees would charge him with profanity and blasphemy, Jesus moved deftly.

> He entered the temple and began to drive out those who sold and those who bought in the temple, and he overturned the tables of the moneychangers and the seats of those who sold pigeons; and he would not allow any one to carry anything through the temple. And he taught, and said to them, "Is it not written, 'My house shall be called a house of prayer for all the nations'? But you have made it a den of robbers' " (Mark 11:15-17).

The money changers were in the outer courts of the temple.[15] Here they exchanged common coins for the "pure" ones required for temple offerings. The animal jockeys sold sheep and goats for sacrifices to pilgrims. The outer courts, a place of worship, had been turned into a lucrative cattle market and bank. Tables cluttered the area. The stench of animal dung hung in the air. Prayer was not what the setting inspired.

We don't know if Jesus merely chased a few sellers out or if he completely purged the area. A major disturbance would have certainly activated the Roman cohort, stirring his immediate arrest. Regardless of the scope of the purge, the religious leaders certainly regarded it as outrageous profanity in the hallowed courts of God. It did more than open up the outer court so Gentiles could pray.[16] It did more than refocus temple activities on the holy of holies. It signified the impending destruction of the temple, which Jesus prophesied would happen because Jewish leaders wouldn't accept his message (Matthew 23:38; 24:2). This flagrant act of deviance cost Jesus his life.

Mark sandwiches the temple purge between two episodes of a fig tree cursing (Mark 11:12-14; 20-26). Before entering Jerusalem for the dramatic act, Jesus spotted a fig tree. He was hungry and reached for figs. Finding the tree empty, he cursed it. The day after the temple episode, the tree's roots had withered. The fig tree represents the temple, the center of Jewish worship. As the curse shriveled the roots of the tree, so the prophetic purge shriveled the temple's functions.

Jesus' bold move symbolically opened the temple once more for Gentiles and signaled that the new kingdom welcomed all—regardless of race or nationality. We have here the Prophet, full of rich symbolism, striking at the nerve center of Jewish religion. In one decisive act, he shuts the temple down.[17] He points to a new age, a time when a new offering will be made, a body. A permanent sacrifice will be given. Each person's heart will be a vessel for the Holy Spirit. In Jewish eyes this is a daring move. But the Prophet is fearless in the face of Roman soldiers and Sadducean authorities. He acts definitively, striking the religious economy which oppressed the poor for the sake of profit.

Jesus is not only Lord of the Sabbath and Lord of the oral tradition; he is also Lord of the temple. He ends its sacrificial ritual in preparation for the new kingdom. Jesus has returned to the temple! Not in a miraculous parachute, but as lord of its functions. In a single moment he critiques human religion and points to a new age.

The temple purge had sweeping consequences. Flipping over a few tables in a backstreet inn would have been bad enough. But in the sacred courts the table turnover was a deliberate attack on the well-heeled Sadducees. Jesus had boldly challenged the authority of the priestly families who ran the temple for lucrative gain. The Sanhedrin—that mighty Jewish court—met a few blocks down the street. Out in rural Galilee a little blasphemy and a little Sabbath naughtiness might slip by. But not here. Not in the sacred temple, not by the doors of the mighty Sanhedrin, not under the nose of the high priest. Institutionalized piety can't permit such irreverence.

In Mark's Gospel the plot to kill Jesus now flares up more openly than any time since his Sabbath clash back in Galilee. Jesus has galvanized the hatred of chief priests and scribes. They must destroy him. Jerusalem, the place of life and worship, becomes the stage for death and revenge.

Given the danger of anti-Semitism and our growing understanding that Jesus was truly a Jew, we should note here that what Jesus critiques is finally *human* religion, not *Jewish* religion. Jesus cleanses the temple not because it's Jewish but because it's corrupt. If he were to return in the flesh today might he overturn some tables in our Christian temples?

Pompous Piety

If irreverence wasn't enough, Jesus scolded the religious leaders with a volley of indictments and parables. Although much of his talk condemned the religious leaders, a few accepted or at least befriended him. Some amiable Pharisees warned Jesus that Herod Antipas wanted to kill him (Luke 13:31). The Pharisee Simon entertained Jesus in his house (Luke 7:36). Nicodemus, a Pharisee who perhaps sat on the Sanhedrin, chatted warmly with Jesus one evening (John 3:1). We may not have an objective picture of what Jesus said about the Pharisees because Jewish-Christian conflicts raged as the Gospels were being written. The Gospel accounts reflect one side of the story. Written *after* Jews and Christians had become bitter enemies, the Gospels cast the Pharisees in a negative light. Keeping this bias in mind, what do the Gospels report Jesus saying to the religious establishment?

The social glory of the Pharisees was at the root of Jesus' scathing criticism. They offered their sacrifices on the altar of social status. The demands of God mattered little. What counted was how their piety appeared to others. Would their prayers, fasting, and tithes enhance their status in the eyes of their peers? Although he doesn't mention the Pharisees specifically in Matthew 6:1, Jesus debunks their clamor for social applause. "Beware of practicing your piety before men in order to be seen by them; for then you will have no reward from your Father who is in heaven."

Two kinds of public piety were particularly irksome. Trumpets were blown in streets and synagogues when the religious leaders gave a tithe in order to "be praised by men." And the leaders vied for the best seats in the synagogue and wore ostentatious garb. They sewed long fringes on their robes and wanted seats of honor at feasts. They preferred dignified greetings in the streets (Matthew 23:5-7; Luke 11:43; 20:46). Mark (12:40) and Luke (20:47) say the scribes made long prayers for the sake of social display. The leaders did all these things, Matthew (23:5) says, for a social audience, "to be seen by men." Luke calls them lovers of money who justify themselves before men (Luke 16:14-15). Such religiosity, oriented toward the applause of others, is an abomination in God's eyes.

John (12:42-43) notes that some of the authorities who believed in Jesus were afraid to admit it because "they loved the praise of men more than the praise of God." In Matthew's Gospel, Jesus lumps the scribes and Pharisees together in a fiery critique.[18] They are like filthy cups which appear clean on the outside and like polished tombs which stink on the inside. "So you also outwardly appear righteous to men, but within you are full of hypocrisy and iniquity" (Matthew 23:28).

In the three synoptic Gospels Jesus warns his disciples to watch out for the leaven of the Pharisees (Matthew 16:11-12; Mark 8:15; Luke 12:1). Luke calls their cancerous leaven hypocrisy. Although we often associate the word *hypocrisy* with the Pharisees, the issue, as one scholar points out, wasn't really hypocrisy. The Pharisees were actually sincere and devout. The issue was *what* they were sincere about.[19]

The verbal attack on the Pharisees continues. They talk but don't walk, preach but don't practice, theologize but don't obey. Consumed with the details of cleaning pots, they forget the agony of the sick and poor. In a satirical comment, Jesus advised the crowd to "practice and observe whatever they *tell* you, but not what they *do*; for they preach, but do not practice" (Matthew 23:3, emphasis added).

Another time, after the elders had questioned Jesus' authority, he made the same point in a biting parable (Matthew 21:28-31). A man had two sons. He asked them to work in the vineyard. The first one said, "No, I won't," but afterward he repented and went. The second son said, "Yes, Dad," but never went. The scribes and Pharisees were like the second son. They were always promising smoothly, "Yes, Dad," but never getting to the vineyard.

The religious leaders were like the brothers of the rich man in the Lazarus story. They had Moses and the prophets, yet refused to practice Jubilee. They remembered trivia but forgot justice, mercy, and faith. Foolishly trying to strain a mosquito out of their tea, they overlooked swallowing a camel (Matthew 23:23-24; Luke 11:42). They observed pious regulations but foreclosed on widows' houses (Luke 20:47; Mark 12:40). With the vow of corban they thwarted the law of love by pushing the elderly into poverty (Mark 7:9-12). Their verbiage produced no action and their sweet God-talk camouflaged economic injustice as they merrily went on their way tithing herbs.

How Great Thou Art

Careful observance of religious dogma breeds pride. The Pharisees were like the person singing "How Great Thou Art" in front of the mirror each morning. In a pithy little parable Jesus condemns their arrogance.[20] A tax collector and a Pharisee walk to the temple to offer their prayers (Luke 18:9-14). The devout one finds his prominent place and offers a prayer of thanks. He thanks God that he's not a cheat, he's not unjust, he doesn't fool around with other women. Peeking out of the corner of his eye he notes that he's especially thankful he's not contaminated like this tax collector who robs the poor.

The Pharisee offers his righteous deeds to God. Although the law calls for an annual fast on the Day of Atonement, he voluntarily adds a fast every Monday and

Thursday. He gives tithes on everything he buys from the shopkeepers. If the grower has previously paid a tithe of the products, he tithes again to make sure everything he uses is holy. This man represents the epitome of Hebrew orthodoxy. He stands at the top of the religious ladder.

The tax collector, ostracized by decent people, is considered a robber with no civil rights. He can barely reach the ladder's bottom rung. He stays at the edge of the temple court, not venturing to a prominent spot. In contrast to the proud Pharisee, the tax collector doesn't lift his hands heavenward. Instead he pounds his chest, a sign of deep contrition. He cries out to God in despair, overwhelmed by the gulf of separation. Repentance for this man doesn't mean pleasant smiles. It means leaving his profession and starting over. It means repaying fivefold all the people he has cheated. He doesn't even know how many he has swindled. This is an impossible situation, so he cries for mercy.

Unexpectedly, the upside-down movement strikes. In a surprising reversal, the penitent tax collector is commended—not the devout Pharisee. This social bandit, this betrayor of the nation, has found favor with God. The Almighty has accepted the tax collector's sacrifice of a broken and contrite heart. He returns home justified.

This sounded upside down indeed to Jesus' audience. Those who arrogantly trust in themselves and despise others have rejected God despite their religious motions. Self-centered worship sneers at others rather than taking personal inventory. It derives false piety from social comparison. The barbs of the parable stung the haughty Pharisees.

Keep Out

Condescending pride turns churches into exclusive clubs. Shunning outsiders and mocking their ignorance wasn't the Pharisees' only fault. They used a barricade of trivial rules to bar sinners from the table of salvation. Jesus detested this exclusive spirit.

> They bind heavy burdens, hard to bear, and lay them on men's shoulders; but they themselves will not move them with their finger. . . . But woe to you, scribes and Pharisees, hypocrites! because you shut the kingdom of heaven against men; for you neither enter yourselves, nor allow those who would enter to go in" (Matthew 23:4, 13-15; Luke 11:45-52).

In contrast to the burden of rules which crushed devout Jews, Jesus offered a light load. "For my yoke is easy, and my burden is light" (Matthew 11:30). In their attempt to translate the five books of Moses into daily practice, they had mistakenly thrown away the key to the kingdom. They had locked themselves inside the synagogue of their own ritual and sealed out others. Ceremonial religion not only accents ritual; it also creates a gap between insiders and outsiders.

The Last Will Be First

Many of Jesus' parables are a defense of the gospel. His acceptance of sinners embodied the good news. Religious leaders were indignant that Jesus welcomed immoral folks—swindlers and adulterers—into the kingdom. "Sinners" were customarily deprived of civil rights—office holding and serving as a witness in court. They included tax collectors, shepherds, peddlers, tanners, pigeon racers, and others in tarnished occupations.[21] Jesus' message in numerous parables is clear. The religious establishment may toss these people from the kingdom, but God still loves them. Jesus offers such love in table fellowship despite scorn from leading Pharisees. Adding insult to injury, the Pharisees' smug rejection is no flippant matter. Things just might turn upside down. They might find themselves on the outside of the door while repentant sinners feast inside with the prophets.

Yes, God cares for these social outcasts. In four stories Jesus shows how God's forgiving compassion reaches out to rebellious and lost outsiders.

Jesus compares God to a father who waited day after day for his rebellious son to return home. When he returns, the father hugs and kisses him and even throws a party in his honor (Luke 15:11-24). God is like a woman who sweeps every crack of her house searching for a lost coin (Luke 15:8). God can be compared to a shepherd trudging over the hill country looking for a weak lamb caught in the thorns (Luke 15:3-5). Or think of God as a farmer who cared so much about laborers working one hour that he gave them a full day's wage they surely didn't deserve (Matthew 20:1-16).

The parables sizzle into the religious heavyweights: Your attitude is just the opposite of God's. You're like the elder son who grumbles at the sight of a party thrown for his own brother (Luke 15:25-32). You're like the farmhands who work all day, receive their promised wage, then gripe because the latecomers received the same (Matthew 20:11-16). Like the tenants of a vineyard you refused the owner's servants wine from his own vineyard. You killed other servants he sent and finally you had the audacity to kill his only son (Luke 20:9-16). Suddenly the tables are turned. The owner will give that vineyard to others.

The biting stories continue: Like the guests invited to a banquet you refuse to come when the feast begins (Luke 14:15-24; Matthew 22:1-10). Because of your stubbornness God invites others to replace you at the table. God welcomes the poor, the maimed, the blind, and the lame from city streets. God even goes to the countryside and invites others. These spiritual and social outcasts which you spit upon, God welcomes with a royal reception. The moment of judgment strikes! "For I tell you, none of those men who were invited shall taste my banquet" (Luke 14:24).

Jesus clarifies the upside-down reversal in another picture of impending crisis. The judgment will surprise the staunchest defenders of the faith. They will say, "the Lord ate and drank in our presence," but the Lord will reply,

> " 'Depart from me, all you workers of iniquity!' There you will weep and gnash your teeth, when you see Abraham and Isaac and Jacob and all the prophets in the kingdom of God and you yourselves thrust out. And men will come from east and west, and from north and south, and sit at table in the kingdom of God. And behold, some are last who will be first, and some are first who will be last" (Luke 13:27-30).

Speaking to the Pharisees, Jesus ends the parable of the two sons with these terse words: "Truly, I say to you, the tax collectors and the harlots go into the kingdom of God before you" (Matthew 21:31). After blasting the scribes for devouring widows' houses and making long prayers as a pretense, Jesus says they face not only exclusion from the kingdom, but "will receive the greater condemnation" (Mark 12:40; Luke 20:47). The stalwarts of Jewish faith had access to Moses and the prophets. The leaders were given a talent—knowledge of God's law—but so buried it in oral tradition that sinners missed God's call. The human traditions, in fact, repulsed the outcasts and drove them far from God. Jesus restores the day of grace. His table fellowship with the stigmatized signals the dawn of God's salvation. And the impious, social castaways, unlike the Pharisees, embrace God's welcome.

This is tragically upside down. The ones who work so hard to apply the Torah to everyday life are left behind. Their fervor and enthusiasm for ceremonial piety thwarts God's law of love. Those who fought so hard for religion are in jeopardy. The newcomers, meanwhile, are a motley-looking and irreverent crew, but their righteousness exceeds the righteousness of the Pharisees (Matthew 5:20). One of their crowd, Zacchaeus, returns stolen goods. A prostitute who anointed Jesus repents and is forgiven much. The tax collector at the temple penitently beats his breast. A runaway son returns home.

In contrast to the religious elite, these sinners are truly sorry for their sins. They walk the kingdom's red carpet. The tragic message finally penetrates the skulls of the righteous. "When the chief priests and the Pharisees heard his parables, they perceived that he was speaking about them. But when they tried to arrest him, they feared the multitudes, because they held him to be a prophet" (Matthew 21:45-46; Mark 12:12; Luke 20:19).

Brittle Skins and New Patches

What does all this mean for us today? How do kingdom and church intersect? Jesus described the inbreaking of the kingdom with two stories (Mark 2:21-22). Always wash a patch before sewing it on an old garment. Otherwise the patch will shrink after the first laundering and rip the old cloth worse than ever. Moreover, store new, fermenting wine in new and flexible wineskins. Bubbling wine poured into brittle old skins will crack them open and drain away. The wine is the essential, primary substance. The skins are secondary. We can't drink them, but we do need them to store the wine.

In picturesque words Jesus pinpoints the tension between the new wine of the kingdom and the old religious structures. New skins, soft and pliable, are needed for new wine. As the wine ferments the skins expand and contract. The kingdom wine which Jesus brought cracked the brittle skins of the Sadducees, Pharisees, and scribes. The skins of the oral law were too old and brittle to hold the ferment of the new wine. Sinners couldn't even smell the wine. All they could see were the hard, old skins. The wine of the upside-down kingdom requires new skins—

flexible institutional structures.

How do we distinguish between the kingdom and the institutionalized church?[22] Is the kingdom the same as the church? The biblical shift from "kingdom" to "church" between the Gospels and the Epistles reflects a shift from Jewish to Greek culture.[23] One of the difficulties in distinguishing between kingdom and church today lies in the many words that we often use loosely—church, denomination, institution, and people of God.

A careful distinction among three realities—*kingdom, church,* and *structure*—can clarify the conceptual waters.

The kingdom Jesus announced points us to something greater than ourselves and our own structures. We've already said that the *kingdom* refers to the rule of God in our hearts and relationships. God was "at hand" in Jesus, living in the midst of people and calling them to obedience. Today God rules through the Holy Spirit's presence. The Spirit teaches us kingdom ways and ideas. The wine in the parable symbolizes the dynamic power of God infiltrating our lives. Like fresh wine in ferment, the kingdom embodies the dynamic and creative power of God's Spirit. It takes on visible expression in new and exciting ways as people submit their lives to God's rule.

The kingdom entails a new *vision,* a new set of *values,* and a new *openness* to yield to the ways of God. Past and present, now and then, the kingdom is the reign of God in the lives of believers. It becomes visible in form and practice as persons yield to God's dynamic rule.

The *church* is the assembly of persons who have welcomed God's reign in their hearts and relationships. The church consists of the citizens of the kingdom. It's the body of Christ composed of obedient disciples following in the way of Jesus. Or we might say the church is the community of believers—the collective gathering of the people of God. The church isn't a building, a sanctuary, or a program. It's the visible community of those who live by kingdom values.

Finally come the *structures*. The people of God need social vehicles—institutions and programs—to meet their own needs and those of others. The church creates these vehicles or servant structures. Servant structures include the whole gamut of organized church activities. They encompass denominations, schools, liturgical traditions, mission agencies, publishing ventures, camps, and, of course, committees, commissions, and programs galore. These are the social skins, the servant structures the church creates to do its work. They're *not*, however, the church or the kingdom.

The kingdom transcends the church in two ways. It existed before the beginning of the church and will be God's kingly domain at the end of the church's earthly existence. The kingdom is also larger than the church in the present world. It represents the ultimate lordship of Christ over all peoples, principalities, and powers. The church, the body of believers, embraces the rule of God. The structures of the church, designed to express kingdom ways, can become brittle and leak the precious wine. We must periodically overhaul these organized structures, these human creations, to assure they remain servant structures.

This threefold distinction of kingdom, church, and structure provides historical continuity between the kingdom and the church. The church began and existed alongside the kingdom as persons accepted the rule of God in their lives. The kingdom has visible social and political characteristics both in the body of believers who declare Jesus as King and in the structures they create to accomplish their mission. Furthermore, if we view the structures as human creations, not synonymous with the kingdom itself, we less easily sacralize them. The moment we see church structures as identical with the kingdom, they rise to sacred heights. The structures of the church reflect and embody the kingdom but are neither the kingdom nor the church itself.

174 / The Upside-Down Kingdom

Expressing the vision of *one* kingdom, the structures we create will take on *diverse* forms in different cultures. They should, however, not be mere reflections of their culture. Their diverse skins should be culturally relevant but not culturally determined. The kingdom message, anchored in the biblical story, should design the social architecture of the church's program. When cultural rather than kingdom values primarily shape the church's institutional forms, the salt loses its savor.

Sacred Cows or Servant Structures?

The vision of the kingdom breaks in upon us in fresh ways through the ministry of the Holy Spirit. It takes shape in new buildings, new projects, new programs, and new committees. These social structures, however, soon solidify. First-generation participants enthusiastically welcome the new programs. But spontaneous patterns soon gel and become routine. Gradually they're taken for granted. They become "the way things are." They exude a sense of "rightness." No longer are they seen as one of many ways of meeting a need. The second generation sees them as the *only* way. They have, in short, become sacred cows. Structures once created seek their own legitimation. They perpetuate themselves.

The Pharisee temptation is always with us. The one-time spontaneous expression of love solidifies as an organization grows in size and age. The constitution gets longer. The red tape grows thicker. The symbols are idolized. Procedures rigidify. Evangelism yields to ethnicity. Openness to new needs gives way to maintaining the status quo. Exclusive words and symbols emerge. Outsiders feel left out. Policies, structures, and bureaucrats smother the way of love. It's time for new skins.

The genius of the gospel is its seed of self-criticism or self-reformation. Each generation of Christians, like the Pharisees, is tempted to sacralize its programs and freeze

its routines. Jesus showed us that humanly created structures aren't sacred. There are no sacred places, organizations, times, objects, doctrines, or social positions, except
in the sense that all good things are finally sacred.

The altar in a church building is no closer to God's
heart than a rest room. The unfortunate use of the term
"sanctuary" encourages us to view the church building as
a sacred place deserving special reverence. Religious
buildings often witness to our rigidity, pride, and social
status.[24] When Jesus purged the temple, he declared once
and for all that even the most religious buildings aren't
sacred nor due special reverence. They can be dedicated
as one of many tools for proclaiming and celebrating the
good news of the kingdom but they should always be
subservient to the assembly of believers.

The same loving irreverence must apply to doctrine,
objects, social positions, and programs of the church. The
creed which molds a denomination's unique identity can
become an idolatrous manifesto superseding biblical authority. The chair of the board of elders may offer wise
counsel but holds no sacred position. The pastor may offer special insight and understanding but is not a saint set
above the saints we're all called to be. Symbols of faith—
the cross, the pulpit, the altar, the basin—are as mundane
as other everyday objects. They *do* point us to spiritual
meanings. But they aren't sacred *in and of themselves*.

White Elephant Sabbaticals

The institutional programs of the church sometimes become sacred cows—or should we say, white elephants.
Agencies, institutions, and programs, designed as servants, can over time rise up and master us. Their original
purpose met real needs and communicated the gospel effectively. But over the years they turn brittle. The patterned ruts of worship services, youth programs, mission
boards, doctrinal practices, educational agencies, and ser-

vice projects become coercive since they are the "Lord's work."

Organizations are necessary and useful to funnel human activity in effective ways. We need social institutions and will always have them. It's important, however, that we periodically evaluate their role and purpose. Perhaps we should start institutional sabbaticals—periodic times when we review programs and projects. If they no longer serve their original intent, we ought to nudge them back toward servant roles.

The seventh or sabbatical year in the Hebrew calendar provided time not only for rest but also for reflection. Would it be fitting, every seventh year, to call a sabbatical rest for the committees, commissions, and programs making up much of institutional religion today? During this seventh year, extensive study and evaluation could assess the effectiveness of these programs. Some might need a major overhaul. Others might continue in their present form. Still others might need a funeral. Seven-year intervals allow enough time to test a program and also assure periodic review.

Too often the church's white elephants plod on and on. Since they're the "Lord's work" no one dares tamper with them. Service to others and edification of the community of faith is the benchmark for evaluation. When pastors have to urge, cajole, and beg parishioners to participate in a particular program or attend a certain service, it may be the people have sold out to secular priorities. It may also be time for an institutional funeral.

When members of a congregation feel obligated to attend services, they may need to review their priorities. It may also be that the structures have become their masters. When structures serve the true needs of disciplined people, participation is joyous and spontaneous.

Jesus is Lord of the "Sabbaths," those religious structures we create. His Spirit and the perspectives of his kingdom critique our humanly devised skins. The lordship of Christ over these organizational structures prevents them from perverting the gospel and enslaving the faithful. Too often we forget Jesus is Lord of the Sabbath. We too easily equate our own structures with the kingdom. Former servant structures rise up and beckon us to serve them.

How do we evaluate servant structures? The following questions help assess their servant posture.

(1) What are the specific needs which this program is meeting?

(2) Would people create this project anew if it were terminated?

(3) Does it express the spirit and mission of the gospel?

(4) Is this structure designed to serve in the Spirit of Jesus?

(5) Does it promote an exclusive self-righteous posture?

(6) Do people enjoy participating in it?

(7) Is flexibility built into its very structure?

(8) Has a time been designated to evaluate its functions?

(9) Is there a decision-making process to declare an "institutional funeral" if necessary?

(10) Is it clear that the people of God, as led by the Spirit, have the authority to declare its moratorium?

The church is always caught in the tension between the traditional solutions of the past and the fermenting wine of an ever-new kingdom. It's a tension between form and love, structure and gospel, organization and vision. The symbols of the past threaten to become idolatrous. The old rituals assert themselves as absolute. The Spirit of the Jesus who violated Sabbath rules, avoided purity rituals, ate with sinners, and purged the temple is Lord of our structures also. He judges them, critiques them, and makes them pliable for the new wine. Hidden in the excruciating pain of judgment is the germ of renewal. The gospel shapes fresh, elastic skins for the kingdom's ferment. In this process the church reforms itself across the generations.

Questions for Discussion

1. Do we have equivalents of the oral law in the life of the church today?

2. How do you reconcile the "irreverence" of Jesus with his message of love?

3. Are any of Jesus' criticisms of religious leaders applicable to the church today?

4. In what sense might we be Pharisees?

5. Can you distinguish between kingdom, church, and structure in your local context?

6. Identify some brittle skins in your congregation and denomination.

7. In what ways are religious traditions helpful in the life of an individual or congregation?

8. What is your response to the proposal for institutional sabbaticals?

9

LOVABLE ENEMIES

The Foolish Father

Violence is obsolete in the new kingdom. *Agape* love becomes the new mode of governing. Agape in Greek means unconditional love and often defines God's love. Wholly unselfish, upside-down agape love exceeds passion, friendship, and benevolence. It supersedes self-interest. Agape is more than unselfish feeling. It acts. It loves unlovables, even enemies. Compassion, generosity, forgiveness, mercy—these are the essence of agape.[1]

Agape flows from the king of the kingdom, who is like a loving parent. The ruler's subjects aren't slaves, but children. They don't say, "Yes, your Majesty," but fondly call him *abba,* or "Daddy." In this new order the citizens love generously because a gracious Parent has overwhelmed them. The divine love stirs their own. What kind of Parent triggers such love?

Responding to complaints from scribes and Pharisees that he was eating with sinners, Jesus told a story to clarify God's love. God, sinners, and Pharisees are portrayed in the story by a father, a runaway son, and a complaining brother (Luke 15:11-32).[2] What is God like? This is the parable's central question. Jesus suggests God is like a foolish father.

179

According to Jewish custom, the younger of two sons was entitled to one third of his father's property. Wealth could be passed on in two ways: by a will at the father's death or as a gift during the father's lifetime. In contrast to Western culture, if the son received the property as a gift, he did *not* have the right to dispose of it until after the father's death. To dispose of it while the father was living was to treat the father like a corpse. Jewish custom expected children to honor their parents by obeying and supporting them financially.

Indeed, the son's gross disrespect for his father is as sinful as his vice in a foreign country. The young upstart violates cultural customs. He leaves his father and squanders funds that can never support the father again. He treats his father like he's already dead! It was the rudest thing a son could do to his father.

Piling insult upon insult, the son ends up tending swine. Such work was prohibited in Jewish culture, which considered unclean pigs to be the abode of devils. The son not only engages in this degrading job but identifies with the pigs by hungering for their food. He had fallen to the very bottom of the social pit. Imagine the father's embarrassment. The scribes in the village surely sneered at him. Why did he give the son his property at such a young age in the first place? They must have laughed until they cried. The son had shattered his father's reputation, esteem, and honor. Such a father was certainly not fit to give leadership or wise counsel in the synagogue.

To vindicate himself, a good father would at least publicly deplore such behavior. A wise father wouldn't look the other way or approve rank disobedience. He would legally disown the son. Surely, this is what a prudent father would do.

But not this father. He doesn't defend himself. He doesn't retaliate to protect his social status. He doesn't run after the son with a search party. He gives his son the freedom to go. His love for his son is stronger than his own need for social approval. Moreover, he patiently waits for his son to return. He never forgets him. He walks out the lane every day—waiting, hoping, expecting.

Finally the son "comes to himself." In the Aramaic, this phrase suggests repentance. He finally realizes the stupidity of his ways and turns around. He returns home expecting the worst. He knows how harshly fathers react when publicly disgraced. So he comes confessing, begging his father to accept him as mere servant.

We might expect several responses from a Jewish father who sees his son walking home, splattered with pig dung. A reasonable father might close the door, and declare him an alien. He might at least ask his son to wash before launching into a tirade. He might investigate the details of the deviance before taking proper action. Justice would prescribe punishment to teach the boy his lesson. A whipping was perhaps in order. Maybe the knave should serve time as a slave. This would at least permit him to prove his sincerity.

The father rejects all these fair and common-sense solutions. Foolishly he welcomes the scoundrel home, rolling out, in effect eight red carpets.

—He doesn't wait for the son to knock. His compassion compels him to run. It wasn't usual for an older person to run. The father had no idea what the son would say. Running to him might signal endorsement of the son's vices.

—Then the father hugs the boy, breaking another rule of social etiquette. Embracing was considered undignified for an aged person.

—A kiss—the biblical symbol of forgiveness—follows. The father wipes the slate clean. He welcomes the son back from the pigpen, not as slave, not as hired servant—but as son.

—The father's next sign of welcome heralds the son as an honored guest, in fact. The best robe is put around him. This fine garment was a mark of high distinction. It was reserved for royal guests, not disobedient sons.

—He's offered a signet ring symbolizing authority. He returns not as stigmatized parolee but as one worthy of power and prestige.

—The shoes the servants place on his feet also signal his high status. Free men wore shoes. Slaves went barefoot. This reclaimed son would return as a free person. The servants would serve him.

—A fat calf was killed. Steak was reserved for special occasions. The son who yesterday ate with pigs, dines today on steak.

—No whips crack. Instead music soars and dancers twirl. It's time to celebrate a dead son's resurrection. A sinner has come home. Let the party roll!

Such foolish forgiveness offends the older son. He demands justice and fairness. Where is the punishment due this upstart who squandered his father's security? Where is the party, long overdue, for the elder son's years of faithful labor in the fields? Contemptuously, the elder son calls his own brother "this son of yours." "My dear child," the father warmly responds. Like the scribes and Pharisees, the infuriated older son refuses to join the party. And now he's lost, at the very moment the lost is found.

God is like an upside-down parent. God forgives generously as we repent. God is like a Jewish father who rewards his pork-eating son with steak. Instead of spanking the son who brings disgrace, he elevates him to the high post "of most honored guest." God is like a parent who asks no questions, even when treated as though dead. This is limitless, unconditional love with no strings attached.

Such a Parent propels us to act. Like the man who found a treasure in the field, such stunning forgiveness sweeps us off our feet. This dramatic love energizes a chain reaction. The children of such love want to pass it on. Like their Parent, they become merciful. They love as God loved. Because God has forgiven them, they too can forgive.

Grateful response to God is the motive for action in the upside-down kingdom. Deeds of loving kindness, stirred by God's goodness, embody God's caring hug for this world. Meritorious deeds, performed to earn salvation, are as filthy rags. The same deeds triggered by God's love are a sweet offering on the altar of worship.

Get Off Your Donkey

What does agape love look like? If God is like a foolish parent, does agape love look foolish as well? Jesus clarified his kingdom's new Torah of agape with a story. It concretely spells out the radical nature of upside-down love (Luke 10:25-37).[3]

It begins in a believable fashion. A man walks along the winding, desolate road from Jerusalem to Jericho. The audience assumes the walker is a fellow Jew. Bandits living in caves infested the barren countryside along the Jericho road.

A robbery came as no surprise. It was typical for priests and Levites from outlying areas to use this road after performing their week of duties in the Jerusalem temple. And the crowd knew that priests and Levites who followed the purity laws would be contaminated if so much as their shadow touched a corpse.

This traveler, stripped and beaten, appeared nearly dead. Thus a conscientious priest would avoid him. The audience expects the story to end with a scathing criticism of the religious elite. Like many of Jesus' other parables, this one also will criticize callous leaders for lacking compassion. The crowd expects a common farmer will become the hero by rescuing a battered fellow Jew. Such an ending will prick the priests and Levites. A Jewish peasant shows more compassion than religious leaders!

Jesus flips expectations upside down. A *Samaritan*, not a Jew, pops up as hero. The audience is appalled. Why is a Samaritan so shocking?

Bitter tension divided Jews and Samaritans. Samaria was sandwiched between Judea and Galilee. The Samaritans emerged about 400 BCE from mixed marriages between Jews and Gentiles. The Jews regarded them as half-breed bastards. They had their own version of the books of Moses. They had constructed their own temple on Mt. Gerizim north of Jerusalem. They even claimed their temple was the true place of worship. Samaritan priests traced their blood lines back to the royal priestly line in the Old Testament.

To the Jewish mind, the Samaritans were worse than pagans, because they at least knew better. Samaritans, hated and despised by Jews, were at the bottom of the social ladder.[4] The Scripture attests to the belligerent racism between the two groups. John (4:9) reports that "Jews have no dealings with Samaritans." When Samaritans refuse to give Jesus lodging, James and John become so angry they beg Jesus to destroy the village with fire (Luke 9:51-56). Jewish leaders call Jesus a "Samaritan," a derogatory nickname, reserved for the demon-possessed (John 8:48).

When Jesus was about twelve years old, Samaritans sneaked into the Jerusalem temple at night and scattered human bones over the temple sanctuary. This outrageous act inflamed Jewish passions. Jews would not eat unleavened bread made by a Samaritan, nor an animal killed by a Samaritan. One rabbi said, "He who eats the bread of a Samaritan is like one that eats the flesh of swine."[5]

Intermarriage was taboo. Jews thought Samaritan women perpetual menstruants from the cradle and their husbands perpetually unclean. The saliva of a Samaritan woman was unclean. A whole village was declared contaminated if a Samaritan woman stayed there. Any place a Samaritan slept was considered unclean, as was any food or drink which touched the place. Another rabbi said the Samaritans "have no law or even the remains of a law and therefore, they are contemptible and corrupt."[6] Samaritans frequently attacked Galilean Jews making pilgrimages to Jerusalem. The devout Jew saw Samaritans as worse enemies than the Romans because the halfbreeds mocked Jewish faith by practicing a rival religion in the midst of God's holy land.

Jesus shocked Jewish minds when he said a Samaritan, that despicable enemy, stopped to aid the victim. If Jesus merely wanted to teach about neighborly love, the hero of the story could have been another Jew. Better yet, why not tell a story where a Jew rescued a Samaritan? That would have been comforting—good guy helps bad guy. But to turn a rascal into a hero? Unthinkable! Jesus flips the crowd's social world upside down. The good guys— the priests and Levites—turn bad guys. The villain turns hero.

What an earthquake! It shook the crowd's assumptions. Fault lines gaped in prior values. Dogmatic judgments, established conclusions, and conventional assumptions were suddenly overturned.[7] The audience faced contradictory facts. Jewish leaders acted without compassion. A vile Samaritan behaved like a loving neighbor. The priest and Levite, representing the Jewish temple, refused to help because of religious regulations. The Samaritan, representing the rival temple, defied ceremonial prescriptions and offered tenderness.

Oil and wine were often used as a crude ointment and antiseptic. But they were declared contaminated if touched by a Samaritan. The Jerusalem temple contained sacred oil and wine stored in a holy place and used on special occasions as sacrificial elements. Only officiating priests could touch the sacred oil and wine. In the story, a stranger pollutes the sacred emblems with his touch and then uses them to heal a Jewish enemy. This is true worship, genuine sacrament!

The Samaritan lavishly pours the elements on his opponent, not even tithing them according to proper Jewish procedure. Like God's love, the oil and wine aren't restricted to special people in holy places. They are shared freely, even with enemies.

Only twice in the Gospels is Jesus asked how one gains eternal life. The first time, Jesus directs the rich young ruler to sell out to the poor and follow Jesus. The second time Jesus tells the story of the good Samaritan to explain kingdom love to a sophisticated Jewish lawyer. This upside-down story is Jesus' shocking answer to the lawyer's questions, "How do I inherit eternal life?" and "Who is my neighbor?"

The story clarifies agape love in several ways. (1) Agape is *indiscriminate*. Kingdom love mocked the lawyer's question, "Who is my neighbor?" Jesus' disciples love indiscriminately, beyond obligation. Agents of agape don't draw lines of responsibility and exclusion. The answer to the lawyer's question is clear. If even enemies are defined as neighbors, then certainly anyone less hostile deserves agape assistance.

In other words, the question, "Who is my neighbor?" is moot. The story defines *everyone*, even my enemy, as my neighbor. The term "neighbor" is all-inclusive in the upside-down kingdom. The categories of friend and enemy dissolve since everyone is a neighbor. We treat as neighbor even those to whom we have no obligation to act neighborly, even enemies we can rightfully hate. Agape love responds to persons, not to social categories. Jesus reverses things by asking the lawyer, in essence, "Are you acting like a neighbor?"

(2) Agape is *bold*. Religious custom doesn't stymie it. It suspends social norms which might justify callous disin-

terest. Unlike the priest who feared his shadow might touch a corpse, agape values people over religious traditions. Agape penetrates the social barricades which hide people in prisons, hospitals, addiction centers, and ghettos of all sorts.

(3) Agape is *inconvenient*. The priest and Levite "saw and passed by on the other side." The Samaritan had compassion and got off his donkey. He placed the victim on his donkey and walked alongside. It's inconvenient to get off the donkeys which carry us to places of comfortable security.

(4) Agape is *risky*. The whole scene might have been a frame-up. Perhaps the robbers were hiding nearby waiting to pounce on anyone who offered help. By walking instead of riding, the Samaritan made himself more vulnerable to armed attack after the rescue.

(5) Agape *takes time*. The Samaritan merchant's schedule was hampered. Stopping and bandaging the victim, walking alongside him, and stopping at the inn surely delayed his trip.

(6) Agape is *expensive*. The Samaritan paid the innkeeper the equivalent of twenty-four days of lodging and offered a "blank check" for any additional costs. If Jew were helping Jew, a civil court would have likely repaid the helper. But a Jewish court would never reimburse a Samaritan. The Samaritan freely lends finances without hope of return. This is precisely what Jesus prescribes in his formal instruction: "Lend, expecting nothing in return" (Luke 6:35).

(7) Agape *jeopardizes social status*. What happened when the word got back to the Samaritan's hometown that he was aiding Jews? He must have been considered a traitor to the Samaritan cause. His reputation and social status were tarnished. He likely faced ridicule from his own people.

This upside-down parable leaves no doubt about the

nature of agape. It's courageous and aggressive. Agape is more than warm fuzzy feelings. It's more than good attitudes toward others. It doesn't stop with sweet smiles. This foolish love is aggressive. It's costly, both socially and economically.

Although the parable portrays the shape of agape it doesn't answer all our questions. What if the Samaritan had found the robbers beating the victim? How would agape have responded? Would force be used to stop the atrocity? Does agape only apply Band-Aids to the wounded? Did the Samaritan ever get to the root of the problem by going back to the caves and searching for the robbers? If he found them, what did he do to them? What if one sees many battered victims? Which ones receive priority? These questions, unanswered in the parable, greet us in contemporary applications of agape.

One-Legged Law

The Gospels herald agape love as *the* ordinance of the upside-down kingdom. After the great commandment to love God with all our being comes the revolutionary instruction. Love your neighbor in the *same* manner that you love yourself. All three synoptic writers underscore this Christian manifesto (Matthew 22:37-40; Mark 12:28-31; Luke 10:25-27).

The simple phrase is packed with meaning. First, it assumes self-love is appropriate. There is a place for personal respect and dignity. It's all right to have personal aspirations. But there's a catch. The revolutionary phrase calls us to care for our neighbor as intensely as we care for ourselves. We should work as hard to help our neighbors achieve their goals as we work for our own.

The invitation to love our neighbor as ourself collides with selfish individualism. This wise admonition balances the pursuit of self-interest with the needs of others. It celebrates personal needs and desires. But it restrains them by calling for equal attention to others. Selfish individualism is abolished in the upside-down kingdom. Here equal doses of self-love and neighbor love flow from our ultimate love—devotion to God. Such love eradicates pride. Caring for our neighbor's welfare with the same intensity as we care for our own eliminates greedy egoism.

For Jesus, the norm of agape love summed up the *entire* law and the message of the prophets (Matthew 7:12). Although agape was the key to Old Testament righteousness, Jesus called it a new commandment. We're to love others as he loved us. Our expression of love is the sign that we are indeed his disciples (John 13:34-35).

Jesus added new dimensions to the Old Testament understanding. A skeptical Gentile once told a rabbi he would accept the Jewish faith if the rabbi could summarize the Jewish law while the Gentile stood on one leg. The rabbi replied, "Do not do to another what would be hurtful to you." Jesus moved beyond the Jewish maxim, "As you wish that men would do to you, do so to them" (Luke 6:31; Matthew 7:12). Jesus flipped the negative rule upside down and turned it into a directive for action.

Jesus modeled agape. He embodied it by being an advocate for the poor. He violated civil and religious laws in the face of human need. His words and deeds insulted the rich and powerful. They didn't think he was loving. He championed the downtrodden, the outcasts, and the oppressed even when his behavior created a ruckus.

Agape is also firm when responding to exploiters. Although agape willingly suffers, it understands that a firm "no" is also an expression of loving care. The young child, the emotionally disturbed, the adolescent with a character disorder, and the irresponsible adult may need a firm *no* rather than sweet smiles. Kind but firm confrontation can be a deep expression of agape. Such love confronts when others exploit relationships. Saying that agape can be firm and confrontive dare not, however, be an

190 / The Upside-Down Kingdom

excuse to use violent or authoritarian means, even for good ends.

Suggesting that agape is the single ordinance of the kingdom sounds nice. But it's not a panacea. How does one respond when the needs of three or four different neighbors clash? Caring for one neighbor may harm the interests of another one. In an age of aggressive competition, how does a Christian enterprise embody agape in the face of strident competition? Are corporate competitors also "neighbors"? How do we love our neighbor when the neighbor's goals clash with Christian values? Although the questions beg for answers, the agape view does offer new perspectives. It tilts us away from arrogant individualism and prods us to ask the right questions about neighborly love.

Beyond Tit for Tat

Jesus' mode of love cut through the widespread norm of reciprocity. Throughout the world, reciprocity is a basic rule of social life. It shapes expectations for giving and receiving favors—both verbal and material. If I buy you a cup of coffee, this obligates you to say "thank you" and return the favor sometime. The exchange needn't be equal in value or form. A candy bar might be an acceptable thank you for a cup of coffee. The underlying rule, however, is simple: we should appreciate and return favors.

The norm of reciprocity assumes that people should help—and certainly not injure—those who have helped them. Reciprocity maintains a balance of obligations in personal and group ties. We feel awkward if we can't reciprocate a gift. We consider rude those who break the rules of reciprocity. Gift giving and card exchanges at holidays conform to the norm. Gifts need to be of similar value so things won't get unbalanced. Giving a $2.00 gift in exchange for a $25.00 one makes us uncomfortable. We anticipate who will send us holiday cards so we can return one before it's too late. A deliberate, late exchange is embarrassing.

This rule isn't just a seasonal thing. It pervades all aspects of human relations. The little "thank you's" we say and do throughout the day are governed by reciprocity. So is the exchange of labor for wages and fees for services rendered. We can manipulate relationships for personal gain by building up an indebtedness with others. This happens when salespersons "wine and dine" prospective customers—thereby obligating the prospects to return the favor by making a purchase. If we want to ask a favor of others we may take them out to lunch, thus obligating them to help us. Of course, while we're to help those tied into our web of reciprocity, we're not obligated to "go out of our way" to do favors for strangers.

Jesus slices through the norm of reciprocity:

"If you love those who love you, what credit is that to you? For even sinners love those who love them. . . . And if you lend to those from whom you hope to receive, what credit is that to you? Even sinners lend to sinners, to receive as much again" (Luke 6:32-34).

Jesus presses the point by asking, "For if you love those who love you, what reward have you? Do not even the tax collectors do the same? And if you salute only your brethren, what more are you doing than others?" (Matthew 5:46-47). In other words, agape love stretches far beyond simple reciprocity.

Don't be tricked, says Jesus, into thinking that agape love is the same as the norm of reciprocity. Agape isn't returning a smile for a smile or a favor for a favor. Even sinners play by that rule. Pharisees and tax collectors smile back when people smile at them. Pagans return favors to persons who favor them. Gentiles politely conform to these rules of social etiquette. It's no big deal if you simply play by the rules of reciprocity. That's not kingdom love.

Agape is a norm of *excess*. It goes beyond reciprocity. The foolish father didn't play by reciprocity when he welcomed his stinking son home. The Samaritan crossbreed didn't play by reciprocity when he got off his donkey. Your heavenly Parent doesn't play by that rule either. God sends sun and rain on the unjust as well the just (Matthew 5:45). God models the norm of excess. We should be merciful as God is merciful (Luke 6:36). "You received without paying, give without pay" (Matthew 10:8).

God injects a divine dimension into the "tit for tat" formula. God enters the equation of social relationships. God has taken the initiative by doing us a favor. God loved the world so much that God became a human person. God redeemed and saved us through Jesus Christ. As the first actor, God initiates the chain reaction. We've been graciously forgiven. How do we repay? By sharing God's initiative of love with our neighbors. In this network of social relations there are three actors. *God* takes the initiative by extending unconditional love like the foolish father. *We* reciprocate our indebtedness to God by spreading the loving initiative to *others*.

Though we don't earn our salvation, we erase our indebtedness to God by loving others. Paul spells out the workings of this "love debt" succinctly: "Owe no one anything, except to love one another; for he who loves his neighbor has fulfilled the law" (Romans 13:8). Jesus spells it out as clearly when he says: "Truly, I say to you, as you did it to one of the least of these my brethren, you did it to me" (Matthew 25:40). In this context he describes acts of love to the most destitute: the hungry, the thirsty, the sick, the prisoners, the strangers, and the naked. As you love even the least of these, those on the bottom rung of the social ladder—you have repaid me!

The transaction is complete. A new chain reaction begins. The least of these who experience God's care now pass it on. The Jubilee refrain rings in our ears again. As I have liberated you, so liberate others! This isn't a cold, calculating exchange where we seek to "repay" God in some legalistic way. It's impossible to fully repay our enormous debt. This is a joyous Jubilee response—spontaneous gratitude for God's marvelous grace.

Agape love exceeds the norm of reciprocity in three ways. First, the initiative is now ours. Instead of waiting to return a favor, we make the first move because God has already favored us.

Second, agape serves others regardless of their status. It doesn't focus on friends or peers to whom we must "be nice." As the story of the Samaritan suggests, under the reign of agape, strangers, foes, and outcasts are cared for as well as close friends.

Third, agape love doesn't expect a return. Since God has taken the initiative, we've already been paid. In typical upside-down fashion, agape urges a neighbor to pass the love on, offering the favor to someone else rather than returning it.

Jesus articulates this clearly. "When you give a dinner or a banquet, do not invite your friends or your brothers or your kinsmen or rich neighbors, lest they also invite you in return, and you be repaid. But when you give a feast, invite the poor, the maimed, the lame, the blind, and you will be blessed, because they cannot repay you. You will be repaid at the resurrection of the just" (Luke 14:12-14).[8]

Jesus' disciples don't love for personal gain, nor do they expect a return. After mocking those who pride themselves for following the norm of reciprocity, Jesus spells out the vulnerable, boundless nature of agape. "But love your enemies, and do good, and lend, expecting nothing in return; and your reward will be great, and you

194 / The Upside-Down Kingdom

will be sons of the Most High; for he is kind to the ungrateful and the selfish" (Luke 6:35).

The disciples of Jesus are upside-down deviants. They exceed conventional expectations. They take the initiative. They don't discriminate between enemies and neighbors. They expect no return. When we expect a return, we turn the recipients of our gift into clients. When we expect no return, we free them from debt.[9]

It's often difficult to accept a gift. We hate to feel indebted. We worry about how to reciprocate. Our gifts to others may make them feel awkward as well. The agape posture alleviates the awkwardness. When someone gives us a gift and says, "Just pass the favor on," it relieves our indebtedness. It also protects our dignity since we can reciprocate in due time through someone else. Passing on the kindness enlarges the circle of redeeming love.

Beyond a Cut for a Cut

We've looked at the positive side of the norm of reciprocity—do good to those who do good to you. The downside allows us to harm someone who has harmed us. It's fair play to retaliate if someone has deliberately hurt us. In fact, we can go beyond an eye for an eye. If people poke out one of our eyes, we may poke out both of theirs. This negative reciprocity undergirds the spectrum of human behavior from sibling pinches to international war. In brief, if persons take advantage of me, I may take advantage of them.

If someone files suit against me, I may file countersuit. If someone swindles me, I have license to cheat them back. If another nation launches missiles against us, we may counter-launch. In fact, if we *think* they're about to launch, we have the right to launch first. The negative side of reciprocity not only permits self-defense, it legitimates a spiraling cycle of retaliation. The revenge exceeds the original insult to "teach" the aggressor "a lesson." We reflect the negative norm when we say, "She had it coming to her," "He got what he deserved," or "It serves them right."

In upside-down fashion, Jesus overturns the negative rule of reciprocity. His words and actions are forthright. There can be no question. Jesus suspends the negative as well as the positive side of the norm.

> "You have heard that it was said, 'An eye for an eye and a tooth for a tooth.' But I say to you, Do not resist one who is evil. But if any one strikes you on the right cheek, turn to him the other also; and if any one would sue you and take your coat, let him have your cloak as well; and if any one forces you to go one mile, go with him two miles. Give to him who begs from you, and do not refuse him who would borrow from you.
>
> "You have heard that it was said, 'You shall love your neighbor and hate your enemy.' But I say to you, Love your enemies and pray for those who persecute you" (Matthew 5:38-44).

Love our enemies? They're the one category of people that the norm of reciprocity *allows* us to hate.[10] To love our enemies is the ultimate flip-flop, for it demolishes the norm of reciprocity.

In Luke's Gospel Jesus offers upside-down responses to seven types of aggressors (Luke 6:27-30). How should Christians respond when someone else makes an evil move? What treatment does the old norm of reciprocity prescribe for aggressors? An item-by-item contrast between a "fair" response and the upside-down kingdom response is sketched below. The proposed kingdom reactions seem utterly unfair according to the norm of reciprocity.

Type of Person	Fair Response	Kingdom Response
Enemies	Kill	Love
Haters	Hate	Do good
Cursers	Curse	Bless
Abusers	Exploit	Pray
Strikers	Slug	Offer the other cheek
Beggars	Avoid	Give
Thieves	Prosecute	Do not ask for your goods

Matthew (5:39) tells us to turn the other cheek if someone strikes us. A blow on the right cheek had special significance in Jewish culture. It symbolized ultimate contempt. Its punishment was a fine equivalent to a year's wages.[11] In other words, Jesus forbids his disciples to retaliate even in the face of the most abusive insult.

In calling for enemy love, Jesus clashes with the Essenes, the rebels, and the Pharisees. The patriotic rebels, as we've seen, didn't hesitate to kill enemies. The Essenes, living in isolated Dead Sea communities, thought it was their righteous duty to hate sinners. Jewish law, taught by the Pharisees, said it wasn't necessary to love an enemy. Jesus reverses these typical solutions to evil. Revenge and retaliation are obsolete in the new kingdom.

As assertive love supersedes reciprocity, so forgiveness obliterates the tit-for-tat of revenge. Forgiveness is the startling mark of Jesus' disciples. They forgive 490 times a day (Matthew 18:22; Luke 17:3-4). Jesus isn't setting legal limits. With a twinkle in his eye, he suggests that forgiveness is the perpetual mark of kingdom citizenship. His disciples can forgive because they were so graciously forgiven. Those who don't forgive jeopardize their own forgiveness. "If you do not forgive men their trespasses, neither will your Father forgive your trespasses" (Matthew 6:15). Forgiveness replaces retaliation. It's the distinguishing mark of the upside-down way.

Jesus models this bountiful forgiveness when he tells the woman caught in adultery to go and sin no more. According to Jewish law, she could have been stoned on the spot.

Jesus models the upside-down way of forgiveness from the cross. If retaliation is ever in order, this is the time. But in a startling reversal, in the midst of excruciating pain, Jesus pleads, "Father, forgive them" (Luke 23:34). He urges us to "love one another as I have loved you. Greater love has no man than this, that a man lay down his life for his friends" (John 15:12-13).

In the new kingdom we treat enemies as friends. This kind of forgiveness is vulnerable. It brought Jesus death. He invites us to live the same way, forgiving abundantly even at the expense of our lives. There is no witness, no redemption, no love if we play by the old rule of retaliation. The willingness to suffer in the midst of injustice witnesses to the power of divine love. In front of the cross Jesus rejects self-defense. "All who take the sword will perish by the sword" (Matthew 26:52). "If my kingship were of this world, my servants would fight, that I might not be handed over to the Jews" (John 18:36).

In the face of violence this is a sweeping rejection of self-defense, resistance, and retaliation. The agonizing prayer in Gethsemane, "Nevertheless not my will, but thine, be done" (Luke 22:42), wasn't mere submission to a programmed sequence of events. It was a commitment to continue living the way of forgiving love even in the shadow of impending doom. God wills that we embody forgiveness in the midst of hatred. Even Jesus found that difficult as he struggled with the prospect of death in the garden of Gethsemane.

The message of Jesus is clear, blunt, and unequivocal. The use of violence, whether physical or emotional, is evil. By suspending the norm of reciprocity Jesus negates the validity of violence. By refusing to cheer the revolutionary rebels, Jesus even rejects using violence to protect others from violence. The Romans were oppressors. They assaulted the people with physical brutality and excessive taxes. Jesus rejected violence even in the face of such oppression. He modeled God's new way. The Torah of love in the new kingdom heralds forgiveness, not violent self-defense and retaliation.

Detours Around Agape

Jesus' call to love enemies has baffled human logic down through the centuries. Even the church has found it difficult.[12] Christians have evaded the message of the Prince of Peace in several ways. First, some have prostituted the gospel by justifying military crusades with God's blessing. This blatant contradiction of the gospel sees God smiling warmly on military endeavors.

The use of God-talk to justify militarism spans the centuries from holy crusades to modern claims that "the greatest way to serve God is to sacrifice one's life in defense of the nation."[13] Many songs of American patriotism imply that God "protects" the nation. Coins inscribed with "In God We Trust" are an outright mockery when we spend billions of dollars for defense. We obviously trust weapons, not God.

A second tempting detour around Jesus' plea for agape is Old Testament warfare. Didn't God command warfare in the Old Testament? Modern warfare modeled on the Old Testament pattern would have dire consequences. When Yahweh commanded Israel to engage in military action, it was clear Yahweh was the warrior. Thus military force was deliberately scaled down so any victory would be miraculous and attributed to Yahweh's divine intervention. If we took the Old Testament pattern seriously, our modern armies would dramatically reduce their size and firepower and rely on God's miraculous intervention for victory!

Above all, Jesus, as God's final and definitive revelation, is the interpretive norm of Scripture. Jesus has the final word in God's progressive revelation. Jesus offers a new way superseding the Old Testament norm of tit-for-tat.

A third detour suggests Jesus only calls us to love personal enemies. Jesus' words apply only to interpersonal ties. If government is instituted by God, we're obligated to obey the call of conscription and defend the country. We should love personal enemies, yes, but not national ones. This view elevates national allegiance above kingdom loyalty. The classic Christian text that calls for submission to government (Romans 13:1-7) is sandwiched between two ardent pleas by the apostle Paul for suffering love. Often interpreting it out of context, we use this passage to justify ranking national loyalties above kingdom values, thus negating Jesus' words and example.

We take a fourth detour when our churches affirm the way of peace in public statements but view it as an appendage to the gospel. Instead of seeing forgiveness and all its social implications as the core of salvation, we see it as a peripheral option. It's merely one of many higher rungs on the Christian maturity ladder. Furthermore, we deem it a question of "individual conscience," not a gospel mandate. We can take it or leave it.

We would never baptize prostitutes or bank robbers and allow them to continue their professions. Yet baptizing new converts who join the military and prepare to kill others doesn't trouble us. Military service is a matter of "individual conscience," we say. Would we say the same about prostitution and robbing banks? Which is worse?

A final detour affirms Jesus "nonresistant love" but not his assertive agape. The nonresistant view sees only a passive and mild Jesus—a wimp stooping under the cross. This image blurs the fact that Jesus' three years of active ministry triggered his death. It was precisely *because* of his assertive love that the cross came about in the first place. Jesus acted decisively and forcefully, eating with sinners, healing the sick on the Sabbath, and confronting religious leaders. To face evil serenely isn't to be forever mild and passive. Jesus didn't call us to be passive peace-*keepers* who merely preserve the status quo. His blessing falls on active peace*makers* (Matthew 5:9).

We often think of peace as the absence of violent conflict. *Shalom*, the Old Testament word for peace, is closely connected with ideas of justice, righteousness, and salvation. It refers to a pervasive sense of well-being in personal, social, economic, and political spheres.[14] There is no peace when greedy systems oppress the poor. Peace vanishes when the stigmatized find no justice in the courts. The "peace" which hangs on a precarious balance of nuclear warheads isn't shalom. An individualism which cares only about number one destroys peace. Christians who plan and execute war forfeit the role of peacemaker.

Shalom comes when there are right relationships among people in all realms of life. The Scriptures tell us peace is God's gift. Through Jesus Christ we have peace with God and our neighbors. Shalom is God's design for the created order. God is a God of peace. Jesus is the Prince of peace. The Holy Spirit is the Spirit of peace. The kingdom of God pivots on justice, peace, and joy. The children of God are peacemakers. The gospel is the good news of peace. Shalom is the core, not the caboose, of God's salvation.

Facing Up to Nuclear War

Talk of lovable enemies is hard to hear in a world loaded with nuclear weapons.[15] The overkill potential of modern weapons is astonishing. The superpower nations have long had the capacity to pulverize each other many times over. A single Trident submarine *alone* has the capacity to destroy 408 separate cities with a blast five times stronger than Hiroshima. Weapon after weapon, system after system—the overkill capacity is mind boggling. Our preparations for nuclear war in the name of defense threaten the very people we mean to protect. They also rob the world's poor of basic necessities, such as food, shelter, and health care. Our very preparation for nuclear war is sinful! Even if we somehow avoid a nuclear nightmare, building and deploying nuclear weapons is an outrageous waste of resources when one fourth of the world community lives in squalor.

Many churches and individual Christians have been strangely silent about this threatening menace. What will it take for us to speak up? If a nuclear warhead pulverizes one more city, will we then speak up? What will we say when our children ask why we remained silent for so long? The preparation for nuclear war is an abomination against a God who loves the whole world.

In the midst of worldwide violence, the Carpenter's appeal to love enemies sounds like good advice. Doesn't it make more sense to learn to live with our enemies than to kill ourselves with nuclear weapons while trying to defend our country? Christians in every land must insist that madness in the name of peace is really death in disguise. A peace that holds millions of people hostage to fear isn't peace. A peace built on military threats, bluffing, and bullying isn't peace. Preserving freedom by threatening to use nuclear weapons is slavery to death.

The shalom of God comes not by military strength but by forgiveness. It comes not by threats of violence but by negotiation. War spoils God's shalom. The disciples of Jesus reject war and its preparation without any ifs, ands, or buts!

202 / *The Upside-Down Kingdom*

Questions for Discussion

1. What types of persons in our contemporary world might represent the "Samaritan" in the parable of the good Samaritan?

2. What are the implications of saying that everyone is my neighbor?

3. Does the term neighbor refer to business competitors as well as individual persons?

4. Identify instances where persons or organizations have exceeded the norm of reciprocity.

5. Is it possible to live the way of agape and be successful in a competitive society?

6. Why have many denominations and individuals placed national allegiance above kingdom values?

7. How have many Christians explained participation in military efforts?

8. Are there any conditions when it's appropriate for the disciples of Jesus to use force? Violence?

10

INSIDE OUTSIDERS

Birds of a Feather

The last chapter explored Jesus' teaching on agape. How does agape translate into social interaction? A sage once said, "Birds of a feather flock together." Similar people cluster together. We enjoy those with whom we have things in common. We feel awkward in unfamiliar settings with folks from strange backgrounds. We like those who think as we do. And we begin to think like people we respect. But don't opposites attract? They do on an emotional level. When it comes to beliefs, however, opposites repel and birds of a feather do flock together.

Many social factors bind humans together—income, education, occupation, race, religion, politics, lifestyle, family, ethnic background, and national heritage. We migrate toward similar people and feel most comfortable with those whose education matches our own. It's easier to "talk shop" with persons in similar occupations. It's pleasant to be around those whose social views mirror ours. We seek similar companions to gain reinforcement and support for our ideas. Without objective yardsticks to confirm ideas, we find security among friends who agree. Strange ideas may threaten our beliefs and force us to rethink our convictions. We might even need to change!

The "birds of a feather" principle not only governs personal relationships, it also shapes group interaction. People with similar educational backgrounds and jobs often live in the same area. If we know a person lives on "the hill," in "the ward," or on "the lower side," we can often predict their race, income, and job prestige. We can venture safe estimates of lifestyle, political views, and education if we know someone lives in "Walnut Hill Estate" or "Executive Manor." Congregations and parishes often attract similar people as well. There are, of course, exceptions to these patterns. But they don't erase the fact that in most places, most of the time, most people flock with birds of a common feather.

The Social Checkerboard

Human communities draw lines. They create boundaries that separate good from evil, clean from dirty, stigma from respect, insiders from outsiders. A checkerboard helps us visualize the lines that organize social interaction. Each square on the board can represent a particular kind of person. The boxes and lines limit and define social interaction. We drink coffee, ski, vacation, dine, travel, and swim with folks from our own or nearby squares. It's a rare occasion indeed to relate intimately with someone whose box is on the other side of the board. We treat "inbox" members as friends and neighbors. We invite people from similar boxes to our house. These familiar patterns eliminate worries about dealing with weird people from distant squares. This normal clustering on social squares orders life and makes it predictable.

Individuals as well as groups occupy boxes on the board. Most people occupy several boxes. I'm a father, husband, teacher, neighbor, and writer. Some of our boxes we inherit without choice—race, sex, and nationality. We put ourselves in others—occupation, religion, politics, and education. Each box includes certain rights, privileges, and obligations. The social definition of a box determines to a large extent how we perceive ourselves and how we think others should respond to us. The label on the box tells those on the outside how to relate to the boxholder. Take a police uniform. It reminds the officers themselves to behave properly. But the officers also expect citizens to relate to them with respect when they wear it.

Playing Social Checkers

We carry social checkerboards around in our minds. As we meet people we sort them into social boxes or bins. It's impossible to collect intricate data quickly on each new person. Lacking personalized details, we simply toss persons into a box based on their external appearance. They're white, oriental, sloppy, preppy, nurse, or trucker. In other situations more data may allow us to tag them: fundamentalist, Jew, good guy, born again, liberal, politician, drug addict, or gay.

In addition to boxing people, we generalize about the behavior we expect from people in a particular bin. We stereotype. We assume a particular person behaves like *we think* other people in that box do. We assume charismatics try to get people to speak in tongues. Theological liberals, of course, don't believe in the Virgin Birth. Puerto Ricans are lazy. Blacks are on welfare. Fundamentalists care not a whit for social justice. Republicans are fiscally conservative. Jews are tight. Wealthy folks are indifferent and callous. Salespersons are tricky. Women are emotional. Teenagers are irresponsible. And parents are rigid.

We make serious errors when we play social checkers. We easily place people in the wrong box. Our generalizations about behavior often flow from myth rather than fact. Even if a stereotype is true, a particular person may transcend the patterns associated with the box. Boxing has tragic effects. We relate to others by labels instead of meeting them as real people. We may avoid folks because their tag says deaf, ex-convict, disabled, prostitute, or homosexual. Boxing people isn't entirely harmful, however. It stabilizes social life, making it orderly and predictable.

Jesus models creative ways of penetrating boxes. He crosses lines. He walks over boundaries and deals with the real person. He spurns the rules governing the social checkerboard in Palestine. He walks through barricades erected between adversaries. Wandering over the social checkerboard of his time, he pays little attention to the "No Trespassing" and "Stay Out" signs hanging around the necks of many.

Jesus ignores the social norms specifying the who, when, and where of social interaction. In fact, when the Herodians and Pharisees try to trap Jesus on the question of taxes, they preface their tricky question with some flattery: "For you do not regard the *position* of men, but truly teach the way of God" (Mark 12:14, emphasis added). In other words, Jesus ignored social boxes.

Purebred Pedigrees

One of the boxes Jesus shattered was ethnic purity. Racial purity was important in Palestinian culture.[1] Tidy genealogical histories preserved untainted bloodlines. People were careful not to contaminate family lines by marrying someone with bad blood. Pure pedigrees weren't just a genealogical hobby. They determined one's civil rights in Hebrew culture. A clean pedigree was required to participate in court and to hold a public office. In short, a pure family tree was a necessary ticket to power and influence.

The thoroughbreds—priests, Levites, and others who could prove their pure lineage—lived at the top of the checkerboard. A box below were slightly blemished Jews, often illegitimate descendants of priests and proselytes.

Third were those gravely blemished—bastards, eunuchs, and persons without known fathers. Gentile slaves were exiled to a box by themselves. Although circumcised, they weren't an integral part of the Jewish community. Relegated to the worst box on the ethnic checkerboard were Samaritans and Gentiles.

The Gentile Box

Overlapping these social rankings were two major boxes—Jew and Gentile. Jews treated Gentiles with the same contempt and animosity as they did Samaritans. The Gentiles were unclean outsiders. They were pagans who contaminated the purity of Hebrew ceremonial ritual. Jews avoided Gentiles, whom they called "wild dogs." They were careful not to let Gentiles tarnish them in everyday life. The Old Testament envisions Abraham's blessing touching all nations. In the early pages of the books of Moses, Gentiles receive the divine blessing. By the time of Jesus, however, the vision had vanished. To most Jews, Gentiles were pagan dogs who polluted Jewish purity.

We left a riddle dangling in an earlier chapter. Luke reports that after Jesus' inaugural speech, "All in the synagogue were filled with wrath. And they rose up and put him out of the city, and led him to the brow of the hill on which their city was built, that they might throw him down headlong" (Luke 4:28-29). Why did the crowd explode with anger? Jesus reminded them that a prophet is not acceptable in his own country, and then he told two stories. There were many widows in Israel in the days of Elijah, he said. But in the time of famine Elijah wasn't sent to a pedigreed Jewish widow. He was sent to a Gentile widow in the land of Sidon for help. The second story has the same opening and punch line. There were many lepers in Israel at the time of Elisha the prophet. But it was Naaman, a Gentile Syrian, who was cleansed.

The message sliced through Jewish pride. Belonging to Israel gives no one a special right to be healed. Having a pure pedigree offers no special right to the gospel. Jubilee news is good news for all. In two swift strokes Jesus cut through the crowd's ethnicity. He shattered their tribal pride.

The Old Testament Jubilee applied only to Hebrews. Gentile slaves and debts weren't released in the seventh year. Hebrews could charge Gentiles interest on loans. Jews wanted God's vengeance to fall on Gentiles. Now in a split second, Jesus puts the Gentile community on par with Israel.[2] Exclusive membership cards are unthinkable in the upside-down kingdom. God's favorable year, the day of salvation, applies to *all*. Jesus shreds the patriotism of the synagogue audience. His words sting. They cut so deeply the crowd tries to shove him over a cliff to his death.[3]

The implications are clear. The Gentiles are on board. Again in Mark's Gospel, Jesus includes Gentiles in the kingdom. Couched between Mark 6:30 and 8:30 are symbolic signs of Gentile inclusion in the kingdom.[4] The sequence begins with Jesus feeding the five thousand. Later that night, he walks on the water and announces, "It is I." The Messiah is here. The water-walking astonishes the disciples. But they miss the spiritual meaning of the picnic.

Next the Pharisees quarrel with Jesus for refusing to wash before eating. Then Jesus enters Gentile territory. A widow rebuffs him when he refuses to heal her child. In her reply she calls him Lord. Amazed that she recognizes his lordship, he casts the demon out of her child.

Now a new sequence begins. Jesus moves to a Gentile region on the east side of Lake Galilee and heals a deaf mute. There's another feeding of 4,000, another controversy with the Pharisees over a sign, and another discussion with the disciples about bread. Jesus asks his disciples if they understand the significance of the numbers. A blind man receives sight after two touches from Jesus. This is followed by Peter's declaration: Jesus is the Christ!

The incidents in these chapters come in twos. Two feedings. Two sides of the lake. Two boat rides. Two discussions of bread. Two controversies with the Pharisees. Two healings. Two touches. Two sets of numbers with two feedings. What do the numbers mean?

The first feeding of five thousand involves five loaves. Twelve baskets are left over. It's on the western side of the lake—the Jewish side. There are five books of Moses and twelve tribes of Israel. This is the Jewish feeding. Everyday bread is broken for the hungry five thousand. Yet the bread's significance is profound. It's prophetic bread. The Messiah's own life is about to be broken for the life of his own Jewish people. After this feeding Jesus announces on the water, "It is I" (Mark 6:50). The same utterance appears in Exodus 3:14 when God declares, "I AM WHO I AM." According to Mark, Jesus is telling the disciples Almighty God is here. The Messiah is among them! Had they understood the symbolic feeding, the Messiah's walking on water wouldn't have shocked them. But they missed the signals.

The next episode finds the Pharisees quarreling with Jesus about washing. They reject this prophet who mocks their ceremonial traditions. So Jesus moves on to Gentile turf in the land of Tyre and Sidon (Mark 7:24-30; Matthew 15:21-28). He tries to evade the public eye but a courageous woman begs him to exorcise a demon from her daughter. She pleads with Jesus to heal her child. He stalls and turns away. She persists. Finally Jesus defends his hesitation with a Jewish proverb, "It is not right to take the children's bread and throw it to the dogs," meaning the Gentiles. Jesus tells her it's unwise to share the Jewish Messiah with Gentiles. But she courageously

210 / *The Upside-Down Kingdom*

uses his own proverb to argue back: "Yes, Lord; yet even the dogs under the table eat the children's crumbs" (Mark 7:28). She calls him Lord and Jesus heals her child. The upside-down moment, filled with irony and paradox, arrives. A Gentile, of all people, calls him Lord!

In the feeding of the five thousand Jesus symbolically announces his messianic mission. Both the disciples and the Pharisees are blind. They're deaf to the good news. But on Gentile turf, a pagan woman realizes he's the Messiah. She sees and she hears! Then Jesus pushes eastward to the Decapolis, a circle of ten Gentile cities. Here he heals a deaf mute, another sign that the Gentiles hear. This miracle leads to the second feeding.

The new feeding involves a new set of numbers—seven loaves, seven baskets of leftovers, and four thousand people. Is it just another feeding? In contrast to the first one, this luncheon is on the eastern side of the lake—the Gentile side. Seven is the biblical symbol for wholeness, completeness, and perfection. It completes the Jubilee cycle. Four represents the four corners of the earth. It signifies the time when people from east, west, north, and south will come to eat the salvation banquet. In the second feeding the messianic bread is broken for all humankind. This complete and perfect messianic meal includes the Gentiles and all other peoples.

Irony visits again. After the picnic the Pharisees come to Jesus begging for a sign, for a symbol. In the midst of all these symbols, they don't see; neither do they hear! After breaking Jewish bread for the five thousand, the Pharisees pester Jesus about washing before eating. And now, after the Gentile feeding, they come asking for a sign! The disciples are in the same boat. Like the Pharisees, they too are deaf and blind to the symbolic meaning of the numbers (Mark 8:17-21).

Jesus tries again. A blind man cries out for healing. Jesus touches him and asks, "Do you see anything?" The man replies, "I see men; but they look like trees, walking" (Mark 8:24). Jesus touches him again. Now he sees everything clearly. Two touches: one yields fog, the other sight. The Pharisees and the disciples had foggy eyes and plugged ears. They weren't hearing and seeing the messianic announcement.

Ironically, things were perfectly clear to the Gentile woman, even before the second feeding. Suddenly Peter begins to hear and see. The numbers start to click, the fog clears. "You—" he stammers in amazement. "You are the Christ!" (Mark 8:29).

In the rich symbolism of these passages Mark points us to Jesus' embrace of the Gentiles. Parts of the message arise from Jesus' own words and parts flow from Mark's editorial work. But the message is plain. Jesus has shattered the social boxes. Jews and Gentiles march arm-in-arm into the new kingdom.

In another instance a Roman centurion—commander of 100 men—asks Jesus to heal his servant (Matthew 8:5-13, Luke 7:1-10). The centurion doesn't speak to Jesus directly in Luke's account. But he makes it clear he believes Jesus can heal his assistant from a distance. The commander's faith impresses Jesus. Without going to the man's home, Jesus cures the subordinate and exclaims, "Truly, I say to you, not even in Israel have I found such faith" (Matthew 8:10).

A Gentile army officer displays greater faith than the religious leaders of Israel. This is upside down indeed! At the end of the incident Matthew reports Jesus saying, "I tell you, many will come from east and west and sit at table with Abraham, Isaac, and Jacob in the kingdom of heaven, while the sons of the kingdom will be thrown into the outer darkness; there men will weep and gnash their teeth" (Matthew 8:11-12). In the upside-down kingdom Gentiles come from the four corners of the earth while some sons and daughters of Abraham are locked out of the banquet.

Jesus met another Gentile, the chain-snapping demoniac. He roamed in the country of the Gerasenes, Gentile turf east of the Sea of Galilee. Mark says the demoniac worshiped Jesus and called him "Son of the Most High God." After Jesus exorcises the demons, he tells the man, "Go home to your friends, and tell them how much the Lord has done for you" (Mark 5:19). This contrasts with Jewish healings where Jesus warns the healed to hush up and tell no one!

So we see Jesus ministering to three Gentiles: the Syrophoenician woman, the Roman centurion, and the Gerasene demoniac. Not only were they Gentiles; sex, politics, and illness also stigmatized them. We hear two of them, the woman and the demoniac, confessing Jesus as the Messiah. The centurion receives the "Great Faith" award and Jesus urges the demoniac to spread the good news. The kingdom is breaking in among the Gentiles!

The Gentile vision flashes through the Gospels in other places as well. Jesus sends out seventy missionaries, symbolizing the wholeness and completeness of his mission (Luke 10:1). He instructs the disciples to be light and salt, not just within Judaism but in the whole world (Matthew 5:13-14). He chases the money changers from the temple's outer court so it can be a house of prayer for *all* nations (Mark 11:17). Jesus' earthly sojourn began and ended in "Galilee of the Gentiles" where his disciples received a final mandate to go and make disciples of all nations (Matthew 28:19).

Others also witness to the multiethnic vision of the kingdom. Matthew sees Jesus' ministry fulfilling the words of Isaiah: "I will put my Spirit upon him, and he shall proclaim justice to the Gentiles. . . . And in his name will the Gentiles hope (Matthew 12:18, 21).[5] Devout Simeon, seeing the babe in the temple, said this salvation was "prepared in the presence of *all* peoples, a light for revelation to the Gentiles" (Luke 2:31-32, emphasis added). John the Baptist prepared the way in the wilderness so that *"all* flesh shall see the salvation of God" (Luke 3:6, emphasis added). There can be no doubt. The new kingdom transcended the Jewish box. This is clear in the Acts of the Apostles as well. Paul's concept of justification involves social reconciliation of Jew and Gentile in the community of faith.[6] The social barricades between Jew and Gentile crumbled in the presence of Jesus, the Messiah. They continued to erode in the life of the early church.

The Samaritan Box

We've already noted the barrier separating Jews and Samaritans. Jesus shattered this ethnic wall as well. Striking at Jewish pride, Jesus held up a "good" Samaritan as the supreme example of agape love. The implication, of course, is that Samaritans were, by definition, "bad." Another Samaritan, whom Jesus called a foreigner, was *the* only one of ten lepers to return and give thanks. This thankful half-breed was sole recipient of Jesus' blessing (Luke 17:16-19).

Jesus refused to comply when some of his disciples, "the Sons of Thunder," asked him to torch a Samaritan village (Luke 9:55). Some Samaritans incensed the disciples by denying Jesus lodging. The box-conscious Samaritans couldn't permit a Jew in their village, especially one heading for the rival temple in Jerusalem. So they kicked him out. The last place a Jewish rabbi wanted to be found was in a Samaritan village. Jesus, the upside-down rabbi, took the initiative to enter Samaritan turf. With daring irreverence for social boxes, Jesus strikes up a conversation with a sleazy Samaritan woman (John 4:7).

The record is clear. Jesus doesn't bypass Samaritans just because of their name tags. He willingly meets them. He boldly walks on their turf because he loves them.

The Female Box

It's difficult for us to grasp the meager status in Hebrew culture of women, stashed at the bottom of the heap with slaves and children. Male and female boxes were different as day and night.[7] One of the six major divisions of the Mishnah is devoted entirely to rules about women. None of the divisions, of course, deal exclusively with men. The Mishnah section on uncleanness has seventy-nine legal paragraphs on the ritual contamination caused by menstruation!

Women were excluded from public life. When walking outside the house, they covered themselves with two veils to conceal their identity. A chief priest in Jerusalem didn't even recognize his own mother when he accused her of adultery. Strict women covered themselves at home so even the rafters wouldn't see a hair of their head! Women in public places were to remain unseen. Social custom prohibited men from being alone with women. Men dared not look at married women or even greet them in the street. A woman could be divorced for talking to a man on the street. Women were to stay inside. Public life belonged to men.

Young girls were engaged around twelve years of age and married a year later. A father could sell his daughter into slavery or force her to marry anyone of his choice before she was twelve. After this age she couldn't be married against her will. The father of the bride received a considerable gift of money from his new son-in-law. Because of this, daughters were considered a source of cheap labor and profit.

In the house, the woman was confined to domestic chores. She was virtually a slave to her husband, washing his face, hands, and feet. Considered the same as a Gentile slave, a wife was obligated to obey her husband as she would a master. If death threatened, the husband's life must be saved first. Under Jewish law, the husband alone had the right to divorce.

The wife's most important function was making male babies. The absence of children was considered divine punishment. There was joy in the home at the birth of a boy. Sorrow greeted a baby girl. A daily prayer repeated by men intoned "Blessed be God that hath not made me a woman."[8] A woman was subject to most of the taboos in the Torah. Girls could not study the Holy Law—the Torah. Women couldn't approach the Holy of Holies in the temple. They couldn't go beyond a special outer court designated for women. During their monthly purification from menstruation they were excluded from even the outer court.

Women were forbidden to teach. They couldn't pronounce the benediction after a meal. They couldn't serve as witnesses in court, for they were generally considered liars. Even the linguistic structure reflected the low status of females. The Hebrew adjectives for "pious," "just," and "holy" do not have a feminine form in the Old Testament.

In this context, Jesus knowingly overturns social custom when he allows women to follow him in public.[9] His treatment of women implies he views them as equal with men before God. In a stunning upheaval, he declares that female harlots will enter the kingdom of God before righteous Jewish males (Matthew 21:31). The prominence of women in the Gospels as well as Jesus' interaction with them confirms his irreverence for sexual boxes. He doesn't hesitate to violate social norms to elevate women to a new dignity and a higher status.

Consider a few examples of Jesus' upside-down attitude toward women. The most striking is his talk with the Samaritan woman at Jacob's well (John 4:1-42). Samaria was sandwiched between two Jewish areas: Galilee to the north and Judea to the south. Jews moving between these areas often bypassed Samaria to avoid attack.

In this instance, Jesus takes the shortcut and walks through Samaria. He waits alone, by a well, while the disciples try to buy food in a nearby village. A person approaches with three stigmas hanging around her neck: woman, Samaritan, flirt. Jesus asks her for a drink. In a split second he shatters all the social norms designed to prevent such behavior.

Jesus isn't merely being friendly to a woman. His simple request slices through five social rules. In the first place, Jesus violates turf rules. He has no business being here. Samaria is outside the Jewish box. Jesus has wandered into enemy territory and a rival religion.

Second, she's a woman. Men weren't to even look at married women in public, much less talk with them. The rabbis said, "A man should hold no conversation with a woman in the street, not even with his own wife, still less with any other woman, lest men should gossip."[10] Woman she may be, but Jesus addresses her. This makes him vulnerable. Anyone walking around the corner and seeing the conversation could ruin his reputation. He doesn't care. He cares more for the person than his reputation.

Third, this isn't just another woman. She's having her sixth affair. She's a promiscuous flirt. Everyone in town knows her number. Rabbis and holy men scurry from such women. Jesus doesn't run. He takes a risk; he puts his career on the line by asking for her help.

Fourth, she's not only promiscuous, she's a Samaritan. Jewish rabbis said Samaritan women were menstruants from the cradle and thus perpetually unclean. Jewish social norms were clear: look the other way. Avoid her. Act as though you don't see her. Jesus boldly shatters the social barricades. He addresses her.

Finally, and worst of all, he deliberately defiles himself. As a supposed menstruant from the cradle, she was unclean. Anything she touched became unclean. A whole Jewish village was declared unclean if a Samaritan woman entered it. By asking for water she had touched, Jesus was intentionally polluting himself. The religious rule said, "Stay as far away as possible from unclean things." His brief request mocked the norms of purity. Jesus was completely out of place, doing the wrong thing with the wrong person in the wrong place. Yes, merely saying, "Give me a drink," shattered five social norms imprisoning this woman in a tight cultural box.

Such unprecedented behavior startled the woman and the disciples. In her words, "How is it that you, a Jew, ask a drink of me, a woman of Samaria?" When the disciples returned, they "marveled that he was talking with a woman" (John 4:9, 27). The conversation obliterated the social trappings that separate people and lock them in boxes.

It began with water—the one element of life all humans need, regardless of their box. When it comes to water we're all equals. As the living water, Jesus provides life for all. No other person stands out as clearly in the Gospels as having received Jesus' private disclosure of his messianic identity. Jesus reveals himself not to the chief priests in Jerusalem, not to the members of the San-hedrin, nor to the scribes—but to this promiscuous half-breed. She asks about the Messiah. And Jesus tersely responds, "I who speak to you am he."

How upside down! A defiled woman from a rival religion receives the incomparable honor of hearing the Messiah identify himself in first person. Jesus not only cuts through social red tape to ask for a drink. He lifts this defiled woman up to the privileged holy of holies and whispers, "I am the Messiah." Truly a flip-flop!

This miracle moves Samaritan villagers to beg Jesus to stay with them. The unheard-of happens. Enemies fellow-ship and eat together. Many believe. They switch temples, not from Mt. Gerizim to Jerusalem, but to the temple of spirit and truth. And it is this new church of Samaritan

half-breeds that declares, "This is indeed the Savior of
the world" (John 4:42). Not the Savior of the Jews but
the Savior of *all*. The despised, the outlaws, the enemies—Jesus pulls from their boxes and elevates them to
authentic personhood and dignity in his unusual kingdom.

In another meeting with a woman already noted, we
find things upside down again. A prostitute anoints Jesus
at a Pharisee luncheon. The term "Messiah" means "The
Anointed One." Jesus, the Messiah, is anointed by a
woman—a prostitute. The woman, overwhelmed by his
forgiving love, takes the tainted perfume of her trade
(worth a year's wages) and anoints him. Perfume was
used to prepare bodies for burial. This outcast simultaneously anoints the Messiah and signals his death. A
woman has the honor of anointing the Messiah! The religious boxes shatter again!

On another occasion, a woman with a twelve-year hem-
orrhage (Mark 5:25-34) touches Jesus. Mark reports she
suffered under many physicians, had spent all her money,
and was getting worse. Such a person was considered
filthy and ceremonially unclean. Old Testament purity
laws viewed her as a perpetual menstruant (Leviticus
15:26-27). Her touch infected others. Moreover, anyone
touching what she touched became polluted. The contamination could only be removed by ceremonial washing.
She finds a different attitude in Jesus. In a daring move,
she touched the edge of his coat and was healed.

The typical rabbi would have cursed the filthy woman
and run for ceremonial cleansing. Jesus invites her to
come forward not for a rebuke, but for a blessing.
"Daughter, your faith has made you well; go in peace,
and be healed of your disease" (Mark 5:34). Jesus understands her agony. Despite her social stigma, he loved her.

In another episode, Luke reports Jesus' compassion for
a widow as he comes upon a funeral procession. The

dead man is the widow's only son. When a man died, his property went to the eldest son, not the wife. If there were no sons, the youngest brother of the dead husband often married the widow; but he had the right to refuse. In that case the widow became an object of charity with no means of support. The death of this widow's only son means financial uncertainty for her—possibly poverty. Jesus, moved with compassion, raises her son to life.

Luke, who seems to have a special interest in Jesus' relationship with women, tells another story (Luke 10:38-42). Jesus is about to dine with Martha and Mary. Like a good Jewish domestic, Martha is engulfed in kitchen duties. Women were household servants; they weren't to study the Torah nor to converse with rabbis. Mary breaks from her culturally prescribed role. She forgets the kitchen. She enjoys Jesus' teaching. This peeves Martha. Mary's impropriety and perhaps Martha's double kitchen duty angers her.

In a few words, Jesus redefines the role of Jewish women. He chides Martha for fretting about Mary's deviance. Mary, he says, has chosen the "good portion." She is fully human, entitled to think, to engage in intellectual discourse. The message is clear: women belong in the human box. They're more than domestic servants.

Some women accompanied Jesus' band of disciples. As he preached the good news of the kingdom, Mary Magdalene, Joanna, and Susanna were among the many who accompanied him. The women helped support the disciples financially (Luke 8:1-3). The Greek wording of this passage suggests the women were deaconesses.

By permitting women to travel with him in public and listen to his teaching, Jesus was overturning social boulders. The folkways said women were only to walk in public if they were on domestic errands. They weren't to wander in the countryside. They had no business studying and discussing religious matters.

Finally, to travel in a mixed group made them sexually suspect. The other great rabbis never permitted women to follow them or listen to their teaching. One teacher said it was better to burn the law than to let a woman study it. By permitting women to join his disciple band, Jesus upset social and religious protocol. Female boxes crumbled in the kingdom.

Moreover, in the Gospels women are the most loyal disciples. Tough Peter swore he'd never chicken out. Then he denied his association with Jesus as the rooster crowed. The male disciples scampered away when the crunch came in Gethsemane (Mark 14:50). The women persisted to the bitter end. All four Gospels note that the women, who followed from Galilee, watched the bloody crucifixion (Matthew 27:55; Mark 15:40; Luke 23:49; John 19:25). The women didn't abandon Jesus in the moment of crisis and they had their reward. The resurrection was announced first to them. Mary Magdalene was honored as the first person to see Jesus after the crucifixion (John 20:11-18). When the disciples heard the women report Jesus was alive, "These words seemed to them an idle tale, and they did not believe them" (Luke 24:11).

The upside-down moment visits again. Women, barred from Jewish courts because they were considered liars, are the first witnesses to the resurrection. "Liars" certify the triumphant resurrection. They're given the distinctive honor of announcing the victory. Untrustworthy women become the heralds of the upside-down kingdom. Meanwhile, the male disciples refuse to believe the resurrection news.

Beyond his face-to-face encounters with women, Jesus also includes them in his teaching. In an earlier chapter we saw him highlight a widow as a model giver. He uses female imagery to describe his compassion for Jerusalem. "How often would I have gathered your children together as a hen gathers her brood under her wings, and you would not!" (Matthew 23:37). In another instance Jesus compares God to a woman looking for a coin (Luke 15:8-10). Male interpreters have overemphasized the lostness of the coin. But there's another side to this coin. God is like a woman who diligently searches—who doesn't give up looking until she finds it.

By word and by deed Jesus confers a new dignity on women. One confesses him as Lord (Matthew 15:22-28). He reveals his messianic identity to another (John 4:26). A woman is the only person to anoint him as Messiah (Luke 7:38). And women, of all people, are chosen as the first witnesses to the resurrection. In a male-dominated culture these were powerful signs that women had a new status in the upside-down kingdom.

Other Outsiders

The calling of the twelve apostles offers a fascinating instance of unboxing. In this motley crew we find Matthew, the former tax collector. Jewish tax collectors, working for the Romans, were considered outright traitors—especially by patriotic rebels. Another disciple was Simon the Zealot (Luke 6:15). It's possible that other disciples were former rebels or at least shared their sympathies. James and John, "Sons of Thunder," Judas Iscariot, and Simon Peter are possible candidates.

In any event, Simon the Zealot was likely a zealous political rebel, eager to use violence against the Romans. Matthew stopped collecting taxes when he followed Jesus, for he left all (Luke 5:28). Joining the disciple group required repentance and a change of loyalties. Matthew the tax collector and Simon the Zealot came from opposite ends of the political checkerboard. Simon may have harassed his share of tax collectors.

Now, political opponents are walking and sleeping together. Unheard of! Unbelievable! What a mighty witness to the unboxing that occurs when Jesus is Lord. Old labels and tags are torn off. Former enemies stand together as friends under Jesus' lordship.

Political adversaries also come together at the cross of Jesus. Law breaker and law keeper find themselves face-to-face with Jesus between them. One of the criminals hanging beside Jesus is moved by his forgiving love. This insurrectionist believes and asks Jesus to remember him. That very day, Jesus assures him, he will be in paradise (Luke 23:43). The crucifixion overwhelms the Roman centurion, that exterminator of Jewish rebels. He is terrified and exclaims: "Truly this was the Son of God!" (Matthew 27:54).

The boxes of occupation, power, and wealth often overlap. Jesus moves around the Palestinian checkerboard with little care for social labels. He converses with Nicodemus, a ruler of the Pharisees. Joseph of Arimathea, a rich, silent sympathizer, donates a tomb. The daughter of Jairus, the ruler of the synagogue, is healed. The Roman centurion's request is honored. Zacchaeus has a surprise guest. Doctors of the law debate with him. The rich young ruler engages him in dialogue. Magi, astrologers from the East, visit the manger. Men of wealth, prestige, and influence seek him out. They perceive an unusual openness. Jesus accepts them, regardless of the tag on their social box.

Jesus also interacts with the lowly. Shepherds as well as wise men visit the manger. Herding sheep was a dirty and despised occupation. The wealthy living in Jerusalem hired shepherds to watch their flocks in the countryside. But shepherds were distrusted. They were considered dishonest because they often led their flocks on other people's land. They sometimes sold milk and young animals on the sly and pocketed the money. It was forbidden to buy wool, milk, and kids from them because they often embezzled the money. Some rabbis said herding was the most disreputable occupation.[11]

By now the surprise should no longer surprise us. The good news of God's incarnation is announced not to the chief priests in the Jerusalem temple, but to dishonest shepherds in a Bethlehem field.

From beginning to end, from start to finish, the thread of inversion and irony weaves its ways through the gospel. Mary believes the angel but Zechariah doubts the angel's message. Shepherds hear the good news first. Women are the resurrection's first witnesses. In parabolic form Jesus compares God to a shepherd who wanders through a maze of obstructions to find a lost lamb. Jesus calls himself the Good Shepherd. Stigmatized occupations are honored in the upside-down kingdom.

Jesus accompanies fishermen who enjoy moderate prestige. He pounds nails himself as a respected carpenter. But he spends most of his time with the masses—the poor and the sick. Although he relates to all sorts of people, the Gospels show his unequivocal commitment to those branded with social stigmas. Jesus' people are the demoniacs, the blind, the deaf, the lame, the diseased, the paralyzed, prostitutes, tax collectors, sinners, adulterers, widows, lepers, Samaritans, women, and Gentiles. Jesus spans the Hebrew checkerboard, but his focus is primarily on these outcasts. These were the social throwaways—dumped on the human trash pile. Instead of spitting on them, as the rest of society does, Jesus touches them, loves them, and names them God's people.

Jesus' words underscore his commitment. Again and again Jesus mentions the same catalog of people: the poor, the blind, the lame, the oppressed. They pop up in his inaugural sermon. He mentions them when John the Baptist's disciples probe his messianic identity. He welcomes them at the banquet when the invited guests refuse to come. He tells us to invite them, instead of friends, to meals.

In the final judgment scene they appear once again.

People are rewarded or damned for their response to the hungry, the thirsty, the naked, the stranger, the prisoner, and the sick (Matthew 25:31-46). In the East these words stir images of the dead.[12] These are folks without hope. Life for them is too miserable to be called life. Jesus brings life to these who are as good as dead. He brings healing, hearing, walking, talking, sanity, purity, and freedom. These images of transformation signal the age of salvation. The Messiah is here. Restoration is complete. Now is the favorable year of the Lord.

The spirit of Jesus penetrates social boxes. Barricades of suspicion, mistrust, stigma, and hate crumble in his presence. He calls us to see the human beings behind stigmatized social labels. His kingdom transcends all boundaries. He welcomes people from all boxes. His love overpowers the social customs which divide, separate, and isolate.

Jesus' welcome to *all* is at the heart of the gospel. Reconciliation is the core of the gospel. It melts spiritual barriers between humans and God and lowers social barriers between diverse people. The agape of Jesus reaches out to boxed-up people, telling them God's love washes away their stigma and welcomes them into a new community.[13]

The Dog and the Checkerboard Tail

Once again a dog-and-tail question faces us. How does the dog of faith relate to the tail of social interaction? Does our faith make a difference in our social relationships? Or do customary social patterns wag our theology? Does our Christian faith nudge us toward boxes marked "Keep Out" and "Stigma"? Or do we play social checkers like everybody else—interacting with those who are like us and politely obeying the "No Trespassing" signs hanging around the necks of odd folks? Do our pious slogans keep us from others—"To each his own" or "Never trust a stranger"? When this happens, the tail of social custom wags the dog of faith.

God has created us as social beings. Boxing and labeling others are natural social processes. They organize social life and make it predictable. But these social routines can become demeaning when they dehumanize others. The Holy Spirit can redeem our attitudes and enable us to see the people behind the labels. In this way God transforms our social interaction. This doesn't mean we'll live without boxes. It does mean we'll not allow social labels to obstruct genuine care for others.

How do the people of God relate to each other? How are our social relations transformed? Do we categorize others like everyone else? Do holy turfs and stigmatized labels pervade the church? Many of the labels we acquire outside the church follow us inside as well. We often relate to other members of the body of Christ on the basis of their social tags. They become doctors, secretaries, professors, Mexicans, students, Republicans, or females rather than siblings in the family of God. These external labels often shape our interaction even in the church.

Informal networks in the church form around common occupational, educational, and theological interests. Charismatics cling to each other. Members of the local country club huddle and chat after the worship service. The college crowd sticks together. The elderly sit in the same section of pews. The snowmobilers and waterskiers flock together. "Committed members," involved in the work of church committees, interact with each other. Clusters and cliques emerge. The number and type of subgroups vary from parish to parish. A careful observer can detect them in virtually every religious setting. Beneath the surface, these informal networks regulate the social interaction of congregational life.

Subgroup formation isn't all bad. Even mature, birds of a common feather need to flock together. We need ties of commonality to feel secure. But we also need to redeem and transform social clusters in our congregations. They offer us needed security, but they can also fragment congregational life. They can become divisive ghettos of gossip and exclusive cliques. Controversies related to pastoral leadership, buildings, theology, educational curriculum, and the like often stem from these subgroupings.

Several steps can hasten the redemption of divisive cliques. First, we need to openly recognize informal clusters and their inevitability.

Second, teaching and preaching ministries ought to call people to a common faith in Jesus Christ that transcends social ties. Is our common bond of unity in Christ stronger than the social glue that holds us together? This is precisely the genius of the gospel. Diverse people from all sorts of boxes are reconciled together in Jesus Christ.

This doesn't mean people jump completely out of their boxes. It does mean that in the new kingdom social boxes mesh in a complementary way. Fellow Christians realize they need each other. The intellectuals need the charismatics. The fundamentalists need the social activists. The young need the old. The complementary nature of the different clusters builds up the whole community so the entire body matures in Jesus Christ. The apostle Paul's analogy of the body applies to subgroups as well as to individuals. Social clusters need each other to keep things in balance.

Third, we can as individuals seek ways to crisscross established boundaries. We can venture beyond our boxes. We can sit in different pews in the worship service. Invite people from other boxes to our homes. Join in churchwide activities. Visit folks with labels different than our own.

Finally, we can alter patterns of congregational life to open our boxes. Time for social interaction is necessary to get behind masks and labels. Weekend or daylong congregational retreats in a camp setting are an excellent way to discover each other. More unboxing can happen in a

three-day retreat than in fifty-two Sundays of bench sit-
ting. Work projects can involve a variety of ages.

In an age of specialization the church has developed
specialized activities of all sorts for those with special
needs—the elderly, teens, adoptive parents, singles, hand-
icapped, professionals, and the like. Although these are
helpful, we also need to create deliberate times when
folks of all stripes mix together in congregational life.

One congregation upset the routine in their Sunday
school. They devoted one quarter of each year to Sunday
school classes formed around common birthdays. All the
October babies, for example, met together for twelve Sundays. In this way young and old, male and female, conservative and liberal studied together. The rest of the
year they returned to their typical classes. Such creative
ventures promote the reconciliation of boxes and embellish the common life of the entire body.

Although we must unlatch the doors that shut us off
from others, we do need social boxes for our emotional
well-being. We need caring networks of others who listen
to our frustrations, doubts, and hassles. We usually find
acceptance among those most like us. They understand
and care best because they identify with our problems.
Although Jesus straddled the social checkerboard of his
day, he related more intimately to an inner circle of
three. Peter, James, and John witnessed the transfiguration and huddled closely with Jesus in Gethsemane. We
too need the close fellowship of similar others as we use
our special gifts to minister to the whole body. We need
a healthy tension between our natural tendency to snug-
gle up to similar others and Jesus' mandate to accept others regardless of their status.

Unboxing Churches

Social boxes also play a role in the church's commission to evangelize. Churches as well as people carry la-

bels. Denominations carve out unique historical identities. Denominational founders are esteemed. Songs, books, and creeds articulate a denominations' history and its unique contribution to the larger church. Some denominations have museums and conduct tours to historical sites. Denominational schools, publications, and annual conferences sharpen the consciousness of a people. A particular denominational image emerges. Catholics act so and so. A good Presbyterian should think so and so.

Specialized words in a denomination's culture acquire secret meanings, known only to the insiders—"Confirmation," "second work of grace," "neo-evangelicalism," and "discipleship." These code words stir the passions of insiders who know their secret meanings, but they leave outsiders cold. It's normal and natural for churches to cultivate a sense of common solidarity and identity. It sharpens the participants' sense of belonging. They know who they are, where they're from, and where they're going. Members have a place, a group—a people.

This religious ethnicity, as sociologists call it, also creates problems. It can become idolatrous, demanding more respect than the Scriptures themselves. It then clouds the centrality of Jesus Christ. The biblical Jesus can easily become a denominational Jesus. He becomes our Baptist Savior, our Mennonite Lord. Denominational glue can clog the free exchange of love and cooperation among denominations.

Most seriously, denominational boxing can barricade others from the kingdom. We've already heard Jesus' indictment of the Pharisees. Too much denominational glue frightens others away. Strange words, odd rites, and obsolete traditions obscure the welcome sign. A sharp theological identity is essential for a vigorous church, but we must balance this with programs that welcome newcomers.

One of the dilemmas faced by growing churches is that

birds of a common feather do flock together. Lower-class folk feel at home in congregations with those of kindred class. Upscale congregations attract individuals from upper-class backgrounds. Hispanics feel most at home in worship services rooted in Hispanic culture. Professionals migrate toward congregations which endorse heady intellectual exchange.

Should congregations focus their efforts on homogeneous neighborhoods that match the congregation's racial, social, and economic profile? This is a sound strategy if the only goal is a surge in attendance. Although the easiest route to growth involves attracting similar people, it's urgent that the message of reconciliation not be lost. Simply getting the same kind of people together is no great feat. It happens all the time in all sorts of organizations and service clubs. If the gospel transforms social relationships, if the church is more than just another Rotary Club, spiritual and social reconciliation need to be at the forefront of its ministry.

In the genius of the gospel, when people declare Jesus as Lord, they experience a new unity that transcends social boxes. True church growth uses the best insights from social science to call different kinds of people together under a common Lord. A gospel which only attracts similar people blurs the good news bonding Jew and Gentile, male and female, black and white. This doesn't mean we ignore social characteristics. Just the opposite. We take them seriously as real ingredients in congregational life. We need to search for the delicate balance between sameness and difference. Our natural tendency is to flock toward other birds like ourselves. The good news of Jesus Christ, however, welcomes all, regardless of their feathers.

Questions for Discussion

1. In what ways does the "birds of a common feather" principle operate in your own life?

2. Consider the persons you've invited to your home over the past six months. How many of these came from boxes different than your own?

3. Identify some of the stigmatized boxes in your community. How might your church open new doors to these persons and groups?

4. What kind of boxes exist inside your church fellowship? How can they be lessened?

5. What rules of social etiquette might citizens of the upside-down kingdom violate if they take social boxes less seriously?

6. When have you felt especially close to folks from different cultural backgrounds because of your common faith in Jesus Christ?

7. What are some ways the mission of the church can strike a delicate balance between sameness and difference?

11

LOW IS HIGH

The Social Ladder

In the last chapter we viewed human interaction on a social checkerboard. Social life, however, isn't flat. Indeed, the social checkerboard stands on its edge with the squares stacked on each other like mailboxes in a post office lobby. Some boxes are considerably higher than others. We capture this vertical dimension of life when we talk of pecking orders and social ladders. Such word pictures reflect the fact that society isn't flat. People aren't equal. Some are more important and distinguished than others. Stratification is the technical term for social ranking. This chapter explores Christian perspectives on power and stratification.

Some folks prefer to smile sweetly and think that, after all, everyone *is* equal. A little thinking should convince anyone that stratification does exist. A father with a daughter who graduates from law school bubbles with pride when he talks with friends about her achievement. The same father is embarrassed to report that another child has dropped out of high school.

Let's face it—the chair of a committee has more power than rank-and-file members. Episcopalians are higher on the prestige ladder of denominations than Pentecostals. Jews, as an ethnic group, wield more political influence on American politics than the Amish. Nations, churches, ethnic groups, occupations, and persons are ranked and layered in our minds. Pecking orders emerge in all societies. They're deeply embedded in human experience throughout the world.

Social ranking shrinks the value of some people and expands the worth of others. We value folks for their ability to perform a certain job. Presidents, doctors, and managers are valuable. Shoe shiners, dishwashers, and typists are less so.

Our weekly paychecks underscore this harsh fact. We're paid according to socially determined values. Our paycheck reminds us how much we're worth. It's difficult to sort out the difference between one's *personal* and *financial* value. Our view of others leans heavily on their financial value as a wage earner. We can *tell* people they're very important, but if we turn around and *pay* them half as much as others, they know jolly well what we think.

One sociologist has noted that we should choose our mothers carefully, for our birth determines our niche in the system of stratification. The height of our rung on the social ladder has an immense impact on our life chances. Being born into a wealthy family or into a destitute one makes a world of difference. It influences whether we'll experience malnutrition, infant mortality, college, prison, and mental torture. The quality of our life—medical care, education, work, shelter, even the length of our life itself—to a great degree hinges on our birth rung.

Social Muscle

Social power rises and falls with the relative height of the rungs on the social ladder. In a broad sense, power is the ability to affect social life. It's the capacity to "make things happen." To make things happen we need resources. We need knowledge, money, and position. Those who own and control resources can make things happen more easily than those who don't.

Four major types of power flow from our resources. (1) *Financial* power is rooted in economic resources. Money makes things happen. It's one of the most important sources of power.

(2) *Expert* power stems from extensive knowledge or special information. Doctors and lawyers exercise expert power because they control special knowledge in medicine and law.

(3) *Organizational* power arises from a person's position within an organization. An executive vice-president has more power than a typist because the executive has a higher position in the organizational flow chart.

(4) *Personal* power emerges from personal appearance and personality traits. Certain people attract us because of their pleasant interpersonal style and manner. Their charm appeals to us.

When individuals or institutions have access to all four types of power, they wield enormous clout. To be president, personable, wealthy, and smart is to be exceedingly powerful! Power isn't necessarily bad. All of us exercise some of it every day. It is a natural part of social life. We do, however, need to grapple with how we use and disburse it. What are proper and improper ways to flex power from a Christian perspective?

Joe Down and Doc Up

An illustration from the academic world sharpens the inequalities produced by social stratification. We'll compare Dr. Up, a full professor on a university campus, with Joe Down, a janitor who cleans Dr. Up's office.

First, Joe and Doc share opposite ends of the campus hierarchy. Doc is near the top of the "professional" community. Joe is part of the lowly maintenance crew. The status difference is present in their titles. Dr. Up is "prof," "doctor"—and sometimes "Mr. Up" to disrespectful students. Dr. Up's name and title hang on a plate outside his office.

Joe doesn't have a title. He's simply called "Joe." He has no office or nameplate. Clothing confirms the status differences. Joe wears old jeans, T-shirts, and tattered sneakers. Dr. Up wears a tie and coat, and chews Certs. He grooms his hair frequently in front of the private mirror in the closet in his office. Joe, of course, has no private closet or mirror.

Second, Joe and Doc part ways when it comes to power. Doc can ask Joe to work for him in the office—hanging pictures, rearranging furniture, and dusting cobwebs. If the air conditioner is turned up too high, Doc yells for Joe to turn it down. If Doc forgets the key to his door, he calls for Joe to open it. Joe even makes the coffee for Dr. Up and his colleagues. If Joe doesn't obey his requests, Dr. Up sends a memo to Joe's supervisor. Bingo, that's the end of any raise for Joe.

Joe has no control over Doc. He might ask Doc for a favor, but he has no real power. He certainly can't reward or punish Doc. Doctor Up knows the university president personally and sometimes asks for special favors. The president doesn't even know Joe's name, let alone hand out favors to "some old janitor."

Third, when it comes to prestige, there's also a wide gulf. When Doc strides down the hall students greet him with smiles and choruses of "Hello, Doc." They politely step out of his way if he's in a hurry. The president always shakes Doc's hand and smiles warmly. When students bring their parents on campus they drop by Doc's office for introductions. Doc likes telling friends in the community that he's a college professor. It's a respectable job.

When Joe comes down the hall, the most he gets is a nod or a "Hi, Joe," from professors who know him. He's not normally entitled to warm smiles from the president or introductions to parents. And he really doesn't like to tell people what he does. He knows it's the kind of thing any old Tom, Dick, or Harry could do.

Finally, when it comes to privilege, things are quite different. Salary is Doc's most obvious advantage. He makes three times as much as Joe for only eight months of work. Joe, on the other hand, gets one week of vacation, several personal days, and one third of Doc's salary. Doc's fringe benefits exceed Joe's. His retirement perks are much higher since they're tied to a percentage of his salary.

Doc controls his schedule. He arrives in the morning when he feels like it and leaves when he needs to. If something important turns up, Doc can cancel his classes for the day with an "out of town" note. As long as he doesn't miss classes, Doc can take off for medical appointments or a snack with an out-of-state friend without telling anyone. He goes off campus for coffee breaks at a good downtown shop. Doc has a desk and private office all his own.

For Joe things are different. Morning and evening he must punch the time clock. He must schedule vacation days at least two months in advance. Coffee breaks stay on campus since Joe must be ready to work at any moment. About the only privilege Joe has is the opportunity to read everyone's junk mail as he empties wastebaskets. Despite all their differences, Doc Up and Joe Down pay the same price for bread, gas, and household utilities.

A U.S. Senator describes the prestige and privilege which accompany the status of senator:

> My every move through the Senate perpetuates this ego message. When I leave my office to go to the Senate

floor, an elevator comes immediately at senatorial command, reversing its direction if necessary and bypassing the floors of the other bewildered passengers aboard in order to get me to the basement. As I walk down the corridor, a policeman notices me coming and rings for a subway car to wait for my arrival and take me to the Capitol Building. The elevator operator, the Capitol policeman, and the subway drivers all deferentially greet me. On the subway car I may take the front seat, which is reserved for Senators who may ride alone; tourists already seated there are removed by a policeman unless I insist otherwise. At the Capitol another elevator marked FOR SENATORS ONLY takes me to the Senate floor. There at the raising of an eyebrow a page comes to give me a glass of water, deliver a message, or get whatever I need. Aides scurry about telling me when votes will occur on which bills, although no one bothers me with all the details unless I ask.[1]

Says Who?

Stratification isn't unique to the modern world. Stratification language peppers the Gospels. Jesus was aware of the realities of social ranking. The angel told Mary that Jesus would be called son of the Most High and the power of the Most High would overshadow her (Luke 1:32, 35). Zechariah prophesied his son John would be a prophet of the Most High (Luke 1:76). Jesus promised we'll be sons of the Most High if we love our enemies, do good, and lend, expecting nothing in return (Luke 6:35). A demoniac called Jesus son of the "Most High God" (Mark 5:7). Most High is used in the Scriptures as another name for God, suggesting that God tops the highest ladder.

The word *authority* is frequently on the lips of Jesus. Luke begins with Jesus rejecting the "authority" and the "glory" of the kingdoms of the world (Luke 4:6). Later in the same chapter, Jesus expels a demon and the people are all amazed. They ask, "What is this word? For with authority and power he commands the unclean spirits, and they come out" (Luke 4:36).

Jesus turned his back on the legal right to rule by political authority, but he didn't reject authority outright. His right to rule comes not from coercive political force but from the Most High. He doesn't command armies, but he does command demons. Although his authority doesn't come from white horses, chariots, tanks, and military victories, the people recognize its authenticity. "And when Jesus finished these sayings, the crowds were astonished at his teaching, for he taught them as one who had authority, and not as their scribes (Matthew 7:28-29; Mark 1:22).

Ironically, Jesus comes to the people without the traditional trappings of authority. He doesn't have any political clout nor the necessary training to be a scribe. Following a teaching session, "The Jews marveled at it, saying, 'How is it that this man has learning, when he has never studied?' " (John 7:15). Without a scribe's license he's not merely teaching, but teaching in a compelling way. His words earn their own authority. The audience certifies his authority, not a board of theological experts in Jerusalem.

The crowds aren't the only ones who ratify his authority. When the centurion approaches Jesus to request healing for his servant, Jesus begins to walk toward the centurion's home. The centurion hedges, saying he isn't worthy to have Jesus enter his house. "Only say the word, and my servant will be healed. For I am a man under authority, with soldiers under me; and I say to one, 'Go,' and he goes, and to another, 'Come,' and he comes, and to my slave, 'Do this,' and he does it" (Matthew 8:8-9). When Jesus hears this he marvels and heals the servant. The soldiers and slaves under the centurion jump at his words.

Why does Jesus marvel when the officer describes his powerful position? Is he threatening Jesus—heal my ser-

238 / The Upside-Down Kingdom

vant or else? Rather, the centurion is comparing Jesus' authority to his own. This Gentile understands that Jesus, like himself, is a man of authority. This is a Gentile confession of faith, not a military threat. He acknowledges that Jesus has the power to heal his servant even from a distance. Jesus marvels that this Gentile has such a full understanding of his authority and power.

Ironically, the peasants and the centurion understood the nature of Jesus' authority while the religious authorities remained perplexed. One day the chief priests and elders interrupted his teaching and asked, "By what authority are you doing these things, and who gave you this authority?" (Matthew 21:23 and Mark 11:28). In other words, who said so? Who gave Jesus the right to teach? Who signed his ordination papers?

Jesus answered by posing a question. Where did John's baptism come from? The heavyweights were in a jam. If they said John's authority came from heaven, then why had they refused to listen to John? If they said John's authority merely came from his personal powers of persuasion, the crowd would be angry because they thought John was a prophet. Jesus didn't answer their question because they couldn't answer his. In asking the question about the Baptist he aligned himself with John. The questions and answers about the authority of John's ministry also fit his own. The Pharisees had earlier charged that Jesus' authority came from Beelzebub. Now the chief priests were faced with two options. Either Jesus had the endorsement of the Most High, or he was an astute crowd charmer.

In John's Gospel, Jesus clarifies the source of his authority.

> I can do nothing on my own authority . . . I seek not my own will but the will of him who sent me. John 5:30.
> The Father . . . has granted the Son . . . authority to execute judgment. John 5:26-27.

My teaching is not mine, but his who sent me. John 7:16.

I do nothing on my own authority but speak thus as the Father taught me. John 8:28.

For I have not spoken on my own authority; the Father who sent me has himself given me commandment what to say and what to speak. John 12:49.

Again and again Jesus underscores the root of his authority. It's not his own. He is steward of God's authority. He has the power of attorney. He acts on God's behalf. His Parent has given him the "right" to speak about the kingdom. This is fundamental. The one who speaks on behalf of another directs people to the other. Self-appointed leaders who speak on their own authority point others back to themselves. Jesus understands this well when he says, "He who speaks on his own authority seeks his own glory" (John 7:18). After Jesus healed the paralytic, the crowds "were afraid, and they glorified God, who had given such authority to men" (Matthew 9:8). Jesus uses his authority in a way that clearly points to God. He's not a self-acclaimed prophet basking in the crowd's applause.

In summary, several themes lace Jesus' understanding of authority. (1) There is no question that he saw himself as a steward of God's power. It was God who gave him the right to speak. (2) He was careful to use his authority in a way that didn't bring personal prestige. His words and acts reflected God's desires. (3) He used his authority to serve and help others. They were the beneficiaries of his power. (4) Although his ordination wasn't certified through proper channels, the crowds felt the authenticity of his message and gave it grass-roots accreditation.

Stop Climbing

Jesus rebukes the ladder-climbing leaders throughout the synoptic Gospels. He pinpoints three ways religious

240 / *The Upside-Down Kingdom*

leaders polished their eminent rungs on the Jewish ladder. First, ostentatious clothing charmed them. In the words of Jesus, they made their robes long, their phylacteries broad, and added fringes to their robes (Matthew 23:5; Mark 12:38; Luke 20:46). The Pharisees used extravagant clothing to remind people of their superior niche in the social system.

Second, the synagogue held a special place for prominent dignitaries. A scribe would sit on the seat of Moses at the front of the room, facing the people. Everyone could see him and admire his special seat. Jesus derides the scribes for seeking prestigious seats in the house of worship (Matthew 23:6; Mark 12:39; Luke 20:46). The scribes also scrambled for the best seats at feasts, the distinguished positions on the right-hand side of the host. Jesus made it clear such maneuvering in public meetings isn't fitting in the upside-down kingdom.

Third, the scribes used language to polish their prestige. They insisted on being called rabbi (Matthew 23:8). Since a greeting represented a communication of peace, strict ceremonial rules governed to whom and how a greeting was given.[2] Jesus knew that titles reinforce social ranking by calling attention to status. They remind us everyone isn't equal.

In one stroke Jesus wipes out titles. "You are not to be called rabbi, for you have one teacher, and you are all brethren. And call no man your father on earth, for you have one Father, who is in heaven. Neither be called masters, for you have one master, the Christ" (Matthew 23:8-10). Tagging each other with titles has no place in the upside-down kingdom. In his critique of those hankering after prestige, Jesus debunks the hunger for status which drives many facets of social life.

Growing Down

Clamoring after status wasn't only a Pharisee problem.

It also snared the disciples. One day they began arguing about who was the greatest (Mark 9:33-34). Peter felt he should be number one since he was the first to understand Jesus was the Messiah. James and John, however, thought they should be first because they had seen the transfiguration. James and John were so anxious about their status that they pulled Jesus aside and pleaded, "Do for us whatever we ask of you" (Mark 10:35). They wanted to sit in the best seats, on the right- and left-hand side of Jesus, in his kingdom.

Matthew reports that their mother encouraged their request (Matthew 20:20-21). In any event, we find the old autocratic spirit of "do this and do that" in the midst of the disciples. The bossing mentality ranks people from greatest to least. Jesus rebuked their clamoring for status and power by taking a child in his arms. "Whoever receives one such child in my name receives me; and whoever receives me, receives not me but him who sent me" (Mark 9:37).

A few days later, as the disciples were screening visitors, they pushed aside children who wanted to touch Jesus. He was furious with this power play (Mark 10:13-14).[3] To the disciples, these children were social nobodies. They held no prominent positions. They wouldn't help the cause. Jesus should spend his time with influential folks. The children would divert Jesus from his mission.

The disciples still hadn't absorbed the upside-down logic. To Jesus, children were as important as adults. He not only spent time with these little ones, he held them up as model kingdom citizens. "For to such belongs the kingdom of God. Truly, I say to you, whoever does not receive the kingdom of God like a child shall not enter it" (Mark 10:14, 15).

As the disciples vied for status and pushed children away, Jesus used a child to symbolize kingdom living.

242 / The Upside-Down Kingdom

Typically we tell people to grow up and "act their age." Jesus reverses the logic. He tells us to grow down and regress to childlike behavior. Why is this? How can children instruct kingdom learners? Why does Jesus go to the very bottom of the social ladder for an example?

Children rank low in status and power. Totally dependent on others, they're economic liabilities. Children make few social distinctions. They don't put others in boxes. They haven't learned to play by adult social rules. They're friendly to strangers before their parents tell them how dumb that is. They haven't yet learned racist and ethnic slurs. Color, nationality, title, and sexual boxes mean little to the young. They have no sense of bureaucratic structures and hierarchies.

The use and manipulation of power is foreign to a baby. Its cry certainly makes things happen. Parents do come running. Cries, however, are a response to biological needs, not a cunning power which maneuvers and manipulates others. Children learn the tactics of power as they grow older. In early years they exhibit trusting confidence. A child of good parents trusts them completely.

Jesus invites kingdom citizens to babyhood in all these areas. Instead of pursuing the number one spot, he prods us to ignore hierarchy as children do. He tells us to become infants who overlook status differences, seeing *all* others as equally significant despite their social rank and function. Instead of clamoring for more and more power, we followers of Jesus happily share it. We welcome interdependence. Rather than claiming self-sufficiency, we acknowledge our need for community and dependence on others. Blind to social distinctions, dependent on others, we live as children, for of such is the kingdom of God.

Bottom Up

The disciples remain baffled. As they sit around the table during the Last Supper, an argument about greatness breaks out. After all the teaching on babyhood, in the midst of a sacred event, the disciples bicker about who is the greatest. Like typical human beings, they wonder how they stack up with each other.

Jesus tries again. He revamps the meaning of *greatness*.

"The kings of the Gentiles exercise lordship over them; and those in authority over them are called benefactors. But not so with you; rather let the greatest among you become as the youngest, and the leader as one who serves. For which is the greater, one who sits at table, or one who serves? Is it not the one who sits at table? But I am among you as one who serves" (Luke 22:25-27).

Again Jesus flips our social worlds upside down. He reverses our assumptions and expectations. He radically redefines greatness. These words strike at the root of domination in all social groupings. Our typical assumptions about greatness flow together in the following equation:

Greatness = Top, powerful, master, first, ruler, adult.

Jesus radically inverts the equation to read:

Greatness = Bottom, servant, slave, last, child.

There can be no misunderstanding here. Jesus turns our conventional definition of greatness upside down. Pagans lord it over their subjects. They develop hierarchies of power. "Not so among you," whispers Jesus. In the upside-down kingdom greatness isn't measured by how much power we exercise over others. Upside-down prestige isn't calculated by our rank on the social ladder. In God's inverted kingdom, greatness is determined by our willingness to serve. Service to others is the yardstick of status in the new kingdom.

Then Jesus poses a profound question. Who is greater, the chief executive officer of a Fortune 500 company seated in the executive dining hall? Or the waiter who serves her? The president of the country flying in a private jet? Or the stewardess who serves him? The executive and the president are more important, of course. Waitresses and waiters are a dime a dozen. Anyone can do their work. The chief executive has years of special training and experience. Any nitwit knows an executive is more important than a waiter or waitress.

Not in my kingdom, says Jesus. For I'm among you as a waiter, a slave, a servant, not a boss. Instead of giving orders and directives down the hierarchy, Jesus is looking up the hierarchy, asking how he can serve. The Jesus way looks up from the bottom, not down from the top. Such a posture flies in the face of modern individualism, which gives the rights, privileges, and self-fulfillment of the individual precedence over all else. Jesus invites humble servanthood, not assertive individualism. Rather than asking how we can get ahead, meet our needs, and develop ourselves, disciples ask how we can best serve others.

Modern talk of service often falls short of Jesus' way. We often use service slogans not so much to serve as to seduce others into buying products or "services" they really don't need. When this happens, the so-called servant turns artful manipulator. She or he becomes an ad agent, using the language of service to promote selfish interests. Many "professional service" folks, quite high on the status ladder, look at their clients from a "top down" perspective. They'll "serve" their clients as long as their service pays well in both dollars and prestige. But when client needs run counter to the professional's interests, the "service" abruptly ends. Such "service" is hardly Christian.

In contrast, the servanthood of Jesus ended on the cross. He was willing to serve the needs of the sick on the Sabbath even though it placed his own life at risk. He announced forgiveness of sins when such blasphemous words were sure to trigger his death. Jesus' style of service brought neither financial gain nor social prestige. Quite the opposite. His service outraged the authorities and resulted in violent death. For Jesus, serving didn't mean catering to the well-to-do, who could pay high prices.

Jesus served the "least of these," those at the bottom. The least of the least can't pay back. Serving them will undoubtedly tarnish a professional's reputation in the professional community. After all, only incompetent lawyers, doctors, and teachers serve the stigmatized. And they do it only when they can't develop a profitable practice among the respectable. The disciples of Jesus don't worry about this. They give a cup of cold water in his name even to the little ones who have little power or social prestige (Matthew 10:42).

Jesus has redefined greatness. But what does he mean? How are the least among us the greatest in the kingdom? He understands that social greatness rises with access to power. In modern culture, we consider great those who boss and lord it over others. The president, the chief executive officer, the department head are applauded—by society at large, if not necessarily by their subordinates.

Is Jesus suggesting that janitors, day laborers, part timers, the weak, the poor, and the stigmatized are automatically at the top of his kingdom? Is he calling for a complete flip-flop where the top rungers of this world exchange places with the bottom rungers in the kingdom of God? Likely not. Instead of turning the hierarchy upside down and making a new one, Jesus questions the very need for hierarchy. He declares it unconstitutional for his people. He also proposes new criteria for evaluating greatness.

Describing John the Baptist, Jesus says, "I tell you,

among those born of women none is greater than John; yet he who is least in the kingdom of God is greater than he" (Luke 7:28). What do these baffling words mean? Jesus is comparing two orders of stratification. Among persons born in the flesh, none is greater than John. He is the greatest, the last of the prophets.

But in the kingdom, among those born of the Spirit, even the least is greater than John. If the least of kingdom citizens is greater than John, the rest are obviously also greater. Jesus isn't mocking John's significance. He's merely saying that everyone born of the Spirit is as great as the greatest prophet. His eyes twinkle. He's arguing that in the upside-down kingdom, everyone is the greatest! There are, in short, *no* little people in this kingdom.

Jesus is spoofing the language of "greatest and least." That kind of talk has no place in kingdom conversations. Rather than exchanging a new hierarchy for an old one, Jesus flattens hierarchies.[4] He understands that hierarchies too easily begin to function as deities. Humans bow down, worship, and obey them. Jesus once and for all disarms the authority of hierarchies to act like gods. He calls us to participate in a flat kingdom where everyone is the greatest. In this kingdom the values of service and compassion replace dominance and command. In this flat family, the greatest are those who teach and do the commandments of God (Matthew 5:19). They love God and others as much as themselves.

Looking Down

Arrogance rides with power and prestige. Some who make it to the top pride themselves in "their great accomplishments." They bask in the limelight of celebrity status.

Jesus tells the story of a man at a feast who carefully inspects the prestige value of all the seats. He picks a distinguished one to display his prominence. The seats fill up. An eminent guest arrives a few minutes late after all the top seats are taken. The toastmaster asks the earlier guest to take a lowly seat away from the head table.

It's better, Jesus says, to select the bottom seat unless the master of ceremonies motions you to another one. Inversion visits again. "Every one who exalts himself will be humbled, and he who humbles himself will be exalted" (Luke 14:11). Jesus repeats this rule of thumb after the parable of the breast-beating tax collector and haughty Pharisee (Luke 18:14) and after he rebukes the Pharisees for seeking status with clothing and titles (Matthew 23:12).

What does this riddle on humility mean? Jesus doesn't intend it to teach dining etiquette. Our normal tendency is to pursue positions of honor. Enjoying the oh's and ah's of other people, we take it for granted that upward is better. Rather than endorsing such upward flight, Jesus calls us to downward mobility. He asks us to take the seats at the bottom. His disciples defer to others, happily yielding up the good seats. They're so busy waiting on tables, in fact, that they have little time to sit. Serving, not jockeying for seats, is their occupation. Those who exalt themselves will have a backseat in the kingdom. Those who confess their pride and quietly serve others are exalted in the upside-down kingdom.

Contrary to kingdom thinking, we typically look down the social ladder and mutter, "If I did it, they can do it too. If the poor would just work a little harder and be more responsible they could pull themselves up by their bootstraps, too." Proud top rungers often assume their own hard work and motivation pushed them to the top. We like to think our hard work is the sole factor behind our success. In reality, at least seven factors in one way or another place us on a particular rung of social life. We control some factors; others elude control. The unique mix of these factors—reflecting time, providence, place, and people—carves out our special niche.

What are these formative factors?

(1) *Biological constraints* shape our place in life. Physical traits, intelligence, energy levels, skin color, sex, and some diseases are obviously inherited. We don't control them. A retarded child doesn't choose to be stigmatized. These genetic handcuffs limit some and favor others.

(2) *Cultural values* also condition our experience. In some cultures, children are taught to work hard. They even enjoy it. In others, hard work is ridiculed. Those who work hard can hardly thank themselves if they happened to be born into a culture which taught them to enjoy hard work.

(3) *Personal motivation* often has biological and cultural roots. The amount of personal gumption, drive, and sheer persistence modulates the impact of other factors.

(4) *Community assets* also make a difference. The cards of life are stacked in favor of children born into upper-class communities with topnotch jobs, schools, and hospitals. No matter how hard they work, children plunked into a destitute neighborhood face enormous hurdles.

(5) *Family stability* shapes a child's emotional makeup. Lifelong insecurities may nag the children of emotionally disturbed homes. Happy children have a head start in the race of life.

(6) *Financial inheritance* can boost a child into prominence. Inheriting a business, fortune, or political name puts many into powerful positions they probably could not attain on their own.

(7) *Chance* also carves our niche in life. Some make it rich because real estate prices triple overnight. Others lose everything through social or financial catastrophe. Being in the right place with the right people at the right time makes all the difference.

The relative influence and the unique mix of these factors varies greatly. A bit of reflection makes it obvious we don't choose our parents, our birthright, our communities, or our cultures. Many factors molding our place in life are simply beyond our control. This doesn't mean we're mere robots or puppets yanked up and down by mysterious forces. Choices and decisions do shape our destinies. Personal motivation does make a difference. Hard work matters.

Contrary to the cult of individualism, however, ambition isn't the only factor. Individualism breeds unfounded pride in one's "personal" achievements and a contempt for others who stand on lower rungs, often for reasons beyond their control. It's arrogant for people to assume that they "made it" just because they worked hard. The cult of haughty individualism takes personal credit for all personal achievement, neglecting the fixed advantages or constraints which also play a role.

Looking down the social ladder moves the followers of Jesus to compassion. Humility touches them. They understand that they stand where they do, only by the grace of God. They also realize that not sloth, but capricious social, economic, and genetic factors have stranded many of those below them. This doesn't negate the value of personal initiative. But it does put personal initiative in perspective as *one* of many streams of influence in our destiny. A realistic grasp of how we arrive at different rungs on the social ladder wipes away arrogance and propels the people of God toward sympathetic understanding.

Upside-Down Power

Jesus wasn't a typical king. He didn't bark orders to his generals nor threaten his subjects. He didn't command a religious or political dynasty. On the organizational charts, he was powerless. He commanded no armies. For heroes he holds up the young, the last, and the least. He acclaims the child, the servant, and the slave as ideal kingdom citizens. He describes himself as gentle and lowly in heart, saying his yoke is easy and his burden light

(Matthew 11:29-30). He reveals his truth to babes rather than to wise intellectuals (Matthew 11:25). Was Jesus, in the end, a wishy-washy wimp?

Jesus didn't run from power. He exercised a great deal of it. Had he stayed in the desert and quietly taught his disciples in a serene hideaway, he wouldn't have threatened the ruling powers. Although he held no formal seat of power, Jesus certainly wasn't powerless. Far from it. He was so powerful, able to make things happen so quickly, that he was killed. His power unnerved the religious and political authorities.

Why was Jesus a threat? His very life and message menaced political and religious authorities. Designating himself a waiter, he criticized the scribes' pursuit of prestige. He condemned the rich for dominating the poor. By challenging the oral law and purging the temple he assaulted the citadel of religious power. His appeal to servanthood offered an alternate model of power.

The inbreaking reign of God in the life of Jesus cut the muscle of the reigning powers.[5] The authorities killed him because they couldn't cope with political instability. Indeed, they had to be careful how they removed him. He not only had a small band of devoted followers but drew large crowds. His clout over the masses was so strong the authorities feared revolution. If they weren't careful how they treated Jesus, the authorities knew they would have a revolt on their hands (Luke 22:2). They arrested him under cover of darkness to prevent a tumult.

Jesus had power, but he didn't exploit it. Did he keep his messianic identity a secret to prevent the crowd from declaring him king? When he thought they might make him king by force he escaped to the hills (John 6:15). His power over the crowd didn't flow from formal positions or credentials. The masses chose to follow him because he had genuine authority, authenticated by his willingness to reject conventional symbols of status and power.

Jesus exhibited both expert and personal power. His knowledge of the law and his penetrating spiritual insights were the base of his expert power. He controlled the secrets of the kingdom.

Jesus' personal power came not from physical charm but from his notable compassion for all. He had no financial or organizational power. He exercised power through influence, never coercion and control. His teaching style wasn't that of an irrational demagogue. Even here he sought to gain the assent of people through rational influence, not emotional manipulation.[6]

Jesus had no access to soldiers. Nor could he use pay raises to prod his followers. He simply spoke the truth and allowed individuals to make free choices. He described himself as the good Shepherd. He didn't chase or drive his sheep, he called them. Those who recognized his voice followed (John 10:4).

Jesus added mighty acts to his potent word. By breaking social norms—Sabbath healings, eating with sinners, talking with women, purging the temple—he heralded a new set of values in a new kingdom. Here was a man with the wisdom of a prophet who readily violated social custom when it oppressed people. His power was grounded not in coercion or violence but in radical obedience to God's reign. This allegiance pushed all other gods aside. Jesus wasn't about to salute another king. It was this utter abandon to the reign of God, even in death's face, that made the authorities jittery.

The hallmark of Jesus' upside-down power was his willingness to spurn what was rightfully his. Instead of mimicking a typical king, Jesus worked from the bottom up. Rather than demanding service, he served. Rather than dominating, he invited. As servant, waiter, and janitor, he ministered to those strewn on the human dump. The powerful weren't amused. They responded with their kind of power—a violent cross.

Jesus wasn't powerless. But he rejected domination and hierarchy in social governance. Three factors undergird his use of power.

(1) Influence, not control, was his primary mode. He beckons individuals to follow him. His words and acts create a crisis and invite us to make a choice, a voluntary decision.

(2) His use of power focused on the needs of others. He mobilized resources to serve the needs of the hurting and the stigmatized.

(3) Jesus didn't use power for self-gain or glory. He willingly suspended his own rights and served at the bottom of the ladder. Defying social custom, he redefined *rights* and *expectations*.

From There to Here

What can we learn from Jesus' understanding of power? For the sake of discussion, let me suggest several propositions.

(1) We should use power to empower others.[7] This is the opposite of what normally happens. Power usually snowballs. Powerful persons and institutions seek more and more power, often at the expense of others. The exercise of power perpetuates and increases power inequities. The powerful become more powerful as the weaker ones dwindle. The upside-down perspective seeks to use power to empower others. It wants to provide them with the resources for self-determination.

(2) We should distribute power as widely as possible. Power tends to gravitate to the hands of a few. Those in the hub of an organization have more clout than those on the sidelines. There will always be power differentials. Christians, however, will work to share and decentralize power as much as possible.

(3) We should minimize hierarchy in social governance. As organizations grow, they increase the number

of rungs on their social ladders. Although they're necessary, we should shorten ladders as much as possible. As this happens, coordination replaces domination. Collapsing ladders is another way of diffusing power.

(4) Followers should freely give authority for leadership. Leadership should be neither self-appointed nor imposed on a group by an outside agency. Leadership is only worthy of allegiance when the led freely give it to the leader in response to the leader's servant posture.[8]

(5) The Christian perspective looks down the ladder. Our normal tendency is to scramble up ladders as fast as possible. The disciple of Jesus works to serve the powerless at the bottom. This may be through personal ministry or by remodelling social structures. Modeling the posture of Jesus, we're more concerned about the plight of those at the bottom than about advancing our own positions.

Historically the Christian church has often perpetuated rigid systems of hierarchy and stratification. In the context of church life, we sometimes sanctify with pious language chains of command and domination. It's difficult to use the posture of Jesus to justify sacred hierarchies. Let's be clear, however, on one thing. This isn't a call for anarchy, disorder, or confusion. The Spirit of God brings orderliness to the life of God's people. But the search for order doesn't require blind adoption of secular bureaucratic modes. The form and shape of the church's corporate life, if patterned on the principles of Jesus, will likely take a different twist from typical bureaucratic styles.

We will use consensus whenever possible to make decisions. This encourages participation and collective ownership. It gives all members access to the decision-making process, not simply a small group of elites.

Firm and decisive leadership is critical for the health and well-being of a robust group. But firm and decisive servant leaders won't dictate the goals and strategies of the group. They'll instead facilitate the accomplishment of common goals. Rather than declaring "I think this and I think that," servant leaders ask, "Where do *we* want to go?" "What are *we* saying?" and "What direction are *we* sensing?" Servant leaders will use their power to help members discern the Spirit's will for the group.

Large size is the friend of bureaucracy and hierarchy. Decision-making that involves all members happens best in groups of less than 150 persons. Growing congregations might consider multiplying into smaller units to permit fuller participation in their corporate life, rather than allowing bureaucratic structures to spiral.

The Holy Spirit endows each of us with unique gifts and abilities. We use these gifts in various ways to build up and minister to the total body. We should equally esteem each contribution, whether preaching, washing windows, or setting up chairs. In a flat kingdom, each job is of equal importance.

If people are equal and their jobs considered equivalent, should we give similar pay when remuneration is necessary? What do we say about the personal worth of the minister and the janitor if we place them on different pay scales?

Titles are foreign to the body of Christ. Doctor, Reverend, Mister, and Sister perpetuate status differences that clash with the spirit of Christ. Titles pay tribute to position, degree, and status rather than to personhood. Members of flat kingdoms call each other, as our sign of highest respect, by our first names.

Kingdom members involved in business, education, and public life will use influence to nudge organizations in flat directions. Christians in upper-level management and those in professional life will seek to express power through servanthood, not domination.

The bottom-up perspective doesn't mean teachers will sweep floors and lawyers will shine shoes. There's a beauty in finding the proper match between personal abilities and vocational slots. Good matches bring personal fulfillment and meet legitimate needs.

The key question is how we pursue a particular vocation or interest. A medical doctor can practice in a plush suburban area with an excess of physicians. Or she can defy the tug of upward mobility and work in a poor community for a bare-bone salary. A truck driver can take high pay and cross-country runs which tear the family apart. Or he can accept local hauls which hold the family intact. A business executive can expand a subsidiary into a community with a dependable labor supply and a low unemployment rate. Or she can place the new plant in an area which desperately needs new jobs.

Regardless of vocation, place, or position, disciples of Jesus must ask: Are we using our gifts and training to perpetuate inequality and self-advancement? Or are we using them to truly serve others?

Questions for Discussion

1. What ladders of social stratification are important in your community? In your congregation?

2. What are some of the consequences of allowing paychecks to determine the value and importance of persons?

3. What kinds of power are prominent in the life of your congregation?

4. In what situations is it proper for Christians to exercise control?

5. In what ways are Jesus' understanding of power and authority relevant to us today?

6. In what specific ways does your congregation embody flat kingdom ideals?

7. How have the seven factors of stratification influenced your own position and place in life?

8. Identify specific ways to pursue flat kingdom principles in your work, congregation, and community.

12

SUCCESSFUL FAILURES

The Politics of the Basin

We've seen that Jesus steered an independent course from the existing religious parties in Palestine. He didn't endorse the "realistic" Sadducees' working hand-in-hand with the Romans. He also rejected the rituals of conventional religion spearheaded by the progressive Pharisees. Serene life in an Essene commune didn't lure Jesus either. And we've seen that he gave an emphatic *no* to the revolutionary violence of patriotic rebels. These four strategies for dealing with Rome's domination Jesus rejected. Temple, oral law, wilderness, and sword are absent from his kingdom. Although Jesus didn't embrace these political options, he did stay in the middle of things.

Kingdoms fly flags. Mere pieces of cloth, they stir emotional loyalties and spur us to action. Flags represent the collective identity of a kingdom. The flags of the upside-down kingdom are upside down indeed! They're not the symbols which typically swirl around right-side-up kings. The flags of our kingdom are a manger, stable, donkey, basin, thorns, cross, and tomb. These aren't the signs of successful kings born in the V.I.P. suites of prominent hospitals. Their signs are armored limousines, golden crowns, and international applause.

But don't be mistaken. Jesus *is* King. He doesn't walk into Jerusalem; he rides like a king. His mount, however, isn't the white stallion of a commander-in-chief but the poor man's donkey. Jewish prophecy saw the donkey as a royal mount for a gentle and peaceful king (Zechariah 9:9-10). Jesus is King, yes, but a most unusual one indeed.

The cross has become the preeminent symbol—the flag—of the Christian church. It embodies the atoning sacrifice of God's beloved Son for the sins of the world. It also symbolizes the nonresistant way of Jesus in the cruel face of evil. A preoccupation with the cross, however, can detract from its very reason for being. Three upside-down symbols flow together in the gospel story: the basin, the cross, and the tomb. The *basin* is actually the foremost Christian symbol. Jesus himself voluntarily used a basin to represent his ministry. The *cross* was a Roman symbol, a harsh sign of the state's power to execute criminals. The ruling powers used the cross, an instrument of death, to respond to the servanthood initiatives of the basin. The *empty tomb* was God's final word. It stands through the ages as a sign that God will defeat the forces of evil.

In the context of the Last Supper, as his earthly ministry was about to conclude, Jesus hoisted the flag of his upside-down kingdom. "He . . . laid aside his garments, and girded himself with a towel. Then he poured water into a basin, and began to wash the disciples' feet, and to wipe them with the towel. . ."(John 13:3-5).

The towel and the basin are the tools of the slave.[1] This upside-down King uses the instruments of the servant. Instead of the royal symbols of sword, chariot, and white stallion, Jesus scrapes the tools of service off the floor. It was customary in Palestinian culture for a household slave to wash the feet of guests as they reclined on couches while eating. As master of his disciples, Jesus has the traditional right to expect them to wash his feet. He forfeits his privileges. Instead of demanding service he serves. As Jesus kneels to wash, the disciple sits in the master's seat.

Foot washing isn't a pleasant task. It means bending over and facing dirty feet. The bending symbolizes obedient service, so foreign from the arrogant "I'll serve you if you pay me well" attitude. The servant touches feet splattered with filth and mud. Normally a master washed his own hands and face but not his crusty feet. That was slave's work. The slave concentrated on his master's feet, ignoring his own hunger. Jesus voluntarily bends over and does the dirty work. No one forces him. He chooses to serve. He's willing to take orders. The towel he uses is flexible. It gives personal care by adjusting to the size of the other's foot.

The towel and the basin have been called the tools and agents of *shalom*.[2] They're not empty symbols. They're the means by which something is actually done. The tools define our trade. The towel and basin are slave tools. They do the work a professional or a master would never do. These tools place us in the lower position, serving and raising the other to a superior one. In this simple act Jesus turns our old social hierarchies upside down and replaces them with a new one. As we become servants and take turns washing each other's feet, the distinction between master and servant ends. As we all become servants to each other, we're all simultaneously the greatest in the kingdom.

This wasn't the first time our King had touched bottom. King Jesus had washed feet all his life. Towel and basin behavior characterized his entire mission. Jesus had used the basin for three years, but not to exclude others like the Pharisees did. His basin was the basin of assertive love. It took responsibility for others and welcomed them into the flat kingdom. Make no mistake—it was his basin work which set the stage for the cross.

The cross didn't drop miraculously from the sky. Jesus could have avoided it. The cross was the natural social response of evil forces to the presence of the basin. It was the violent tool of the powerful trying to crush his basin ministry. With no basin there would have been no cross. In other words, we must distinguish between the cross and what led up to it.[3]

We've already seen the shape of the basin ministry. Jesus rankled the rich who oppressed the poor. He healed and shelled grain on the Sabbath. He ate with sinners and loved tax collectors. He committed blasphemy, calling God his *abba*, his daddy, and forgiving sins. He violated and condemned the oral law. He welcomed a prostitute's anointing touch. He traveled with women in public. He stung religious leaders with his parables. He talked freely with Samaritans and Gentiles. He healed the sick. He blessed the helpless. He touched lepers. He entered pagan homes. He purged the sacred temple. He stirred up large crowds.

In almost every instance he challenged the conventional definitions of religious behavior. In short, he upset the bedrock assumptions of the pious. He actively used the basin and towel to serve the helpless regardless of social custom. He realized such deviant behavior might trigger his death. But harassment from the authorities and the threat of death didn't stifle his assertive love.

His behavior threatened the entrenched powers. The chief priests and Pharisees said, "If we let him go on thus, every one will believe in him, and the Romans will come and destroy both our holy place and our nation" (John 11:48). Many of the charges at his trial were false. But there can be no question that Jewish leaders thought his new teaching was breaking Palestine's fragile peace.

The Romans, likewise, were nervous about any turmoil that might disturb their control of Palestine. So, hand-in-hand, religious and political leaders joined to execute him. He was more dangerous than Barabbas, the political insurrectionist. Tersely they summarized his kingly, political threat on a tag they tacked to his cross—"King of the Jews."

After washing the disciples' feet in the upper room, Jesus invited them to follow his example: "If I then, your Lord and Teacher, have washed your feet, you also ought to wash one another's feet. For I have given you an example, that you also should do as I have done to you" (John 13:14-15).

Jesus extends his invitation to us. He welcomes us to join the basin trade. He invites us to more than periodic, ceremonial ritual, however. Jesus invites us to follow his example into lives of service, of forgiving and cleansing others as he cleanses us. The Gospels make it clear the Master calls us to follow him by doing the work of his kingdom. He calls us into a kingdom of basin folk, not saints who sit on rocking chairs pondering the mystery of God's salvation. The word and event become one in Jesus Christ. The Word has become flesh and lives among us. We incarnate the Word by acting in Christ's name. Words without acts are empty. Acts authenticate words.

The greatest disciples in the kingdom are the ones who *do* and teach the commandments (Matthew 5:19). "Not every one who says to me, 'Lord, Lord,' shall enter the kingdom of heaven, but he who *does* the will of my Father" (Matthew 7:21, emphasis added). The sheep and goats are separated at the judgment on the basis of such behaviors as clothing, feeding, visiting, and welcoming (Matthew 25:31-46). Members of the family of God are those who *do* his will (Mark 3:35).

Jesus compares the one who hears and *does* his words to a wise man. "Why do you call me 'Lord, Lord,' and not

do what I tell you?" he says (Luke 6:46). He tells the lawyer he will live if he *does* the Great Commandment (Luke
10:28). After telling the good Samaritan story, Jesus instructs us to go and *do* likewise (Luke 10:37). In parabolic
form Jesus tells us that the servant who knows his
master's will, but doesn't *do* it, will receive a severe beating (Luke 12:47, emphasis added in above verses). This
call to an active basin ministry permeates the Gospels.
We're asked to sell, give, love, forgive, lend, teach, serve,
and go. There is only one caution. An assertive basin
ministry can lead to a cross.

Expensive Decisions

"If any man would come after me, let him deny himself
and take up his cross daily and follow me. For whoever
would save his life will lose it; and whoever loses his life
for my sake, he will save it. For what does it profit a man
if he gains the whole world and loses or forfeits himself?
For whoever is ashamed of me and of my words, of him
will the Son of man be ashamed when he comes in his
glory and the glory of the Father and of the holy angels"
(Luke 9:23-26).

For some years I assumed a cross was a symbol of suffering. Thus any kind of personal suffering was a personal cross I needed to bear. I saw tragedy, misfortune, acci-
dent, or physical disease as a cross. It was something I
couldn't avoid, something which God, in his divine providence, allowed to befall me. As a disciple of Jesus, bearing my cross meant accepting my tragedy and enduring
my sufferings without complaint or bitterness. God does
walk with us through our personal tragedies. The God
who counts each hair on our heads must certainly count
each tear. But to think we carry our cross primarily
through our personal pains is to grossly misunderstand
the biblical meaning of the cross.[4]
    A cross isn't something God puts on us. It's not an ac-
cident or tragedy beyond our control. A cross is some-

thing we deliberately choose. We can decide if we want to accept a cross or not. Jesus' use of the words, "If any man," implies a free, deliberate choice. The cross for Jesus wasn't something which God forced on him. The cross was the natural, legal, and political result of his basin ministry.

Long before Gethsemane, Jesus realized a cross was the inevitable outcome of his aggressive basin ministry. He repeatedly warned his disciples he would eventually suffer and die. Even in Gethsemane the plea to "take this cup from me" wasn't primarily a struggle with a predetermined divine plan. It was a struggle to willingly continue living the way of love even in the midst of physical violence. It was the temptation to run, to fight, to retaliate in the face of the ugly cross.

To view the cross as less than a voluntary choice makes a farce of Jesus' temptation in the wilderness. Moreover, it makes a thoughtless puppet of Jesus and mocks the integrity of his entire life.

A cross is an expensive decision. It has costly social consequences. We might paraphrase Jesus by saying, "Take up your basin with the full awareness that it may bring suffering, rejection, punishment, and apparent failure." Jesus clarifies the social consequences of cross-bearing in three ways. First, we must be willing to deny personal ambition before we can pick up a cross. The values our society applauds shape personal ambition. Denying ourselves doesn't mean belittling or demeaning ourselves, however. It means refusing to allow the values of our secular environment to mold our ambition.

Second, Jesus says that if we follow his way it may look like we've "lost" our lives in this world. We may seem to be social failures if we engage in significant basin ministries. Since the tools of our trade are the tools of a slave, and slaves are deemed failures, we may appear to have "lost" our life by this world's standards.

Jesus' words articulate the most fundamental inversion of the upside-down kingdom. He says, in essence, if we pick up our basin and towel for his sake the world will likely write us off. On the other hand, if we play by the rules of this world's game and appear successful we may have "lost" our lives in the kingdom of God. Such a direct clash between the values of the kingdom and the values of the world is a hard saying indeed. But fair exegesis can hardly yield a different meaning.

Jesus hints at the third social consequence of the cross when he talks about shame. Shame is a social concept. He notes that we may be ashamed to engage in a basin ministry which bucks prevailing social currents. We may for a time use our towel and basin. Then ridicule may tempt us to give them up and play by the old rules. And so he concludes, if we're ashamed of him and his words, so will the Son be ashamed of us (Luke 9:26). "Whoever denies me before men, I also will deny before my Father who is in heaven" (Matthew 10:33).

These three clues point to the fact that Jesus wasn't talking about an inner, spiritualized, or mystical cross. Nor was he talking about accidents. He was describing expensive decisions, decisions entailing real social and daily results (Luke 9:23). His own decision to enter Jerusalem and cleanse the temple brought violent death on the cross.

Cost Analysis

The life of discipleship was for Jesus a serious commitment. It ruptured all other loyalties and ties. "So therefore, whoever of you does not renounce all that he has cannot be my disciple" (Luke 14:33). He understood that the way of the basin was costly. He feared that enthusiastic joiners might misinterpret the cost of following him. One day as a multitude of enthusiasts were surging after him, he told two parables to underscore the cost (Luke 14:25-33).

A farmer builds a magnificent tower. He sits down and calculates the price of the materials before he starts building. If he stops midway through the construction because his funds run out, the neighbors will mock him and ridicule his stupidity. Likewise, disciples who don't carefully count the social cost of following Jesus will look like fools if they break their commitment.

In the second story, a king prepares for battle with another king. He sits down and calculates the strength of both forces to see if he has a reasonable chance of winning. If he miscalculates the opponent's strength and enters the battle with too few soldiers, his army will be crushed. Disciples should likewise calculate the cost of following Jesus.

On another occasion two bright-eyed enthusiasts ran up and asked to join the disciple crowd. Jesus reminded the first one that a disciple's life brings insecurity and social ostracism. "The Son of man has nowhere to lay his head" (Luke 9:58).

Another potential recruit wanted to go home to say farewell. Jesus reminded him, "No one who puts his hand to the plow and looks back is fit for the kingdom of God" (Luke 9:62). One hand guides the light Palestinian plow.[5] The other hand, usually the right, carries a six-foot stick with a spike on the end to prod the oxen. The left hand regulates the depth of the plow, lifts it over the rocks, and keeps it upright. The farmer continually watches the legs of the oxen to keep the furrow in sight. A farmer who loses concentration ends up meandering in circles on the field. Such confusion awaits the disciple not fully engrossed in basin ministry.

In another instance, Jesus asks someone to follow him. The prospect wants to go home for the six-day mourning ceremony for his dead father. Jesus tells him to come immediately, proclaim the kingdom, and let the dead bury the dead (Luke 9:60).

In all these instances Jesus is saying two things. First, following him will be socially expensive. When the disciples decided to follow Jesus they "left everything" (Luke 5:11, 28). Second, he expects prospective disciples to sit down and calculate the cost of following him before they decide. They should follow only after completing a deliberate cost analysis. Otherwise they'll end up ridiculed, confused, and devastated.

No hocus-pocus is involved here. Disciples follow Jesus' way fully aware they may be embarrassed or lose a promotion. We deliberately love and serve even when this triggers ridicule and social harassment. Picking up the cross means we engage in an active basin ministry knowing it may bring ostracism and rejection.

The number and kind of crosses depends on the social and political setting. The same act of love in one political context may bring frowns and gossip. In another it may bring imprisonment, torture, or even death. Regardless of the shape or form of the cross, the disciple, following the example of Jesus, doesn't retaliate or seek revenge.

Cross-bearing isn't a one-time decision. It's a daily assessment of our willingness to make expensive decisions for the sake of Christ. Again and again, day after day, the call comes, "Whoever does not bear his own cross and come after me, cannot be my disciple" (Luke 14:27). "He who does not take his cross and follow me is not worthy of me" (Matthew 10:38).

Following in the way of Jesus doesn't mean going barefoot, remaining celibate, or camping in rural areas. We follow him by engaging in basin ministries and accepting their concrete social consequences. We follow by making expensive decisions.

A Cold Prickly

Like cotton candy, Christian faith too easily evaporates into pious fluff. We're tempted to sugarcoat Christian faith. We slice off the call to discipleship and focus on spiritual fluff, froth, and fizz. We sometimes tell each other, "just believe in Jesus and everything will turn out fine."

But the *substance* of Christian faith lies in our willingness to walk in the way of the cross. The expensive decisions called for in the Gospels collide with a fluffy faith that worships the God of success. Just follow Jesus, we are told, and we'll be successful in almost everything. Just give our hearts to him and we'll rise to the top of the ladder. Be "born again" and we'll win more beauty contests, hit more home runs, make more sales, and receive more awards.

No! Such theology pours pious sauce over hard words. Such a Jesus doesn't flatten old status ladders. He helps us climb them as long as we're sure to "give him all the honor and glory." This froth and fizz approach merely coats the old social order with a religious veneer.

The Jesus of the New Testament calls us to costly discipleship—to expensive decisions. Following Jesus means not only turning over personal habits and attitudes, but turning to a new way of thinking. This new logic of the upside-down kingdom counters much of what we take for granted. Jesus calls for a basic revision of values, behavior, and thinking. Simply baptizing the old logic and the old structures with a new vocabulary isn't enough. To follow Jesus, to be converted, means revising the assumptions and habits of the dominant culture. It means the creation of a counter-community. It means choosing an alternate way of life.

This is clear when Jesus tells us his followers may appear to have lost their lives in this world. Our overriding temptation is to save our lives in both systems. We want to save our life in this world and in the community of God's people. We want to succeed by secular standards *and* by kingdom values. Making it in the kingdoms of this world often requires accommodation and compromise.

It's easy to dilute the scandalous nature of the gospel so it blends with the success symbols of modern culture. If the gospel of Jesus threatens the bastions of power, his disciples won't be a popular crowd—much less successful. Jesus appears to draw a hard line when he says that those who truly save their lives according to the values of the upside-down kingdom may indeed lose them in the kingdoms of this world.

In the midst of such hard talk shines a big word of hope. The cross is *not* the last word. It's the middle word in the threefold sequence of basin, cross, and tomb. The cross isn't the symbol of ultimate defeat as it first seems.

God's *final* word is the empty tomb. The cross exposes the nasty power of evil in all its brutality and violence. The resurrection symbolizes God's final victory over the principalities of darkness. Now Christians can live in hope, for God has triumphed over sin. With hope we now pick up basins which bring crosses. Light shines at the end of the tunnel. We followers of Jesus have strength to suffer in the face of evil because the empty tomb tells us God has already won the victory.

The Upside-Down Community

The power of the upside-down kingdom lies in the corporate life of its citizens.[6] Kingdom life means doing God's thing together. Jesus would have been less of a threat if he hadn't gathered a community of followers around him. A wandering vagabond dropping wise sayings doesn't threaten the established order. Jesus' words on riches, power, love, and compassion assume his people share a corporate life together. He calls us to repent and join a disciple group characterized by spiritual, emotional, and economic interdependence.

Leaving ambitions behind, kingdom citizens use their gifts to embellish and enrich the body of Christ. An incarnational community, they embody the life-giving reign of God in the midst of cultures bent on death, destruction, and violence. The distinctive character of this new community erupted with joy in the early church at Pentecost.

Congregational life wanes sometimes to little more than periodic attendance at Sunday worship and other occasional meetings. Commitments to occupation, profession, hobbies, or leisure often take first priority. Church attendance is nice, if we have time. It's occasionally necessary for social window dressing. Jesus' call to discipleship raises the corporate life of his people above other involvements. In fact, our other commitments ought to throb with the pulse of the discerning Christian community. The shape and pattern of Christian communities may span a spectrum from communal experiences to more traditional modes. But life in the body of Christ won't be the caboose of our commitments. It will be the locomotive energizing our other involvements.

The task of rebuilding the church is a new and urgent mandate for every generation.[7] Creating a corporate life based on kingdom values is more critical than having all the right answers to political and economic questions.[8] The creation of Christian community is a political act itself since it represents a distinct new social reality. As one scholar flatly declares, "This is the original revolution; the creation of a distinct community with its own deviant set of values."[9]

This isn't a gathering where a few Christians occasionally come together to worship. This rather is the creation of a counter-community, a new order that follows the beat of a different drummer. As the disciples of Jesus come together, their agenda and corporate life may appear upside down alongside the autocratic hierarchies of even some churches.

When it's faithful to its mission—to be in the world, but not of it—the church is a prophetic minority, an alter-

nate subculture. Jesus calls *all* people to discipleship. But
he knows not all will respond. His movement won't create a fully Christian society. Fourteen times Jesus describes the spirit of his age with the words, "this generation."[10] In all but one case Jesus rebukes "this generation." It is evil, unfaithful, entrenched in unbelief, adul-
terous (breaking its covenant with God), and peevish.
This generation, according to Jesus, is the broad way
leading to destruction. His followers walk the narrow way
pointing to life.

But the narrow way isn't separated physically from the
broad one. The narrow way is not *of* but *in* the world. As
salt, light, and leaven, the community of disciples penetrates and enriches the world. These images used by Jesus symbolize a distinctive subculture, an alternative social reality. The community of God isn't at odds with all
prevailing cultural values nor is it peculiar just to be different. The members of the new kingdom have a different
vision, a different set of values. They pledge allegiance to
a different King. And at times that allegiance will mean
they sail against the prevailing social winds.

The people of God are tempted to absorb the values
around them. It's easy to temper the gospel by making it
pleasant to the majority. And before we know it, we borrow the ideology, the logic, and the bureaucratic structures of our neighbors. We might put a little religious
Teflon on top, but underneath the values and procedures
clash with the way of Jesus. The organizational structures
of our churches must be functional and relevant to our
cultural context without being determined by it. The moment the church capitulates to the world, the light is
dimmed, the salt turns tasteless, and the leaven leaves.

Participation in Christian community undergirds our
spiritual and emotional well-being. Following the beat of
a different drummer requires a community of others to
provide needed support and affirmation. Christian com-

munity can facilitate economic sharing of various sorts. Different parts of the body can lean on each other in times of need. The community cultivates a commitment to care for each other's spiritual as well as economic needs. The practicing of Jubilee becomes possible in the context of this kind of community.

The community of disciples offers a corporate witness to God's love and grace. Without the community the lone disciple is seen as "just another do-gooder." The witness of corporate love and caring is a remarkable feat in the midst of cultures where ruthless revenge is the norm. The Christian community embodies God's design for human integrity, wholeness, and shalom.

Sharing in the corporate life of God's people aids us in sorting out the substance from the chaff of modern life. As individuals we can easily be snookered by the glitz and glamour of modern media selling the sugarcoated demons of materialism. The Holy Spirit in the community of faith helps us discern the times in which we live. In the context of corporate life the Spirit shapes the values and the strategies of the kingdom. As we discern the times and our gifts, we're mobilized for significant ministries. True worship and sincere praise erupt in service to others. God's faithful people engage in a balanced rhythm, a dialogue of worship and service.

The strategies of kingdom folk will vary. The agenda of the kingdom is more critical than a particular strategy. In some cases the Christian community may develop and operate ministries under its own auspices. In other scenarios kingdom people will provide social and legal services to the needy through a variety of institutional umbrellas. Still others will engage in social action to modify unjust social structures. Kingdom folks will also be involved in political and corporate worlds as long as they can faithfully pursue the upside-down agenda. Other Christian siblings will oppose militarism, economic oppression, racism, authoritarianism, and other forms of sin and evil. They will, however, always do so under the flag of King Jesus. And they will always be more concerned about doing justice than demanding it for themselves.

In all these scenarios the critical issue isn't the shaping of a perfect strategy. The paramount question is this: Will we embrace a basin ministry even if it brings a cross? More important than finely honed strategies are compassionate services flowing from a vital experience of worship and prayer in the Christian community. Finally, all the expressions of ministry and service should point others not to ourselves or to the church. They should instead point ultimately to Jesus, our Savior and Lord.

The Marks of Kingdom People

Kingdom people take this upside-down kingdom seriously. We also know how to laugh. We know we must work at personal discipleship. We've also tasted God's grace. We know our salvation doesn't depend on sober-faced discipleship. We take our crosses seriously. We also splurge. Since God's grace has touched us, we can laugh at ourselves and our efforts. We understand that, as usual, the truth lies somewhere in between—somewhere between radical discipleship and the joyful carelessness that flows from God's own spirit of mercy.

The corporate life of the people of God will be visible and external. These are the folks who engage in conspicuous sharing. We practice Jubilee. Generosity replaces consumption and accumulation. Our faith wags our pocketbooks. We give without expecting a return. We forgive liberally as God forgave us. We overlook the signs of stigma hanging from the unlovely. Genuine compassion for the poor and destitute moves us. We look and move down the ladder. We don't take our own religious structures too seriously; we know Jesus is Lord and Master of religious custom. We serve instead of dominate. We prefer invitation over force.

272 / The Upside-Down Kingdom

Love replaces hate among us. Shalom overcomes revenge. We love even enemies. Basins replace swords in our society. We share power, love assertively, and make peace. We flatten hierarchies and behave like children. Compassion replaces personal ambition among us. Equality replaces competition and achievement. Obedience to Jesus blots out worldly charm. Servant structures replace bureaucracies. We call each other by our first name, for we have one Master and one Lord, Jesus Christ. We join in a common life for worship and support. Here we discern the times and the issues. In the common life we discover the Holy Spirit's direction for our individual and corporate ministries.

Generosity, Jubilee, mercy, compassion—these are the marks of the new community. Freed from the grip of right-side-up kingdoms, we salute a new King and sing a new song. We pledge allegiance to a new and already-present kingdom. We're citizens of a future that is already breaking in. We're the ones who turn the world upside down because we know there is another King named Jesus.

We children of the Most High welcome the reign of God in our lives each day. Along with Jesus we exclaim, "Thy kingdom come. Thy will be done, on earth as it is in heaven." For it indeed is God's kingdom, God's power, and God's glory, forever and ever.

Questions for Discussion

1. What difference does it make when we view the cross as a response to Jesus' basin ministry?

2. Identify some crosses which you are presently facing.

3. In your own words, what does Jesus mean by "saving" and "losing" one's life?

4. In what ways is the church a counterculture—an alternate social reality?

5. Evaluate the various strategies for Christian service and ministry.

6. In what ways are you involved in an upside-down community?

7. How can we maintain a healthy balance between radical discipleship and joyful splurges?

GUIDE FOR DISCUSSION LEADERS

This book is designed for use in small discussion groups and classes in a variety of educational settings. The questions at the end of each chapter should stimulate vigorous discussions. Encourage students to reflect on these in preparation for discussion. Many of the chapters include additional questions embedded in the text which you may also find helpful.

A brief summary of the chapters may aid your preparation and organization. The first chapter introduces the concept of the kingdom of God as well as some of the issues surrounding its interpretations. Chapters 2, 3, and 4 deal with Jesus' temptations in the context of the historical setting. They focus respectively on politics, religion, and economics in first century Palestine. These four chapters provide an essential foundation for the rest of the book.

Chapter 5 deals with the beginning of Jesus' ministry and situates it in the context of the Old Testament Jubilee. Chapter 6 investigates the teachings of Jesus related to economic issues. Chapter 7 focuses on excuses which often serve as contemporary detours around Jesus' teaching on wealth. Jesus' relationship to religious leaders and tradition is summarized in Chapter 8. The theme of agape love and nonretaliation form the bedrock of Chapter 9. Chapter 10 traces Jesus' acceptance of a wide range of diverse people and Chapter 11 grapples with his teaching on status, service, and power. The last chapter focuses on the meaning of the cross and discipleship.

Because the book usually provokes lively discussion,

many groups have found it difficult to cover a chapter in a single, one–hour session. There are a variety of ways in which the chapters might be organized for discussion.

1. The ideal pattern would allot two sessions for each chapter (24 sessions). This permits time for reflection between discussions and allows participants to read more carefully and grapple with issues in more depth.

2. The more typical pattern is to assign one chapter per session (12 sessions).

3. For a six-session sequence, the best combination of chapters would be: 1 and 2; 3 and 8; 4 and 5; 6 and 7; 10 and 11; 9 and 12 (6 sessions).

4. A more abbreviated four-meeting sequence might utilize this pattern: 1–4; 5–7; 8–9; 10–12 (4 sessions).

Let me offer several suggestions to enhance discussion.

(1) Distribute books to participants with a reading assignment *before* the first session.

(2) Encourage students to read key passages directly from the Gospels.

(3) Ask several students to be responsible for subsections of a chapter. They might prepare additional background material on a particular topic.

(4) Consider rotating discussion leaders for some sessions.

(5) Consider breaking large groups into smaller groups of three to six for at least some of the discussion.

(6) Encourage students to write down several questions provoked by the reading prior to the discussion.

(7) Encourage all persons to participate and discourage one or two persons from dominating the conversation.

(8) Near the end of the series, encourage individuals and the group to commit themselves to several specific changes they will make as a result of the study.

(9) Consult other reference works such as Bible dictionaries and one other interpretation of the life of Jesus for the sake of comparison. I especially recommend Marcus Borg's *Jesus: A New Vision.*

NOTES

CHAPTER ONE: DOWN IS UP

    1. Jeremias (1971:97) points out that the terms *kingdom of God* and *kingdom of heaven* have an identical meaning.

    2. New Testament scholars generally agree on the centrality and salience of the kingdom theme in Jesus' teaching. Borg (1987:198-99) in an otherwise excellent introduction to the vision of Jesus, downplays the kingdom theme. In a provocative study, Sheehan (1986) proposes that the essence of the kingdom was distorted as the early church transformed the kingdom into another religion—Christianity.

    3. Verhey (1984) explores the "Great Reversal" theme in an excellent study of ethics and the New Testament. His interpretation of social inversion in the Gospels, although developed independent of my work, coincides in many ways with my perspective.

    4. This is essentially the position taken and more fully developed in Yoder (1972:23).

    5. Jeremias (1971:98). Excellent discussions of the history of the scholarship dealing with the kingdom of God can be found in Chilton (1984:1-26), Chilton and McDonald (1987), Riches (1982:87-111), and Sanders (1985:123-244).

    6. Verhey (1984:13).

    7. The Gospels provide different layers or strata of historical material: the words of Jesus, the views of the redactors, oral traditions, and influences from the early Christian communities. The respective editors of the Gospels, of course, offer different slants, or different views, of Jesus. While I am aware of the multitude of interests shaping the historical text, I am primarily concerned with the synoptic or generic view of Jesus as it has been handed down to us. This homogeneous approach is less sensitive to the nuances of the particular editors but offers a more holistic view of Jesus as it has been transmitted to us. And this holistic view, while not verifiable historically, nonetheless captures in a reliable fashion the essence of the essential Jesus.

    8. Discussions of the timing of the kingdom and its eschatological character have been reviewed by numerous scholars. Chilton and McDonald (1987),

Hiers (1970, 1973), Ladd (1974a, 1974b), Pannenberg (1969), Perrin (1963, 1976), Sanders (1985).

9. Schweitzer (1922) in his now classic study, *The Quest of the Historical Jesus*, first published in 1906, argued that Jesus' apocalyptic view shaped his ethical instruction. More recent advocates of Schweitzer's apocalyptic interpretation of Jesus' teachings include Hiers (1970, 1973) and Sanders (1975).

10. The British theologian, Dodd (1936), was an early proponent of this view, often called "realized eschatology."

11. Ladd (1974b:3). The scholarly consensus has clearly shifted toward multiple temporal meanings associated with the kingdom's timing. See also Bright (1953:216-217), Chilton (1984), Chilton and McDonald (1987), Kraus (1974:32), Perrin (1976), and Sanders (1985:150-56).

12. Ladd (1974b:123).

13. Perrin (1976:29-35) offers this helpful distinction. In the interest of simplicity I have labeled Perrin's steno symbol "specific" and his tensive symbol "general."

14. Ladd (1974b).

15. Sanders (1975:31).

16. Ladd (1974b:303).

17. Sanders (1975:29).

18. Ladd (1974b:302) as well as Birch and Rasmussen (1976) articulate this concern. The growing tendency for scholars to link social ethics with the kingdom of God and the teachings of Jesus is illustrated by the efforts of Cassidy (1978), Hauerwas (1983), Longenecker (1984), Mealand (1981), and Yoder (1972). Chilton and McDonald (1987) and Perkins (1981) argue that the parables provide the best insights into the social ethics of the kingdom.

19. One of the difficulties in shaping modern social ethics from the synoptic Gospels is the fact that Jesus and his disciples were an itinerate band wandering through the rural countryside. They were the incipient stage of a social movement of religious revitalization and were thus not preoccupied with the questions of building and maintaining social institutions which press upon a social movement in its later stages. In the Acts of the apostles as well as the other New Testament letters, the questions of institution building and preservation assume a higher priority.

For a sociological treatment of the itinerate character of Jesus and his disciple band, see Theissen (1978). A discussion of the different social needs that correspond with the institutional stages of a social movement as they apply to the role of wealth in Luke and Acts can be found in Kraybill and Sweetland (1983).

20. Verhey (1984:21) suggests that Jesus' ethic is not one of obedience to the law, but is fundamentally an ethic of repentance.

CHAPTER TWO: MOUNTAIN POLITICS

1. Hengel (1977:17-21) suggests that Jesus took a critical stance against all the political powers of his day. Hengel, however, does not relate this critical posture to the temptation.

2. A number of studies are helpful to reconstruct the political and social history of Palestine in the centuries surrounding the life of Jesus. Bruce (1971), Enslin (1956), Guignebert (1959), Horsley (1987), Horsley and Hanson (1985), Lohse (1976), Martin (1975), Metzger (1965), and Myers (1988).

3. BCE indicates the time period before the common era, that is, before the birth of Christ. CE indicates the common era after Christ's birth.

4. Enslin (1956:8).
5. Lohse (1976:25).
6. Enslin (1956:13-14).
7. Jeremias (1975:124).
8. Enslin (1956:60).
9. Metzger (1965:24).
10. For a discussion of the uprising of 4 BCE, see Freyne (1980) and Horsley (1987:50-54). Freyne (1980, 1988) argues that for the most part, Jewish protest movements were rooted primarily in Judea rather than in Galilee.
11. Hengel (1973:29).
12. It is uncertain whether a formally organized Zealot party developed in 6 CE and continued up to the major Jewish revolt of 66-70 CE. There are three possible scenarios. (1) A Zealot movement, formed about 6 CE, persisted until it actively was involved in the revolt of 66-70 CE. (2) Although formed in 6 CE, the Zealots may have waned and were later revitalized in the major revolt. (3) The Zealots did not emerge as an organized resistance movement until 67-68 CE.

Horsley (1987) and Horsley and Hanson (1985) make a persuasive argument for the third scenario. Three additional ambiguities cloud the discussion. Were the Sicarii (dagger men) the same as the Zealots? Was the revolutionary Judas, son of Hezekiah (4 BCE), the same person as Judas of Galilee (6 CE), founder of the Fourth Philosophy? Was the Fourth Philosophy actually an organized Zealot party? Horsley (1987) and Horsley and Hanson (1985) contend that the historical evidence offers negative answers to all these questions. Freyne (1980:216-29) points out, however, that this Judas might have changed his mind over a ten-year period and indeed be the same person.
13. Hengel (1971:10).
14. Horsley and Hanson (1985:35).
15. Lohse (1976:42).
16. Kelber (1974:78) points out the symbolic significance of the mountain in Mark's Gospel.
17. The most influential argument was advanced by Brandon (1968).
18. Harris (1975:179-203).
19. Cullmann (1970) outlines the issues in chapter 1.
20. Cullmann (1970) and Hengel (1971, 1973) both refute the allegations that Jesus advocated violence. Cassidy (1978) and Ford (1984), using Luke's Gospel, argue that Jesus advocated nonviolence. Myers (1988) in a political reading of Mark, contends that Jesus practiced not only nonviolence, but also resistance—symbolic direct action. By contrast, Horsley (1987:318-26) in his lengthy study of Jesus and violence concludes that there is little evidence that Jesus advocated *either* nonviolence *or* violence. His conclusion rests, however, on a very questionable reading of Jesus' command to "love enemies."

CHAPTER THREE: TEMPLE PIETY
1. Jeremias (1975:25).
2. Martin (1975:78).
3. Jeremias (1975:200-205) provides an excellent summary of the temple operation.
4. Lohse (1976:157).
5. Jeremias (1975:83).
6. Metzger (1965:55).
7. Jeremias (1975:75).

8. *Interpreter's* (1962:4:216).
9. Jeremias (1975:160-212).
10. My discussion of the Torah is based primarily on Guignebert (1959:62-67). For an excellent introduction to the Torah, see Neusner (1979).
11. Jeremias (1975) and Saldarini (1988) are the basic references for this section on the scribes.
12. Jeremias (1975:243).
13. Saldarini (1988:298-307) provides an excellent overview of the sparse data available on the Sadducees. Although many scholars note that the Sadducees opposed the oral law of the Pharisees, Saldarini contends that it is possible the Sadducees had their own oral interpretations as well.
14. For extended discussions of the Pharisees, see Borg (1984), Jeremias (1975:246-67), Moxnes (1988), and Saldarini (1988).
15. Martin (1975:109-16) and Ford (1984:13-36) summarize the revolutionary messianism in the Jewish tradition.

CHAPTER FOUR: WILDERNESS BREAD
1. Yoder (1972:31) suggests this reading of the bread temptation.
2. There are numerous detailed descriptions of the social stratification of first-century Palestine. For an analysis of the Galilee region, see Freyne (1980, 1988). Consult Mealand (1981), Moxnes (1988), Myers (1988), Saldarini (1988), and Stambaugh and Balch (1986) for excellent discussions of social classes and economic stratification. Oakman (1986) provides a detailed description of production and economic distribution in Palestine.
3. Hoehner (1972:73).
4. Jeremias (1975:92-99) and Finkelstein (1962:11-16) describe the affluence of the Jerusalem aristocrats.
5. Sanders (1985:174-211) argues persuasively that the "people of the land" should not be lumped together with "sinners" as is often done by New Testament scholars.
6. Saldarini (1988:52) argues that synagogue buildings devoted solely to worship did not appear until the third century CE in Palestine.
7. Baron (1952:1:275).
8. Enslin (1956:127).
9. Hoehner (1972:70).
10. Trocmé (1973:87-88). Freyne (1980, 1988) contends that in spite of the growth of large estates, some peasants, at least in Galilee, continued to farm their own plots.
11. Oakman (1986:72), in detailed calculations, estimates that on the low side, a farmer paid one half of his crop in taxes and rent and on the high side, two thirds. More importantly, when seed and other costs are added to the taxes, Oakman estimates that at most 1/5—and possibly much less—of the crop was actually available to the farmer for subsistence living.
12. Guignebert (1959:39).
13. Jeremias (1971:110).
14. Neusner (1975:29).
15. Baron (1952:279).
16. This essentially is the thesis developed by Borg (1987).
17. Oakman (1986:176-82) offers a detailed description of the role and work of a carpenter in first-century Palestine.
18. Jeremias (1971:221) and Bately (1972:5-9) argue that Jesus was of the poor class. Freyne (1988:241) demonstrates that Jesus and his followers were

280 / The Upside-Down Kingdom

not landowners, but neither were they destitute beggars. They were among the more economically mobile of the peasant culture. Hengel (1974:27) contends that because of his occupation, Jesus came from the Galilee middle class of skilled workers. Theissen (1978:10-16) maintains that Jesus and his disciples were wandering charismatics who had few if any possessions.

Several issues may clarify these conflicting views. As noted before, while Jesus grew up in a low-class family, it was an artisan family, likely in the upper ranks of the lower class. Second, the teaching and lifestyle of Jesus and his disciples may have been dire because they deliberately rejected their original family status. As Jesus called disciples to follow him, he urged them to leave their occupations. Thus while Jesus and at least some of his disciples had roots in the upper ranks of the lower class, their subsequent behavior during his ministry reflected an embrace of the lifestyle of the poorest of the poor—day-to-day wandering.

19. Bately (1972:5-9).

20. This is essentially Theissen's (1978:10-16) argument in his sociological study.

CHAPTER FIVE: FREE SLAVES

1. It is unclear if Jesus followed an assigned lectionary reading for the day or selected the Isaiah passage himself. Ringe (1985:39) thinks the lectionary hypothesis is suspect.

2. A variety of scholars have provided extensive discussions of the Hebrew Jubilee; Blosser (1978), Ford (1984), Gnuse (1985), Gregarios (1975), North (1954), Sloan (1977), Strobel (1972), Trocmé (1973), and Yoder (1972). Perhaps the best one which links the Jubilee image in Luke 4 to the rest of Jesus' teaching is the excellent work of Ringe (1985). An exception is Vaux (1965:1:176) who rejects the notion that Isaiah 61:1-2 refers to the Jubilee.

3. The key issue which is summarized and discussed cogently by Sloan (1977:166-94) is whether or not Jesus was invoking the Jubilee proclamation with its full socioeconomic and political ramifications, or rather using it in an eschatological mode to call for a response to the announcement of God's salvation.

Yoder (1973) and Trocmé (1973) argue for concrete social meanings of the Jubilee in Jesus' usage whereas Sloan (1977:171-73) opts for a more eschatological interpretation, contending that such a view does not deprive it of social meaning. Edwards (n.d.) rejects the hypothesis that Jesus was explicitly restoring the Jubilee program in Nazareth. Gregorios (1975) also makes a clear case for a Jubilean interpretation of Luke 4:18-19.

4. Apart from the question of the social specificity of Jesus' use of the Jubilee in the Nazareth context, the Jubilean themes of release, liberty, and forgiveness are important in Luke's rendition of Jesus' ministry. Blosser (1978), Sloan (1977), Yoder (1972), and especially Ringe (1985) demonstrate the centrality of the Jubilee motif in Luke's theology.

5. North (1954:129). He suggests that the same year was in a certain sense the fiftieth and also the forty-ninth. The forty-ninth year may have loosely been referred to as the "fiftieth."

6. Neusner (1973:14-18).

7. Trocmé (1973:39) calculates that Jesus preached in Nazareth in a sabbatical year.

8. Strobel (1972) argues that it was not only a sabbatical year—but was actually the Jubilee year itself when Jesus appeared in the Nazareth synagogue. I

am indebted to Walton Z. Moyer for translating Strobel's article for me from the German.
  9. Gregorios (1975:187).
  10. Jeremias (1971:104).
  11. The rejection of Jesus at Nazareth has two plausible scenarios: (1) The crowd shifted from applause to condemnation in the course of the sermon or (2) the audience was astonished with anger throughout the episode. The traditional interpretation has favored the crowd reversal thesis since they at first "spoke well of him, and wondered at the gracious words which proceeded out of his mouth," and later "were filled with wrath." Ford (1984:64), following Jeremias, shows that the crowd may have been angered throughout the incident, especially when Jesus dropped the reference to the Day of Vengeance toward the heathen. Thus it's possible that "they were astonished because he spoke of the mercy of God" (toward Gentiles).
  12. Trocmé (1973:42). Oakman (1986:153-56) argues persuasively for a material meaning of debts in the context of the Lord's Prayer.
  13. This, of course, is an oversimplification of the classic idealist/materialist debate in both philosophy and the social sciences. Rather than a monocausal process, the intricate tie between ideas and their material context is a complicated process of ongoing reciprocity.
  14. Ringe (1985) in careful detail demonstrates how the vocabulary and imagery of Jubilee is threaded throughout much of Jesus' ministry.

CHAPTER SIX: LUXURIOUS POVERTY

  1. For extended discussions of Jesus' analysis and teaching regarding wealth and possessions, consult Hengel (1974), Johnson (1977), Kraybill and Sweetland (1983), Mealand (1981), Moxnes (1988), Myers (1988), Oakman (1986), Pilgrim (1981), and Ringe (1985).
  2. For an exegesis of Jesus' stories and parables that is carefully rooted in the sociocultural context of the Palestine of Jesus' time, I especially recommend Bailey (1983).
  3. Jeremias (1971:236).
  4. Yoder (1972:65-66).
  5. Hunter (1971:28).
  6. Jeremias (1972:183).
  7. Jordan and Doulos (1976:65-66).
  8. Jeremias (1972:184).
  9. Glen (1962:69).
  10. For an excellent exegesis of Luke 16:1-13 situated in the cultural context of Palestine, see the fine work of Bailey (1983:86-118).
  11. Derrett's (1970:48-85) discussion of the parable of the unjust steward gives a detailed picture of the economic norms in Palestine and provides the foundation for my discussion. Building on Derrett's work, Moxnes (1988:139-142) provides a plausible interpretation to this sometimes baffling story which has informed my analysis.
  12. Derrett (1970:62).
  13. See Moxnes (1988) for a thorough investigation of the relationship between the Pharisees and wealth, particularly in the context of Luke's Gospel.
  14. *Interpreter's* (1962:3:234).
  15. Jeremias (1972:165).
  16. *Interpreter's* (1962:3:843).
  17. Jeremias (1971:108-113).

18. Jeremias (1971:112) suggests that the Lucan version is surely the original. Matthew's Gospel was formulated in a church fighting the temptation of Pharisaic self-righteousness. The "poor in spirit" emphasis was a needed corrective.

19. Jeremias (1971:109).

20. *Interpreter's* (1962:3:531). Myers (1988:274-75) argues that this saying must be understood literally as meaning a camel and a needle.

21. Baron (1952:252).

22. Jeremias (1975:311-12).

CHAPTER SEVEN: RIGHT-SIDE-UP DETOURS

1. Jordan and Doulos (1976:118).

2. Birch and Rasmussen (1976:179-182) cite the misinterpretation of this statement as a classic example of the misuse of Scripture of social ethics.

3. Derrett (1970:266-278).

4. Sider (1977:175-178) has proposed this as a creative way of tithing expanding incomes.

5. Hengel (1974:29).

6. Sider (1977:32-37).

7. Sider (1977:40-42).

CHAPTER EIGHT: IMPIOUS PIETY

1. Adler (1963:40-41).

2. Danby (1933).

3. Strack (1969:26-28).

4. Davies (1967).

5. For an excellent analysis of the passion for holiness in the religious milieu in Jesus' time, especially as it was embodied by the Pharisees, consult Borg (1984, 1987).

6. For a contrasting view, see Sanders (1985:245-80) who argues that Jesus did not violate the law except for one or two minor infractions. This view is based partly on little distinction between written and oral law but mostly on the assumption that Jesus' confrontations with the law are later creations of the early church and redactors.

7. Swartley (1983:70) makes this observation and uses the Sabbath for a fascinating case study in comparative biblical hermeneutics.

8. Danby (1933:106).

9. Danby (1933:110).

10. Danby (1933:123-27).

11. Jeremias (1971:144).

12. Borg (1984:78-96) offers an excellent analysis of the meaning of Jesus' table fellowship to which I am indebted.

13. Jeremias (1971:115-16).

14. For extended discussions of Jesus' provocation in the temple, consult Borg (1984:163-200, 1987:174-77), Horsley (1987:285-300), Myers (1988:297-306), and Sanders (1985:61-76).

15. Various outer courts surrounding the temple building itself were used for public worship and designated for particular groups, e.g., the priests' court, and the court of Israel. Borg (1987:174) contends that the "Court of the Gentiles," typically referred to by scholars, is a modern, not ancient, designation.

16. Kelber (1974:97-102) expands the traditional interpretation that the temple cleansing was done primarily to open up the outer court to the Gentiles.

He also suggests that the prohibition to carry vessels had more religious significance than stopping people who were taking a shortcut through the temple. Sanders (1985:61-91) argues that the temple incident was not merely chasing out money changers or "cleansing" the temple for the purpose of restoring it to routine operation; it was rather a defiant public act directed against the temple itself and it was this provocative act that more than any other led to Jesus' death. Myers (1988:297-306) argues that the temple was fundamentally an economic institution. Jesus was taking symbolic direct action against the temple operation.

17. Kelber (1974:101) makes a case that the purge was intended to shut down the temple operation at least in a symbolic if not final sense.

18. Jeremias (1975:253-55) points out that Matthew put scribes and Pharisees into the same category. Jesus denounced the Pharisees primarily for their emphasis on tithes and ritual washing while the scribes or lawyers were criticized for their attention to social status. See Luke 11:37-52.

19. See Borg (1987:157-60) for an excellent discussion on this point.

20. Jeremias (1972:139-44) provides helpful insight into this story.

21. Jeremias (1972:132).

22. For a discussion of the relations between church and kingdom, consult Ladd (1974a:105-19) and Bright (1953), especially Bright's chapter 8, "Between Two Worlds: The Kingdom and the Church."

23. Kraus (1974:34).

24. Snyder (1975:69-73).

CHAPTER NINE: LOVABLE ENEMIES

1. Various interpreters vouch for different themes as the primary one in Jesus' articulation of the kingdom. I have chosen agape. Borg (1987) stresses the compassion of Jesus—or "wombishness" as he likes to call it. For Oakman (1986) the key theme is generosity.

2. Bailey (1983:158-206) and Jeremias (1972:128-32) provide helpful cultural background to this parable, for which I am indebted.

3. See Bailey (1983:33-56) for details of the cultural context.

4. Jeremias (1975:352). For additional background on the Samaritans, consult Coggins (1975) and Ford (1984:79-95).

5. Jeremias (1975:357).

6. Jeremias (1975:358).

7. Crossan (1973:65).

8. Moxnes (1988:129-34) offers an excellent discussion of this hospitality story in the context of reciprocal exchange patterns in Palestinian culture.

9. Moxnes (1988:157).

10. The definition of "enemies" in this biblical passage is crucial. If as Horsley (1987:255-272) contends the enemies that Jesus had in mind were local and personal—not foreign and political—the teaching loses its political impact. Klassen's (1984) careful analysis of this teaching disagrees with Horsley. The examples of enemies which Jesus uses in parable and story suggest a broader definition than the one proposed by Horsley. Schwager (1987:171-80) in a creative analysis discusses enemy love in the context of social psychological theories of scapegoating.

11. Jeremias (1971:239).

12. The literature on the various responses of the church to violence and militarism is voluminous. For an excellent introduction to the contradictory hermeneutical positions taken by various theological traditions, see Swartley (1983:96-149).

13. For a description of the many ways in which civil religion justifies militarism, see Kraybill (1976).

14. See Brueggemann (1982) for an exegesis of the biblical meaning of shalom. Yoder (1987) provides one of the best introductions to the concept of shalom, especially as it relates to salvation and justice.

15. For an indepth discussion of Chrisitan faith and nuclear militarism, see Kraybill (1982).

CHAPTER TEN: INSIDE OUTSIDERS

1. Jeremias (1975) devotes six chapters (12–17) to the maintenance of racial purity in the Hebrew community. My discussion is indebted to his careful research.

2. The extent to which Jesus himself welcomed Gentiles is somewhat ambiguous. Sanders (1985:212-21) contends that Jesus started a movement which "came to see the Gentile mission as a logical extension of itself." But Sanders doubts that Jesus himself welcomed Gentiles.

3. For an elaboration, see Tannehill (1972).

4. I am indebted to Willard M. Swartley, my former instructor, for solving the riddle of the symbols in these three chapters. A comprehensive treatment can be found in Swartley (1973). For a popular treatment see Swartley (1981:94-130). Myers (1988:223-27) concurs with this interpretation.

5. Matthew generally takes a more negative view toward Gentiles than Mark or Luke. Perhaps because he is writing to a Jewish audience, Matthew often depicts Jesus with the typical Jewish attitude. Matthew is the only writer who reports Jesus saying that he is sent only to the lost sheep of the house of Israel (Matthew 10:6; 15:24).

Jesus warns his followers not to pray like the Gentiles who heap up empty phrases (Matthew 6:7). In a derogatory manner, Jesus lumps tax collectors and Gentiles together as negative models for his disciples (Matthew 5:47; 18:17). The Gentiles seek anxiously after things (Matthew 6:32). And the Gentiles have hierarchies of authority (Matthew 20:25). The disciples can expect to be dragged before Gentiles (Matthew 10:18). Jesus himself expects to be mocked before Gentiles (Matthew 20:19). In all these instances the Gentiles are castigated in Matthew's gospel.

6. Yoder (1972) devotes chapter 11 to Paul's concept of justification as it relates to the reconciliation of Jew and Greek.

7. Jeremias (1975) has an excellent discussion on the role of women in Hebrew culture in chapter 18. It is the basic historical source for this section. For several introductory sources on the role of women in the New Testament, consider Evans (1983), Praeder (1988), Ruether (1981), Siddons (1980), and Swartley (1983).

8. Jeremias (1975:375).

9. Jeremias (1975:376).

10. Wahlberg (1975:94).

11. Jeremias (1975:305, 311).

12. Jeremias (1971:104).

13. Longenecker (1984) in several insightful essays argues that the mandate of the gospel as practiced by the early church envisioned a new community where social barriers crumbled between male and female, slave and free, Jew and Greek.

CHAPTER ELEVEN: LOW IS HIGH
1. Hatfield (1976:17).
2. Jeremias (1971:219).
3. Chilton and McDonald (1987:79-90) offer a penetrating analysis of the controversy over children with a special emphasis on its ethical implications.
4. Minear (1976:21) in Chapter 1 provides an especially helpful discussion.
5. Minear (1976:21) and Hengel (1977:18-20).
6. Hengel (1977:21).
7. Redekop (1976:147) suggests this thesis.
8. Greenleaf (1970:4). This is a useful pamphlet on servanthood leadership.

CHAPTER TWELVE: SUCCESSFUL FAILURES
1. I am indebted to Brueggemann's (1982) excellent essay on the tools and trade of the Christian's basin ministry.
2. Brueggemann (1982).
3. Burkholder (1976:134).
4. See Yoder (1972:132-34) for a critique of the way the term "cross" is typically used in Protestant pastoral care.
5. Jeremias (1972:195).
6. Hauerwas (1983) offers a creative vision for the peaceable community of the new kingdom.
7. Wallis (1976) provides an excellent argument for the urgency of rebuilding the church in chapter 5.
8. Ellul (1967:145).
9. Yoder (1971:28).
10. Jeremias (1971:135).

BIBLIOGRAPHY

Adler, Morris
1963   *The World of the Talmud.* 2nd ed. New York: Schocken Books.

Anderson, Norman
1983   *The Teaching of Jesus.* The Jesus Library. Ed. Michael Green. Downers Grove, Ill.: Inter-Varsity Press.

Bailey, Kenneth E.
1983   *Poet & Peasant and Through Peasant Eyes: A Literary-Cultural Approach to the Parables of Luke.* Grand Rapids: Eerdmans.

Baron, Salo Wittmayer
1952   *A Social and Religious History of the Jews.* Vol. 1. New York: Columbia University Press.

Bately, Richard
1972   *Jesus and the Poor.* New York: Harper & Row.

Birch, Bruce C., and Larry L. Rasmussen
1976   *Bible and Ethics in the Christian Life.* Minneapolis: Augsburg.

Blosser, Donald
1978   *Jesus and the Jubilee, Luke 4:16-30: The Year of Jubilee and Its Significance in the Gospel of Luke.* Ph.D. diss., Scotland: University of St. Andrews.

Borg, Marcus J.
1984   *Conflict, Holiness & Politics in the Teachings of Jesus.* Studies in the Bible and Early Christianity, Vol. 5. New York: Edwin Mellen Press.

1987   *Jesus: A New Vision. Spirit, Culture, and the Life of Discipleship.*
        San Francisco: Harper & Row.

Bowman, John
1975   *The Samaritan Problem.* Pittsburgh: Pickwick Press.

Brandon, S. G. F.
1968   *Jesus and the Zealots.* New York: Scribners.

Bright, John
1953   *The Kingdom of God.* Nashville: Abingdon.

Bruce, F. F.
1971   *New Testament History.* New York: Doubleday.

1983   *The Hard Sayings of Jesus.* The Jesus Library. Ed. Michael
        Green. Downers Grove, Ill.: Inter-Varsity Press.

Brueggemann, Walter
1982   *Living Toward a Vision: Biblical Reflections on Shalom.* 2nd ed.
        New York: United Church Press.

Burkholder, J. Lawrence
1976   "Nonresistance, Nonviolent Resistance, and Power." In *King-
        dom, Cross, and Community.* Eds. Calvin Redekop and J. Rich-
        ard Burkholder. Scottdale, Pa.: Herald Press.

Cassidy, Richard J.
1978   *Jesus, Politics, and Society: A Study of Luke's Gospel.* Reprint.
        Maryknoll, N.Y.: Orbis Books.

1987   *Society and Politics in the Acts of the Apostles.* Maryknoll, N.Y.:
        Orbis Books.

Cassidy, Richard J., and Philip J. Scharper
1983   Eds. *Political Issues in Luke-Acts.* Maryknoll, N.Y.: Orbis
        Books.

Chilton, Bruce
1979   *God in Strength: Jesus' Announcement of the Kingdom.* Plochl:
        Freistadt.

1984   Ed. *The Kingdom of God in the Teaching of Jesus.* Philadelphia:
        Fortress.

Chilton, Bruce, and J. I. H. McDonald
1987   *Jesus and the Ethics of the Kingdom.* Grand Rapids: Eerdmans.

Coggins, R. J.
1975   *Samaritans and Jews: The Origins of Samaritanism Reconsidered.*
        Atlanta: John Knox Press.

Crossan, John Dominic
1973   *In Parables*. New York: Harper & Row.

Cullmann, Oscar
1970   *Jesus and the Revolutionaries*. New York: Harper.

Cunningham, Philip A.
1988   *Jesus and the Evangelists: The Ministry of Jesus in the Synoptic Gospels*. New York: Paulist Press.

Danby, Herbert
1933   Trans. *The Mishnah*. London: Oxford University Press.

Davies, W. D.
1967   *Introduction to Pharisaism*. Philadelphia: Fortress.

Derrett, J. Duncan M.
1970   *Law in the New Testament*. London: Darton, Longman, and Todd.

Dodd, C. H.
1936   *The Parables of the Kingdom*. London: Nisbet.

Donahue, John R.
1988   *The Gospel in Parable: Metaphor, Narrative, and Theology in the Synoptic Gospels*. Philadelphia: Fortress.

Edwards, George
n.d.   Biblical Interpretation and the Politics of Jesus (unpublished manuscript).

Ellul, Jacques
1967   *The Presence of the Kingdom*. New York: Seabury.

Enslin, Norton Scott
1956   *Christian Beginnings I and II*. New York: Harper.

Evans, Mary J.
1983   *Women in the Bible: An Overview of All the Crucial Passages on Women's Roles*. Downers Grove, Ill.: InterVarsity Press.

Finkelstein, Louis
1962   *The Pharisees*. Philadelphia: Jewish Publication Society.

Ford, J. Massyngbaerde
1984   *My Enemy Is My Guest: Jesus and Violence in Luke*. Maryknoll, N.Y.: Orbis Books.

Freyne, Sean
1980   *Galilee from Alexander the Great to Hadrian, 323 B.C.E. to 135 C.E.: A Study of Second Temple Judaism*. Wilmington: Michael Glazier, Inc.

1988   *Galilee, Jesus, and the Gospels: Literary Approaches and Historical Investigations*. Philadelphia: Fortress.

Gager, John G.
1975   *Kingdom and Community: The Social World of Early Christianity*. Englewood Cliffs, N.J.: Prentice-Hall.

Glen, John Stanley
1962   *The Parables of Conflict in Luke*. Philadelphia: Westminster.

Gnuse, Robert
1985   *You Shall Not Steal: Community and Property in the Biblical Tradition*. Maryknoll, N.Y.: Orbis Books.

Grant, F. C.
1926   *The Economic Background of the Gospels*. Oxford.

Grant, Robert M.
1977   *Early Christianity and Society*. San Francisco: Harper & Row.

Greenleaf, Robert K.
1970   *The Servant as Leader*. (pamphlet) Cambridge, Mass.: Center for Applied Studies.

Gregorios, Paul
1975   "To Proclaim Liberation." In *To Set at Liberty the Oppressed*. Geneva: World Council of Churches.

Guignebert, Charles
1959   *The Jewish World in the Time of Jesus*. New York: University Books.

Guthrie, Shirley C., Jr.
1968   *Christian Doctrine: Teachings of the Christian Church*. Atlanta: John Knox Press.

Harris, Marvin
1975   *Cows, Pigs, Wars, and Witches*. New York: Random House.

Hatfield, Mark
1976   *Between a Rock and a Hard Place*. Waco, Tex.: Word Books.

Hauerwas, Stanley
1983   *The Peaceable Kingdom: A Primer in Christian Ethics*. Notre Dame: University of Notre Dame Press.

Hauerwas, Stanley and William Willimon
1990   *Resident Aliens: Life in the Christian Colony*. Nashville: Abingdon.

Hengel, Martin
1971   *Was Jesus a Revolutionist*. Philadelphia: Fortress.

1973   *Victory over Violence.* Philadelphia: Fortress.

1974   *Property and Riches in the Early Church: Aspects of a Social History of Early Christianity.* Philadelphia: Fortress.

1977   *Christ and Power.* Philadelphia: Fortress.

Hiers, Richard H.
1970   *The Kingdom in the Synoptic Tradition.* Gainesville: University of Florida Press.

1973   *The Historical Jesus and the Kingdom of God.* Gainesville: University of Florida Press.

Hoehner, Harold
1972   *Herod Antipas.* Cambridge: The University Press.

Hollenbach, Paul
1989   "The Historical Jesus Question in North America Today." *Biblical Theology Bulletin.* 19:11-22.

Horsley, Richard A.
1987   *Jesus and the Spiral of Violence: Popular Jewish Resistance in Roman Palestine.* San Francisco: Harper & Row.

Horsley, Richard A. and John S. Hanson
1985   *Bandits, Prophets, and Messiahs: Popular Movements in the Time of Jesus.* Chicago: Winston Press.

Hunter, Archibald M.
1971   *The Parables Then and Now.* Philadelphia: Westminster.

Interpreter's Dictionary of the Bible, The
1962   4 vols. Nashville: Abingdon.

Interpreter's Dictionary of the Bible, Supplementary Volume
1976   Nashville: Abingdon.

Jeremias, Joachim
1971   *New Testament Theology.* New York: Charles Scribner's Sons.

1972   *The Parables of Jesus.* New York: Charles Scribner's Sons.

1975   *Jerusalem in the Time of Jesus.* Philadelphia: Fortress.

Johnson, Luke T.
1977   *The Literary Function of Possessions in Luke-Acts.* Society of Biblical Literature Dissertation Series, no. 39. Ph.D. diss., Missoula, Montana: Scholars Press.

Jordan, Clarence, and Bill Lane Doulos
1976   *Cotton Patch Parables of Liberation.* Scottdale, Pa.: Herald Press.

Kee, Howard Clark
1980   *Christian Origins in Sociological Perspective: Methods and Resources*. Philadelphia: Westminster.

Kelber, Werner H.
1974   *The Kingdom in Mark*. Philadelphia: Fortress.

1979   *Mark's Story of Jesus*. Philadelphia: Fortress.

Klaassen, Walter
1975   *Anabaptism: Neither Protestant Nor Catholic*. Waterloo, Ont.: Conrad Press.

Klassen, William
1984   *Love of Enemies: The Way to Peace*. Philadelphia: Fortress.

Kraus, C. Norman
1974   *The Community of the Spirit*. Grand Rapids: Eerdmans.

Kraybill, Donald B.
1976   *Our Star-Spangled Faith*. Scottdale, Pa.: Herald Press.

1982   *Facing Nuclear War: A Plea for Christian Witness*. Scottdale, Pa.: Herald Press.

Kraybill, Donald B. and Dennis M. Sweetland
1983   "Possessions in Luke-Acts: A Sociological Perspective." *Perspectives in Religious Studies*. 10:3(Fall).

Kreider, Alan
1987   *Journey Towards Holiness: A Way of Living for God's Nation*. Scottdale, Pa.: Herald Press.

Kreider, Carl
1980   *The Christian Entrepreneur*. Scottdale, Pa.: Herald Press.

1987   *The Rich and the Poor: A Christian Perspective on Global Economics*. Scottdale, Pa.: Herald Press.

Ladd, George E.
1974a *A Theology of the New Testament*. Grand Rapids: Eerdmans.

1974b *The Presence of the Future*. Grand Rapids: Eerdmans.

Lee, Bernard J.
1988   *The Galilean Jewishness of Jesus: Retrieving the Jewish Origins of Christianity*. New York: Paulist Press.

Lohse, Eduard
1976   *The New Testament Environment*. Nashville: Abingdon.

Longenecker, Richard N.
1984   *New Testament Social Ethics for Today*. Grand Rapids: Eerdmans.

Malina, Bruce J.
1981   *The New Testament World: Insights from Cultural Anthropology.*
        Atlanta: John Knox Press.

Martin, Ralph
1975   *New Testament Foundations.* Grand Rapids: Eerdmans.

McClendon, James Wm., Jr.
1986   *Ethics: Systematic Theology.* Vol. 1. Nashville: Abingdon Press.

Mealand, David L.
1981   *Poverty and Expectation in the Gospels.* Reprint. London: SPCK.

Metzger, Bruce
1965   *The New Testament: Its Background, Growth, and Content.* Nash-
        ville: Abingdon.

Meyer, Ben F.
1979   *The Aims of Jesus.* London: SCM Press Ltd.

Michaels, J. Ramsey
1981   *Servant and Son: Jesus in Parable and Gospel.* Atlanta: John
        Knox Press.

Minear, Paul S.
1976   *To Heal and to Reveal.* New York: Seabury Press.

Moxnes, Halvor
1988   *The Economy of the Kingdom: Social Conflict and Economic Rela-
        tions in Luke's Gospel.* Philadelphia: Fortress.

Myers, Ched
1988   *Binding the Strong Man: A Political Reading of Mark's Story of
        Jesus.* Maryknoll, N.Y.: Orbis Books.

Neusner, Jacob
1973   *From Politics to Piety: The Emergence of Pharisaic Judaism.* En-
        glewood Cliffs, N.J.: Prentice Hall.

1975   *First Century Judaism in Crisis.* Nashville: Abingdon.

1979   *The Way of Torah: An Introduction to Judaism.* North Scituate,
        Mass.: Duxbury Press.

North, Robert
1954   *Sociology of the Biblical Jubilee.* Rome: Pontifico Instituto
        Biblico.

Oakman, Douglas E.
1986   *Jesus and the Economic Questions of His Day.* New York: Edwin
        Mellen Press.

Pannenberg, Wolfhart
1969   *Theology and the Kingdom of God.* Philadelphia: Westminster.

Perkins, Pheme
1981   *Hearing the Parables of Jesus.* New York: Paulist Press.

Perrin, Norman
1963   *The Kingdom of God in the Teaching of Jesus.* Philadelphia: Westminster.

1976   *Jesus and the Language of the Kingdom.* Philadelphia: Fortress.

Pilgrim, Walter E.
1981   *Good News to the Poor: Wealth and Poverty in Luke-Acts.* Minneapolis: Augsburg Publishing House.

Praeder, Susan Marie
1988   *The Word in Women's Worlds: Four Parables.* Wilmington: Michael Glazier, Inc.

Redekop, Calvin
1976   "Institutions, Power, and the Gospel." In *Kingdom, Cross, and Community.* Eds. Redekop and J. Richard Burkholder. Scottdale, Pa.: Herald Press.

Riches, John
1982   *Jesus and the Transformation of Judaism.* New York: Seabury Press.

Ringe, Sharon H.
1985   *Jesus, Liberation, and the Biblical Jubilee: Images for Ethics and Christology.* Philadelphia: Fortress.

Ruether, Rosemary Radford
1981   *To Change the World: Christology and Cultural Criticism.* New York: Crossroad.

Sabourin, L.
1981   "Evangelize the Poor." *Religious Studies Bulletin* 1:4 (September):101-108.

Saldarini, Anthony J.
1988   *Pharisees, Scribes and Sadducees in Palestinian Society: A Sociological Approach.* Wilmington: Michael Glazier, Inc.

Sanders, E. P.
1985   *Jesus and Judaism.* Philadelphia: Fortress.

Sanders, Jack T.
1975   *Ethics in the New Testament.* Philadelphia: Fortress.

Sanders, James A.
1987   *From Sacred Story to Sacred Text.* Philadelphia: Fortress.

Schottroff, Willy, and Wolfgang Stegemann
1984   Eds. *God of the Lowly: Socio-Historical Interpretations of the Bible*. Trans. Matthew J. O'Connell. Maryknoll, N.Y.: Orbis Books.

Schwager, Raymund.
1987   *Must There Be Scapegoats? Violence and Redemption in the Bible*. Trans. Maria L. Assad. San Francisco: Harper & Row.

Schweitzer, Albert
1922   *The Quest of the Historical Jesus*. New York: Macmillan.

Sheehan, Thomas
1986   *The First Coming: How the Kingdom of God Became Christianity*. New York: Random House.

Siddons, Philip
1980   *Speaking Out for Women: A Biblical View*. Valley Forge, Pa.: Judson Press.

Sider, Ronald J.
1977   *Rich Christians in an Age of Hunger*. Downers Grove, Ill.: Inter-Varsity Press.

Sloan, Robert B., Jr.
1977   *The Favorable Year of the Lord: A Study of Jubilary Theology in the Gospel of Luke*. Ph.D. diss. Austin, Tex.: Schola Press.

Snyder, Howard
1975   *The Problem of Wine Skins*. Downers Grove, Ill.: InterVarsity Press.

1977   *The Community of the King*. Downers Grove, Ill.: InterVarsity Press.

1983   *Liberating the Church: The Ecology of Church & Kingdom*. Downers Grove, Ill.: InterVarsity Press.

Sobrino, Jon
1978   *Christology at the Crossroads: A Latin American Approach*. New York: Orbis Books.

Stambaugh, John E. and David L. Balch
1986   *The New Testament in Its Social Environment*. Philadelphia: Westminster.

Strack, Hermann L.
1969   *Introduction to the Talmud and Mishnah*. New York: Atheneum.

Strobel, August
1972   *Jesus in Nazareth*. Berlin: Walter de Gruyter.

Swartley, Willard M.
1973   *A Study in Markan Structure: The Influence of Israel's Holy History Upon the Structure of the Gospel of Mark.* Ph.D. diss., Princeton Theological Seminary.

1981   *Mark: The Way for All Nations.* Scottdale, Pa.: Herald Press.

1983   *Slavery, Sabbath, War, and Women: Case Issues in Biblical Interpretation.* Scottdale, Pa.: Herald Press.

Tannehill, Robert C.
1972   "The Mission of Jesus According to Luke." In *Jesus of Nazareth,* Ed. Walther Eltester. Berlin: Walter de Gruyter.

Theissen, Gerd
1978   *Sociology of Early Palestinian Christianity.* Translated by John Bowden. Philadelphia, Pa.: Fortress.

Tidball, Derek
1984   *The Social Context of the New Testament: A Sociological Analysis.* Grand Rapids: Zondervan.

Trocmé, André
1973   *Jesus and the Nonviolent Revolution.* Scottdale, Pa.: Herald Press.

Vaux, Roland de
1965   *Ancient Israel: Social Institutions.* Vol. 1. New York: McGraw Hill.

Verhey, Allen
1984   *The Grand Reversal: Ethics and the New Testament.* Grand Rapids: Eerdmans.

Vermes, Geza
1973   *Jesus the Jew: A Historian's Reading of the Gospels.* New York: Macmillan.

Via, Dan Otto, Jr.
1967   *The Parables.* Philadelphia: Fortress.

Wahlberg, Rachel Conrad
1975   *Jesus According to a Woman.* New York: Paulist Press.

Wallis, Jim
1976   *Agenda for Biblical People.* New York: Harper & Row.

West, Charles C.
1986   The Sharing of Resources: A Biblical Reflection. *The Ecumenical Review* 38:4: 357-369.

Yoder, John Howard
    1971   *The Original Revolution.* Scottdale, Pa.: Herald Press.

    1972   *The Politics of Jesus.* Grand Rapids: Eerdmans.

    1984   *The Priestly Kingdom: Social Ethics as Gospel.* Notre Dame, Ind.:
            University of Notre Dame.

Yoder, Perry B.
    1987   *Shalom: The Bible's Word for Salvation, Justice, and Peace.* New-
            ton, Kans.: Faith and Life Press.

Young, Brad
    1989   *Jesus and His Jewish Parables: Rediscovering the Roots of Jesus'
            Teaching.* New York: Paulist Press.

INDEX OF SCRIPTURE CITED

GENERAL INDEX

temptation, 35–37, 54, 55, 58, 61,
    70–72, 74, 75, 84, 87–89, 174,
    262, 266
tithe, 82, 127, 138, 139, 148, 164,
    167
titles, 234, 240, 247, 254
tomb, 101, 222, 256, 257, 267
Torah, 59, 66–69, 71, 72, 151, 170,
    183, 198, 215, 219

value, 62, 103, 118, 145, 147, 190,
    232, 246, 249, 255
vineyard, 166, 169
violence, 25, 52, 55, 56–59, 84, 90,
    179, 197, 198, 201, 202, 221,
    251, 256, 262, 267, 268

war, 38, 42, 76, 194, 200, 201
wealth, 44, 57, 75, 77, 80, 87, 98,
    107, 108, 110, 111, 115–118,
    120–123, 126, 127, 129, 130,
    132–134, 136, 137, 140, 142,
    143, 146, 147, 150, 180, 222

widows, 126, 166, 170, 207, 223
wilderness, 17, 32, 35, 36, 40, 87,
    213, 256, 262
wineskins, 171
witness, 77, 139, 140, 148, 159,
    168, 175, 197, 212, 221, 270
women, 20, 53, 78, 79, 84, 126,
    166, 184, 205, 214, 215, 216,
    219, 220, 221, 223, 246, 251,
    259
worship, 39, 44, 48, 50, 57, 61, 62,
    65, 66, 69, 72, 78, 115, 135,
    155, 158, 161–163, 167, 175,
    183, 184, 186, 225, 226, 229,
    240, 246, 268, 270–272

Zacchaeus, 30, 81, 121, 123–125,
    128–130, 132, 136, 141, 160,
    171, 222
Zealots, 48, 49, 52, 53, 82

THE CHRISTIAN PEACE SHELF

The Christian Peace Shelf is a selection of Herald Press books and pamphlets devoted to the promotion of Christian peace principles and their applications. The editor (appointed by the Mennonite Central Committee Peace Section) and an inter-Mennonite board represent the historic concern for peace within these constituencies.

For Serious Study

Aukerman, Dale. *Darkening Valley* (1989). An analysis of nuclear war from a biblical perspective calling for all-out resistance to the idolatry of militarism.

Durland, William R. *No King but Caesar?* (1975). A Catholic lawyer looks at Christian violence.

Enz, Jacob J. *The Christian and Warfare* (1972). The roots of pacifism in the Old Testament.

Friesen, Duane K. *Christian Peacemaking and International Conflict* (1986). Realistic pacifism in the context of international conflict.

Hershberger, Guy F. *War, Peace, and Nonresistance* (third edition, 1969). A classic comprehensive work on nonresistance in faith and history.

Hornus, Jean-Michel. *It Is Not Lawful for Me to Fight* (1980). Early Christian attitudes toward war, violence, and the state.

Keim, Al, and Grant Stoltzfus. *Politics of Conscience* (1988). Traces the efforts of the historic peace churches to gain alternative service for conscientious objectors, 1917-1955.

Lassere, Jean. *War and the Gospel* (1962). An analysis of Scriptures related to the ethical problem of war.

Lind, Millard C. *Yahweh Is a Warrior* (1980). The theology of warfare in ancient Israel.

Ramseyer, Robert L. *Mission and the Peace Witness* (1979). Implications of the biblical peace testimony for the evangelizing mission of the church.

Trocmé, André. *Jesus and the Nonviolent Revolution* (1975). The social and political implications of the year of Jubilee in the teachings of Jesus.

Yoder, John H. *The Original Revolution* (1972). Essays on Christian pacifism.

Zehr, Howard J. *Changing Lenses* (1990). Experiential, historical, and biblical paradigms for understanding crime and justice.

For Easy Reading

Beachey, Duane. *Faith in a Nuclear Age* (1983). A Christian response to war.

Drescher, John M. *Why I Am a Conscientious Objector* (1982). A personal summary of basic issues for every Christian facing military involvements.

Eller, Vernard. *War and Peace from Genesis to Revelation* (1981). Explores peace as a consistent theme developing throughout the Old and New Testaments.

Kraybill, Donald B. *Facing Nuclear War* (1982). Relates Christian faith to the chief moral issue of our time.

——————————. *The Upside-Down Kingdom* (1978, 1990). A fresh study of the synoptic Gospels on affluence, war-making, status-seeking, and religious exclusivism.

McSorley, Richard. *New Testament Basis of Peacemaking* (1985). A Jesuit makes the case for biblical pacifism.

Miller, John W. *The Christian Way* (1969). A guide to the Christian life based on the Sermon on the Mount.

Miller, Melissa, and Phil M. Shenk. *The Path of Most Resistance* (1982). Stories of Mennonite conscientious objectors who did not cooperate with the Vietnam draft.

Sider, Ronald J. *Christ and Violence* (1979). A sweeping reappraisal of the church's teaching on violence.

Steiner, Susan Clemmer. *Joining the Army That Sheds No Blood* (1982). The case for biblical pacifism written for teens.

Stoner, John K. and Lois Barrett. *Letters to American Christians* (1989). Pithy essays about who Jesus really is and what his salvation has to do with the nuclear arms race.

Wenger, J. C. *The Way of Peace* (1977). A brief treatment on Christ's teachings and the way of peace through the centuries.

Yoder, John H. *He Came Preaching Peace* (1985). Bible lectures addressed to persons already involved in the Christian peace movement.

_____. *What Would You Do?* (1983). A serious answer to a standard question.

For Children

Bauman, Elizabeth Hershberger. *Coals of Fire* (1954). Stories of people who returned good for evil.

Eitzen, Ruth. *The White Feather* (1987). Based on the experience of a Quaker family who treated the Indians as friends and equals.

Lenski, Lois, and Clyde Robert Bulla. *Sing for Peace* (1985). Simple hymns on the theme of living with others.

Minshull, Evelyn. *The Cornhusk Doll* (1987). Tells how the gift of a cornhusk doll in a pioneer setting brought peace and friendship where there had been hatred and mistrust.

Moore, Joy Hofacker. *Ted Studebaker: A Man Who Loved Peace* (1987). A picture storybook of a conscientious objector who was killed in Vietnam while serving as a volunteer agriculturist.

Moore, Ruth Nulton. *Peace Treaty* (1977). A historical novel on the efforts of Moravian missionary Christian Frederick Post to bring peace to the Ohio Valley in 1758.

Smucker, Barbara Claassen. *Henry's Red Sea* (1955). The dramatic escape of 1,000 Russian Mennonites from Berlin following World War II.

THE AUTHOR

Born in Mount Joy, Pennsylvania, Donald B. Kraybill served as a Mennonite pastor and Voluntary Service administrator before completing his Ph.D. in sociology. He currently directs the Center for the Study of Anabaptist and Pietist Groups at Elizabethtown College (Pa.) where he is professor of sociology.

In addition to the two editions of *The Upside-Down Kingdom*, Kraybill has written these books: *Our Star-Spangled Faith, Facing Nuclear War,* and *The Riddle of Amish Culture.*